ABOUT EUROPE'S MONASTERY & CONVENT GUES....

Serving as the most comprehensive directory ever compiled on Europe's monastery and convent guesthouses, this guidebook features more than two hundred seventy-five places of spiritual retreat located in seventeen countries. It is an excellent resource for travelers, pilgrims, summer vacationers, students, armchair travelers, or anyone interested in monasteries. This handbook provides a key to discovering some of Christianity's most ancient and beloved sites. In these pages you will find famous monasteries and abbeys ranging from Santo Domingo de Silos with its famed Spanish singing monks, to the cheese and beer-making monasteries of Belgium, to the tradition-filled abbeys of France, to the very home of St. Benedict and Western Monasticism in Monte Cassino, Italy.

Inside, you'll find the following information and features:

- A brief history of Christian monasticism
- Stories of the major monastic orders
- Chronicle of Gregorian chant
- Contact information for monasteries, convents, and places of retreat
- Short descriptions of each holy place
- Maps and "How to get there" information
- Listing of monastic-related Web sites and travel resources

WORLD RELIGIOUS TRAVEL ASSOCIATION & WORLD RELIGIOUS TRAVEL EXPO

If you are interested in learning more about faith-based travel and tourism, you can visit the official Web site of the World Religious Travel Association (WRTA) at www.religioustravelassociation.com, the organization founded by author Kevin J. Wright. If you would like to become more involved in faith-based tourism as a group planner, travel ministry leader, or travel professional, you can attend the annual World Religious Travel Expo & Educational Conference; for more information visit www.religioustravelexpo.com. To learn more about The Year of Faith Tourism, visit www.faithtourism2009.com.

Europe's Monastery and Convent Guesthouses

**OTHER TRAVEL BOOKS
FROM LIGUORI PUBLICATIONS
www.liguori.org**

Catholic Shrines of Western Europe
A Pilgrim's Travel Guide
Kevin J. Wright

Every Pilgrim's Guide
to Celtic Britain and Ireland
Andrew Jones

Marian Shrines of the United States
A Pilgrim's Travel Guide
Theresa Santa Czarnopys & Thomas M. Santa

NEW
EDITION

Europe's Monastery and Convent Guesthouses

A Pilgrim's Travel Guide

Kevin J. Wright

Liguori
LIGUORI, MISSOURI

Published by Liguori Publications
Liguori, Missouri
www.liguori.org
Library of Congress Cataloging-in-Publication Data

Library of Congress Cataloging-in-Publication Data

Wright, Kevin J., 1972-
  Europe's monastery and convent guesthouses : a pilgrim's travel guide / Kevin J. Wright.
    p. cm.
  ISBN 978-0-7648-1780-9
    1. Monasteries—Guest accommodations—Europe—Directories. 2. Convents—Guest accommodations—Europe—Directories. 3. Spiritual retreat centers—Europe—Directories. I. Title.
  BX2590.W75 2008
  914.06'1561—dc22

                                                                    2008035489

Liguori Publications, a nonprofit corporation, is an apostolate of the Redemptorists. To learn more about the Redemptorists, visit Redemptorists.com.

Printed in the United States of America
12 11 10 09 08   5 4 3 2 1
New Edition

To all monks, hermits, priests, brothers, nuns, and sisters
who have consecrated their lives to Christ and his Church.
To all travelers and visitors of
monasteries, abbeys, convents, and religious houses.

SPECIAL NOTE In order to update future editions of this book, please notify the author with any changes or additions to the contact information of the monasteries and convents listed in the guidebook. Also, if you would like to see a monastery or convent included in future editions, please contact the author with your suggestions as well.

To contact the author Kevin J. Wright directly, you can email him at kwright@religioustravelassociation.com or write to him c/o of the publisher:

Liguori Publications
Attn: Kevin J. Wright, Author
One Liguori Drive
Liguori, MO 63057-9999
Fax (314) 464-8449

CONTENTS

ACKNOWLEDGEMENTS

WHEN COMPILING A BOOK of this size and magnitude, I find there are so many people to thank. First, I have the incredible pleasure and joy of thanking my dear family friend, Keith Dumm. During our year of working together, Keith provided the spark for the idea to write a guidebook about the monasteries, abbeys, and convent guesthouses of Europe. After that first spark, Keith also gave me much encouragement and support, as well as many tips and ideas. Thank you, Keith, for providing the inspiration behind this book!

I also have the monumental task of thanking every person from each of the various monasteries, abbeys, convents, and other places of retreat who took the time to correspond with me. However, since it is virtually impossible to adequately thank each of you for your efforts personally, please know that all of you remain close in my prayers. This book is dedicated to you. May God bless you a hundredfold throughout all the days of your life, and thank you for not only serving as an image of Christ for us here on earth, but also providing and gracing us travelers and pilgrims with your Christian hospitality.

I would also like to extend a special thanks to Rail Europe (www.raileurope.com), who provided me with the extensive research on train information throughout Europe for many of the monastery cities, villages, and towns listed in this book. In addition, my appreciation also goes out to Krista Miller, who performed much of the very important and necessary research found in this new edition. Krista was integral in making this guidebook an outstanding resource for travelers.

I also wish to thank all our members of the World Religious Travel Association (www.religioustravelassociation.com) who serve as the "infrastructure" and support of the global faith tourism industry. Thanks to you, people from all walks of life can travel the world on pilgrimage while experiencing faith, fun, and fellowship.

Finally, I thank my family, friends, and colleagues who support me in all my endeavors in enriching and expanding faith tourism worldwide—and that includes the writing of this guidebook.

INTRODUCTION
Europe's Monasteries & Convents: An Angel's Paradise

FOR MANY PEOPLE, the idea of staying in a monastery or convent is attractive. With their mysterious yet peaceful atmospheres, they are not only great sources of spiritual refreshment and renewal, but sacred places of transformation. History is filled with stories of people who traveled great distances just to get a taste of monastic life and experience its fruits.

Today, more than ever before, people are traveling to religious sites such as monasteries and convents. In fact, more than three hundred million people today embark on faith-based trips. In North America alone, one in four Americans are interested in taking a "spiritual vacation." With this in mind, monasteries and convents continue to open their doors across Europe and the world to travelers and pilgrims, just as they have done for centuries.

But the thought of staying overnight at a monastery or convent may be accompanied by a multitude of questions, such as: Is it really possible? Do you have to be Catholic? Can you speak with the monks and nuns? Are you expected to participate in religious services? Are the accommodations uncomfortable—or even "penitential"? How does one "make reservations"? Often, the answers to these questions are surprising.

First, it is possible to stay overnight at those particular monasteries and convents which are set up to receive guests. Second, one does not have to be Catholic in order to enjoy the fruit of spending a night at one of these places. In fact, there are no faith-related requirements, but one is expected to respect their customs and traditions since you are being "invited into their home."

Third, one of the wonderful aspects of visiting a monastery or convent is that the monks or nuns will often make themselves available to visitors and guests (at appropriate times) for discussions. Having an opportunity to converse with these men and women who have dedicated their lives to Christ can create mutually treasured and insightful moments that last a lifetime.

With regard to the question, "Are you expected to participate in all religious services?" the answer is essentially twofold. Since the purpose behind staying in a monastery or convent is often to experience the daily rhythm of their and work life, it should come as no surprise that guests are usually strongly encouraged to attend the religious services (for example, Mass, Liturgy of the Hours, and so on). However, since there are certain rituals reserved solely for the practitioners of that particular faith, participation may be dependent upon whatever activity is taking place.

As for the type of accommodations and comfort level you can expect, that depends on each individual monastery and convent. You will actually find everything from "budget-type" accommodations to even almost "deluxe." However, the general rule of thumb is that you can expect your monastic accommodations to be simple, yet clean and comfortable.

Finally, one may wonder how to go about "making a reservation" at a monastery or convent. Essentially, all one needs to do is contact them, either by letter, phone, fax, or e-mail, and express the desire to stay overnight. Even though it may take several attempts, one can usually expect a reply in a reasonable length of time, assuming, of course, that you correspond with them in a language they are able to understand. (For more information about this, please refer to the section entitled "Contacting Monasteries, Convents, and Places of Retreat").

In order to help familiarize you with some aspects of monasticism, I begin this book with a brief study of its history. Then, along with an introduction to some popular names and terms associated with monasticism, I provide you with information about how to make the best of your monastic travels. In Part 3, the core of the guidebook, I provide a listing of monasteries and convents throughout Europe, along with pertinent information about each place. The book concludes with a comprehensive collection of invaluable trip planning Web sites and resources.

When setting out to visit these holy sites, it is very important to keep in mind that these places are not to be considered "cheap hotels." Rather, they are living, breathing sanctuaries which foster the spiritual life, not only of their residents (the monks and nuns) but of their guests as well.

Since many people will use this book to embark on spiritual pilgrimages of their own, I have intentionally designed it to go hand-in-hand with other books including *Catholic Shrines of Western Europe* (www.liguori.org) and *The Christian Travel Planner* (www.christiantravelplanner.com). I encourage you to obtain copies of both of these books, especially if you are looking to make the most of your journeys through Europe.

By writing a book of this nature, I hope to accomplish three objectives: (1) Assist individuals in learning more about the wonderful and important tradition of monastic and consecrated life; (2) Provide a resource and venue for enabling travelers and pilgrims to visit these sacred places of hospitality; (3) Present monasticism and the religious life as possible vocations.

With this directory guidebook, you now have the key to unlock the door to the discovery of some of Christianity's most ancient and beloved sites. Few people ever get the opportunity to experience firsthand the daily rhythm of either the monastic or convent life. Now you can make this dream a reality!

PART 1

Everything You Wanted to Know About Christian Monasticism… But Were Afraid to Ask a Monk

HISTORY OF CHRISTIAN MONASTICISM

FOR THE PAST EIGHTEEN CENTURIES, in various forms, monasticism has existed within the Christian faith. It is a lifestyle where an individual withdraws from society in order to devote oneself entirely to God through prayer, penance, solitude, and self-denial. Throughout the history of the Church, this devotion has adopted two forms: the anchoritic style, whereby the monk lives by himself or herself as a hermit; and the cenobitic, where the monks live in community. Today, monasticism remains one of the oldest and most treasured traditions of the Church. The faith has profited enormously, both spiritually and intellectually, from this tradition.

Although monasticism can be found in other religions throughout history, the origins of Christian monasticism date back to the second half of the third century in Egypt (c. 270). Under the influence of both Clement of Alexandria and Origen, a number of Christians withdrew from society in order to dedicate themselves completely to God and the pursuit of holiness and perfection. Detaching themselves completely from all worldly possessions and relationships, they would spend their

Monasticism has existed in Christianity for the past eighteen centuries. Today, it remains one of the oldest and most treasured traditions of the faith. ©ISTOCKPHOTO.COM/DOUGLAS MCGILVIRAY

days praying, fasting, laboring, studying Scriptures, and performing penitential exercises in order to cleanse both their souls and bodies.

Among these first anchorites, the most famous is Saint Anthony of Egypt (c. 251–356). One of the first to adopt this lifestyle, he attracted a great number of followers through his personal example of living and praying. Today, he is regarded as the Father of Monasticism.

Although the anchorite life flourished in the Egyptian desert, another form of monasticism soon challenged it. This latter form of monasticism, called cenobitism, would eventually play such a major role that it would create the basis for the formal monastic orders founded in later years. This type of monasticism consisted of a group of like-minded men or women coming together to reside in a community under the authority of an abbot or abbess. Saint Pachomius (d. 346), who organized the first monastic communities in upper Egypt, was primarily responsible for the formulation of the cenobitic lifestyle.

Before long, the monastic idea quickly swept across Christian lands as many people chose to pursue this path to holiness. Saint Basil the Great also gave the monastic lifestyle a boost by contributing an extensive theological foundation to it. Furthermore, he fostered the idea that communities such as these should be concerned not only with labor but also with learning. This new way of thinking helped heighten the appeal of monasticism. In time, monasteries soon became important contributors to the intellectual life of the Church.

Although monastic life in the East thrived from earlier on, it took much longer to develop in the West. Loose organizational structures were partly to blame, as many of the monasteries in the West followed the rules of their own individual abbots, thus providing for no uniformity.

However, there was one Italian monk who helped put an end to this problem—Saint Benedict of Nursia (d. c. 480–550). As the leader of his own monastery, he wrote and instituted a very useful, yet flexible rule that captured both the guiding principles of earlier monastic customs as well as addressing the practical day-to-day needs of his monks. The excellence of his rule (Rule of Saint Benedict) was such that it spread across the West, facilitating the rise of the Benedictine Order as a major contributor to the civilization of Europe. Also, the impact of his rule was so great that Saint Benedict would earn the title "The Father of Western Monasticism."

Meanwhile, as monasticism continued to spread to other countries, Ireland soon emerged as one of the truly great centers for monastic life since the Irish monks proved to be so numerous and zealous in their approach to the faith, setting out to convert other lands, including Scotland, parts of Germany, Switzerland, and northern Gaul. In fact, many monastic missionaries, not only from Ireland but also from England and modern-day France, set out to bring the faith to Poland, Hungary, Scandinavia, and elsewhere.

During the Carolingian era, the development of the monastic culture steadily continued. Despite the opposition of Saint Benedict of Aniane (d. 821), the Benedictine houses continued to place heavy emphasis upon learning and culture, including the arts (such as manuscript illumination). Throughout the Carolingian Renaissance, many monasteries became important cultural hubs for both education and economic involvement. As a result of their significant contributions to both society and the Church, monasteries gradually acquired wealth, influence, and prestige, while their abbots received royal favors and political rights.

In 910, a much-needed reform of the monastic life began with the founding of Cluny. This event marked the beginning of what was later considered to be the peak of the development of monasticism in the West, lasting from the tenth through the thirteenth centuries. With its call to greater prayer (choir office) and unity among the houses, the Cluniac Reform quickly found widespread appeal. Since many monasteries and abbeys wished to share in the spiritual vigor of Cluny, the abbey soon found itself extending its jurisdiction over more than one thousand houses. Even the Gregorian Reform of the eleventh century, which served to correct moral abuses within the Church, drew much of its inspiration from Cluny.

During this time, monasteries continued to thrive as rich cultural places. Many monks became well-known historians, chroniclers, advisors, theologians, artisans, and architects. While many agreed that the monasteries played a very positive role within society because of their secular contributions, a significant number of monks began clamoring for a return to the religious and spiritual simplicity of earlier times. As a result, new, stricter orders were born including the Carthusians, Camaldolese, Vallambrosians, and Cistercians.

From the thirteenth century on, Western Monasticism declined, both in membership and appeal. Although there were many causes, some of the decline was due, in part, to the widespread relaxation of rules and poor leadership exhibited by the abbots. However, one major cause of the decline could also be attributed to the rise of the mendicant orders, which included the Dominicans, Franciscans, and Carmelites. Many potential monks joined these new religious orders of the Church.

Although a slight revival of the Benedictine Order took place in the late fourteenth century, it was quickly quelled with the beginning of the Protestant Reformation.

In many of the lands where the Reformation took root, monasteries were suppressed, ransacked, and looted. Monks were either expelled or executed, while cultural and intellectual treasures were stolen, burned, or destroyed. The worst destruction occurred in Scandinavia and England, where King Henry VIII (1509–1547) plundered and dissolved the communities. Martin Luther, himself an Augustinian monk, wrote against some of the abuses taking place within the monasteries.

As Western Monasticism became a quickly sinking ship, a beacon of light eventually emerged when the Catholic Church responded with the Council of Trent (1545–1563) and its own Reformation. Strong decrees of reform, centralization, and revitalization helped not only to save monasticism from obliteration, but to provide it with new energy, vitality, and direction. Among the fruits of this Reformation were the creation of two new monastic congregations: the Maurists (founded in 1621) and the Trappists (founded in 1662).

Although the monasteries would eventually experience a sense of calm, they soon had to once again endure intense struggles as the French Revolution and Napoleonic Wars (1796–1815) almost wiped them off the face of Europe. Because of their destruction, monastic houses throughout France, Switzerland, Germany, and elsewhere virtually vanished overnight.

Fortunately, in the eighteenth century, monasticism began to witness a rebirth as prominent leaders such as Dom Prosper Guéranger (Solesmes, France) oversaw the creation of new houses in France, Belgium, England, America, and Australia. In the nineteenth century, European monastic communities again began to blossom, seeking to open new communities around the world.

Today, monastic orders continue to play a vital role both in the world and the Church. They not only make a great contribution to the intellectual life of society and the Christian faith, more importantly, they continue to pray unceasingly on behalf of all humankind.

ORDER OF SAINT BENEDICT

Recognized as being one of the largest and oldest monastic orders in the Church, the Order of Saint Benedict is comprised of both men and women religious who follow the Rule of Saint Benedict. Almost fifteen centuries old, the order was formally established in the sixth century in an effort to continue the highly influential example for monastic life that was set by Saint Benedict of Nursia (c. 480–c. 550).

As Saint Benedict did not actually found an order, the early history of what is referred to as the Benedictine Order was the simple gathering together of various communities under the Benedictine Rule. Although they all operated independently and practiced autonomy, as a whole, they made a great contribution to the development of monasticism throughout Europe. One major supporter of this movement was Pope Saint Gregory I the Great (who was pope from 590–604), himself a Benedictine. In order to help the spread of monasticism and the faith, he sent missionaries to various lands. One of these missionaries was the famed Saint Augustine of Canterbury. Augustine brought the Benedictine rule to England, where it gradually replaced the more austere Rule of Saint Columbanus.

Before long, monasteries began appearing all over Western Europe—in France, England, Spain, Italy, and so on. However, in 817, due to their terrible disorganization, Emperor Louis decreed that some kind of uniformity be implemented, commanding that all monastic communities within the empire adopt the Benedictine Rule. While such a reform proved difficult to enforce owing to the independence practiced by the houses, most of the communities began calling themselves Benedictines.

In the ninth century, further reforms were enacted which attempted a return to greater austerity and asceticism in the monasteries. One of the chief proponents of this cause was Saint Benedict of Aniane (d. 750–821). In the following century, even further reforms took place, primarily due to the Abbey of Cluny. These reforms, particularly those set by Cluny, triggered the rise in the eleventh century of much stricter orders with more centralized monastic governments. Among these new orders were the Carthusians, Cistercians, and Camaldolese. This brought a general revival of monasticism in the West.

The Benedictines, however, remained steadfast in their opposition to institutional centralization, despite the efforts of the Fourth Lateran Council (1215) and the bull Benedictina (1336) of Pope Benedict XII. They did, however, adopt the system of congregations as a means of reform and revitalization. These national and international unions of houses brought improved organization while still permitting their retention of self-determination and identity. Among the most memorable foundations resulting from this was the Congregation of St. Maur (the Maurists), which began in 1621.

However, in subsequent years, monasticism began to witness a decline. Even though this was due to a number of different factors, much of it resulted from the devastation of the Reformation and the Renaissance period. Throughout the medieval era, however, the Benedictines played a major role in the preservation and advancement of learning in Christian Europe, working almost single-handedly to preserve a flicker of culture and civilization in the West during the Dark Ages. For centuries, they were virtually the sole guardians of learning and classical thought.

The Reformation, however, nearly caused the downfall of the Benedictines, as well as many other monastic orders. In England, not only did King Henry VIII (reigned from 1509–1547) ruthlessly suppress the monasteries, he also destroyed and looted many of them. Monasteries in Germany and Scandinavia suffered much the same fate. In the years that followed, the Benedictines again suffered a great deal due to their oppression during the time of the French Revolution and Napoleonic Wars (1796 and 1815).

Fortunately, in the nineteenth century, they witnessed a revival, thanks primarily to a young monk by the name of Dom Prosper Guéranger. Not only did he establish new monasteries throughout France (including the mother house at Solesmes), but he brought a revival of Gregorian chant to the liturgy.

During the past two centuries, the Benedictines have continued to grow throughout the world. In 1846, the first Benedictine house was founded in the United States (Latrobe, Pennsylvania). Today, there are approximately ten thousand Benedictines worldwide who are organized into a number of congregations, including the American, Cassinese, South American, and English Benedictines, as well as the Camaldolese, Sylvestrine, Subiaco, and Olivetan. The Benedictine nuns, founded in 529 by Saint Benedict's sister (Saint Scholastica), are organized into three federations: Saint Scholastica, Saint Gertrude the Great, and Saint Benedict. During the course of their history, the Benedictines have given us twenty-three popes and a number of saints.

CISTERCIAN AND TRAPPIST ORDERS

In 1098, Saint Robert of Molesmes founded the Cistercian Order. Unlike the Benedictine Order, which received its name based upon its founder, the Cistercian Order was named after its mother house at Cîteaux (in Burgundy, France). The order would retain its Benedictine roots, but institute a much more austere daily program. The order came into being, with just a small group of his fellow monks, when Saint Robert became dissatisfied with the lax attitude of his monastery.

Among the first Cistercian abbots were Saint Robert, Saint Alberic, and the famed Saint Stephen Harding. The latter abbot, who served from 1109–1133, is often called the second founder of the Cistercians. In 1119, Harding wrote the constitution of the order, which was subsequently approved by Pope Callistus II. The constitution, called the Charter of Love, called for manual labor, a simplified liturgy, and strict asceticism.

In 1112, during Harding's tenure as abbot, Saint Bernard of Clairvaux, one of the Church's greatest figures, arrived at his doorstep. With his fame and brilliance, he helped to spread the popularity of the order across the continent of Europe.

Cistercian monks adhere to a rigorous life of work and prayer. Although each house could exercise control over its own affairs, it was their duty to strictly adhere to the regulations that were passed by the annual general chapter. This allowed the monks to maintain discipline and introduce new or needed reforms and innovations.

During the 1100s and 1200s, the Cistercians enjoyed widespread prominence, exerting a profound influence on the monasticism of the time. Commonly referred to as the White Monks, they possessed more than five hundred abbeys at the beginning of the thirteenth century, including the famed house of Rievaulx. Unfortunately, the order eventually lost its stature and, like other monastic orders, suffered greatly from the tribulations of the late Middle Ages, Renaissance, and Reformation.

In the 1600s, a reform movement began that called for the return to a more precise adherence to the rule. Known as the Strict Observance, it found support in many of the French houses. This subsequently led, in France, to a division between those practicing the Strict Observance and the others practicing the Common Observance.

During the late seventeenth and early eighteenth centuries, the Cistercians of the Common Observance suffered terribly because of the French Revolution. Fortunately, they did recover and managed to remain intact. With respect to the Cistercians of the Strict Observance, their rallying point centered around the monastery of La Trappe in France during the Revolution. Although the members of La Trappe were expelled at that time, they returned in 1817. With Augustine Lestrange as their new abbot, they revitalized their austere rule and helped to reestablish it in many of their monasteries which had been closed because of the

Revolution. As the order began to spread throughout both the country and the world, their members became known as the Trappists, a name that is still popularly used for those of the Strict Observance.

In 1898, the year that Cîteaux was returned to the order, its community chose to join the Strict Observance. Today, the abbot of Cîteaux serves as the general for the Cistercians of the Strict Observance, which still remain a separate body from the Order of Cistercians. Currently, there are more than twenty-five hundred Trappist monks in the world, and approximately fifteen hundred Cistercians (including Cistercian nuns of both the Strict and Common observance). Trappists are distinguished by their white habits and black scapulars.

CARTHUSIAN ORDER

Founded in 1084 by Saint Bruno, the Carthusians are a contemplative order of monks who adhere to a strict regimen of prayer, self-denial, and solitude. Similar to the Cistercians, the Carthusians took their name from the place of their origin, the La Grande Chartreuse, a valley near Grenoble, France.

Since Saint Bruno never compiled a formal rule for the order during the early years, members were instructed to adhere, in spirit and custom, to the example of the founder. However, over time, this proved to be rather difficult. In 1127, Guigues du Chastel (the fifth prior of La Grande Chartreuse) laid down the first rule. Five years after Guigues wrote the rule, Pope Innocent II approved it. In 1245, the first Carthusian Order of nuns was started.

In 1258, the order issued a new edition of the rule entitled Statuta Antiqua, and in 1368, they promulgated another called the Statuta Nova. Subsequently, almost one hundred and fifty years later, the order delivered a collection of the various ordinances and a synopsis of the statutes under the title, *Tertia Compilatio*. The following year, Johann Amorback printed the rule for the first time, and in 1581, the *Nova Collectio Statutorum* was published.

Since the time of its foundation, the Carthusian Order has remained one of the strictest and most contemplative orders in the entire Church. Following Saint Bruno's regulations, monks would devote their entire day to silence, prayer, and isolation. With the exception of coming together at morning Mass, vespers, and for the evening office, they would spend the rest of their time laboring, praying, and eating alone. On certain feast days, however, they would come together to share their meals.

Owing to their almost total removal from society, the Carthusians did not share the unhappy fate that other religious orders experienced during the upheavals of the Middle Ages. Most escaped persecution, but certain members did suffer execution under King Henry VIII in England. The French Revolution was even less kind to the order. As anticlerical legislation swept through France during the 1800s and early 1900s, the Carthusians experienced many misfortunes. In places such as Spain and Italy however, they remained a popular favorite. Today, they can be found throughout the world.

According to a story told by the Carthusians, there was once a pope who felt their Rule was too severe, so he asked the monks to modify it. In response, the Carthusians sent a delegation of twenty-seven monks to Rome to plead their case. When the group arrived at the Vatican, the pontiff found that the youngest member of the group was eighty-eight years old, and the oldest ninety-five. As a result, the Holy Father left the Rule intact.

To this day, the Carthusian Order is considered by the Church to be the most perfect model of a penitential and contemplative state.

CAMALDOLESE ORDER

Founded in Italy in 1012 by Saint Romuald, the Camaldolese Order is the fruit of one of the strictest monastic reforms of the tenth century. The Congregation of the Monk Hermits of Camaldoli promotes a very austere form of common life with strict hermetical asceticism. While newer members reside in a stern monastic setting, the more advanced live in the associated hermitage.

Since Saint Romuald never instituted a written rule, in the early years there existed several different variations of the Camaldolese life. For example, some monasteries lived more as a community, while others more as hermits. In 1523, this lead to the founding of a reform group called the Congregation of Monte Corona.

Since its beginning, the Camaldolese Order has been revolutionary in its ability to successfully combine aspects of the hermitic life of Eastern monks with the community life of Western Monasticism. Even though the monks live and pray alone, they join each other for community prayers. Their daily diets are quite severe: They never eat meat; they abstain from everything except bread and water on Fridays. During Lent, products such as milk, cheese, eggs, and butter are forbidden. Each monk has his own room, workshop, and garden, where he labors alone, yet he still maintains a connection with the other monks for the upkeep of the community.

ORDER OF CLUNY

The monastic foundation of the Order of Cluny cannot be omitted if we want to fully understand the history of Christian monasticism. It is here at Cluny, which is located in south-central France, that one of the largest reforms of Western Monasticism took place.

First established in 910 by William the Pious, the Cluny Abbey immediately set out to revive the Benedictine Rule. Their first abbot, Berno of Baume (910–927), brought the lives of the monks into greater balance by reducing manual labor and placing a greater emphasis on prayer and worship, especially the choir office.

As the fame and influence of the monastery grew, Cluny's second abbot, Saint Odo, helped extend the authority of the abbey to other houses while seeking to also change their discipline and organization. In the years that followed, the abbey continued to be blessed with a succession of remarkable leaders, since more monasteries throughout France and Italy requested to be placed under their jurisdiction. This dependence not only helped reform many of the monasteries, but it also revitalized them. In fact, Cluny was so successful that it quickly received papal approval to reach out into Spain, Germany, and England. Many members of the order also earned widespread attention for their expertise in religion and other academic matters, serving as advisors and theologians to kings and popes. As one voice, Cluny spoke out against the evils of the time: lay investiture, simony, and clerical lack of self-restraint.

Although Cluny enjoyed unmitigated success for almost three centuries, by the twelfth century, much of its prestige and influence began to wane. This was due, in large part, to the changing social and political climate, but also to the new reforms launched in the Church elsewhere, especially those of the Cistercians. The fact remains, however, that they had a great impact on monasticism, as well as on all of Western Christendom. At the height of its glory, Cluny boasted more than a thousand houses, contributing four popes to the Church.

HISTORY OF MENDICANT ORDERS

A history lesson about Christian monasticism would not be complete without mentioning the mendicant orders. Who are they? Surprisingly, they include the very priests, brothers, nuns, and sisters which most of us have probably met in our daily lives, including the Franciscans, Dominicans, Carmelites, and Augustinians. Mendicant is a name given to those religious orders who require their members to take a vow of poverty and to place their trust in God's divine Providence.

Begun in the twelfth century, these orders came about in an effort to combat the widespread vice and materialism of the time, both in the Church and in society in general. Individuals who adopted this lifestyle strove to respond to the Church's call for poverty, chastity, obedience, charity, and trust in divine Providence. Among the most prominent figures of the mendicant movement were Saint Francis of Assisi (1181–1226), who founded the Franciscans, and Saint Dominic (1170–1221), who established the Dominicans. Before long, the Carmelites and the Augustinians also joined these two orders by living their evangelical lifestyle.

Although the mendicants initially were the targets of a great deal of opposition from many priests and prelates, their orders quickly grew in popularity among the faithful, especially the poor. After learning of their cause, the papacy warmly embraced them, offering enthusiastic support. As well as bringing about considerable reform in the thirteenth century, these mendicant orders produced some of the most outstanding figures in history: Saint Thomas Aquinas, Saint Bonaventure, Saint Teresa of Ávila, Saint John of the Cross, Saint Francis of Assisi, and Saint Dominic.

AUGUSTINIAN CANONS AND HERMITS

One of the most prominent mendicant orders in the medieval Church was that of the Augustinian Friars. Officially referred to as the Order of the Hermit Friars of Saint Augustine, the order was created from the isolated communities of hermits who strictly adhered to the Rule of Saint Augustine.

In 1256, Pope Alexander IV brought them together, not just for the purpose of organization, but to entrust them with the task of becoming active preachers and religious in society, and to follow a more Dominican lifestyle. As a single unit, the order eventually spread throughout Western Europe, evangelizing and preaching. During this time, other less austere congregations joined them.

Martin Luther, himself an Augustinian monk, belonged to the German Reformed Congregation. Although the Hermits were almost completely crushed by the Reformation, they survived intact. Today they can be found throughout the world. (The more severe Augustinian Recollects were founded in 1588).

There was also another group which belonged to the Augustinian mendicant order called the Canons. Distinct from the Hermits, they were commonly referred to as the "Black Friars," "Black Canons," or

"Regular Canons." They were among the first in the Church to adhere to a common life, yet still follow the Rule of Saint Augustine with its call for poverty, celibacy, obedience, and a strict monastic life. It is believed that the Black Friars originated from communities of diocesan priests in Italy and France, sometime around the twelfth century.

Although they received sanctions at the Lateran Councils of 1059 and 1063, they subsequently became very popular. By the 1100s, most canons of the Church belonged to the Augustinians, but their prestige began to wane as they found it difficult to reconcile their Rule with the turbulent times of the 1400s and 1500s. Unfortunately, many of their houses were suppressed during the Reformation. In time, however, they recovered. To this day, some of these congregations continue to exist, including the Premonstratensian Canons and Victorines.

CARMELITES

Although most commonly referred to as the Carmelites, this mendicant order's full title is the Order of Our Lady of Mt. Carmel. Founded by Saint Berthold in 1154, it is known to be one of the more contemplative mendicant orders. According to tradition, Saint Berthold first established the community in Palestine on Mt. Carmel in the year 1154. Former crusaders, hermits, and pilgrims were said to have made up the group.

In 1209, the Latin patriarch of Jerusalem laid down the first rule for the community. All members were to adhere to a strict regimen of self-mortification, abstinence, and poverty. By the thirteenth century, many of the Carmelites were forced to leave the area because of the downfall of the Crusader States in the Holy Land. In 1247, a majority of them regrouped in England under the influential leadership of Saint Simon Stock. (However, in 1291, all of the Carmelites who had remained in Palestine eventually became martyrs.)

With the election of Saint Simon as prior general of the order, at the first chapter at Aylesford, Kent, the Carmelites experienced a new wave of vitality and growth. Simon played a very instrumental role in the increase in popularity of the order throughout Europe. He modified the rule to fit life in the West, designed the brown scapular (after a vision of the Blessed Virgin), and encouraged his community members to enter the university. Under his leadership, the Carmelites became a mendicant order, which enabled them to spread more quickly throughout all of Christendom. In 1452, the Carmelite nuns, who lived a cloistered life, joined the friars by following the same rule.

By the 1500s, the Carmelite nuns and friars were both in need of a general reform, since many of the communities had become too relaxed in their rules and lifestyles. Hence, two prominent figures, Saint Teresa of Ávila (1515–1582) and Saint John of the Cross (1542–1591) initiated reform efforts. Teresa set out to restore the Primitive Rule to the Carmelite cloisters, while still promoting the contemplative life. John of the Cross attempted to accomplish similar reforms within the communities of friars.

However, they were met with strong opposition by those members who preferred to keep the less severe Mitigated Rule. In 1593, their resistance led to the division of the Carmelites into two congregations, the Discalced Carmelites (those who would adhere to the Primitive Rule) and the Calced Carmelites (those who would follow the Mitigated Rule).

As part of their charism, the Carmelites focus most of their effort and activities on prayer, theology, and missionary work. They possess a special love for the Virgin Mary, are dedicated to praying for priests, and wear a brown habit. Recently, they have come back into the spotlight because one of their members, Saint Thérèse of Lisieux, was named a doctor of the Church. Today, throughout the world, many laypeople belong to the third order of the Carmelites.

DOMINICANS

Correctly referred to as the Order of the Friars Preachers (Ordo Praedicatorum, or O.P.), this mendicant order is more commonly known to us as the Dominicans. Founded in 1216 by Saint Dominic, they were originally established to convert the Albigensian heretics of southern France.

Drawn from all walks of life, the early members of the group traveled throughout the countryside preaching and evangelizing, especially to the Albigensians. In 1215, Dominic received the group's first endorsement from the local bishop, and one year later, received the pope's formal approval and blessing.

In 1217, the order adopted the Augustinian Rule along with some other monastic guidelines. In the years that followed, many of the friars were sent throughout France, Italy, and Spain to preach, attract new candidates, and found new houses. In 1220 and 1221, the Dominicans held two general chapters during which they continued to work out further details about the order's government. During these meetings, they voted to place special emphasis on corporate and individual poverty.

The Dominicans were very innovative in their approach to the contemplative and active life: they accepted many of the principles of monastic life as well as those of the regular clergy. Although they maintained a strong adherence to daily prayer and liturgy, they did not isolate themselves from the world, as they would preach to the people daily. This bold new philosophy helped advance the initiatives of the mendicant orders.

Since they did not reside in monasteries, nor spend much of their time doing manual labor, they were often found to be present in or around universities since they placed much importance on the development of the intellect. In time, they became known for their academic work and were the recipients of high positions within universities. With their keen intellect and strong fidelity to orthodoxy, the Dominican theologians earned the title Domini Canes (Watchdogs of the Lord).

As the Dominicans grew in their membership, so did the number of their houses. By the end of the thirteenth century, they had not only expanded to include more than thirteen thousand friars, but could also be found throughout Europe. In that century alone, the Dominicans also produced two of the greatest intellectual giants in the history of the Church: Saint Thomas Aquinas and Saint Albertus Magnus. The Dominicans not only contributed enormously to the intellectual life of the Church, but also to its overall spiritual well being. Like the Franciscan Order, they sent missionaries to Africa, the Middle East, northern Europe, and the Far East.

Unfortunately, after such a glorious century, the Dominicans experienced a period of decline. Since much of this was due to its rule of poverty, it was further complicated, in 1303, by Pope Boniface VIII's command for them to restrict some of their privileges. However, the order received a boost, in 1475, when Pope Sixtus IV rescinded the order's law regarding corporate poverty.

With a new spark and general renewal about discipline and studies, the Dominican Order again began to grow as they opened new houses in Spain and Rome. By doing this, they were able to accelerate the implementation of Saint Thomas Aquinas' teachings under their own gifted Dominican theologians.

Unfortunately, like most of the other religious orders, they suffered major setbacks during the Reformation and the French Revolution. However, unlike other orders, they received the brunt of it. They were singled out, both because of their traditional excellence in learning, as well as their fierce loyalty to the Holy See. In the nineteenth century, they began to recoup under the leadership of Jean Baptiste Henri Lacordaire.

Today, the Dominican friars number some sixty-five hundred members around the globe. Dominican nuns, founded in 1206 by Saint Dominic, are also found throughout the world today. They are involved in many different apostolic activities, including perpetual adoration, education, hospital work, and the perpetual rosary. Dominicans are most easily recognized by their white habits, which feature a large rosary that hangs from their leather belts. Their habits also include a scapular, white mantle, black cowl, and a black cape.

FRANCISCAN ORDER

Easily the most recognizable of the mendicant orders (both in name and appearance), the Franciscan Order was founded by the renowned Saint Francis of Assisi. Although he never originally set out to establish a new religious community, he attracted a number of followers to his way of life simply by his personal example and holiness.

The origins of the Franciscans date back to 1208, the year when its first members joined Saint Francis in his life of poverty, chastity, and prayer. In the following year, when their number grew to twelve, Francis was inspired to travel to Rome to ask Pope Innocent III (who reigned from 1198–1216) for his approval. The pope consented, and each of the brothers subsequently took vows of poverty, chastity, and obedience. April 16, 1209, marked the official beginning of the Order of Friars Minor.

With a very strong dedication to poverty, the early Franciscans would travel throughout the region preaching and evangelizing. Before long, a number of women, led by Saint Clare of Assisi, expressed the desire to imitate Francis and his followers. Hence, in 1212, a women's order named the Poor Ladies (later to be called the Poor Clares or the Second Order of Saint Francis) was established. Almost ten years later, a group of laypeople wanting to imitate the principles of the Franciscans adopted their own rule. Saint Francis actually wrote the rule himself, but it was then rewritten by Cardinal Ugolino, and eventually approved by Pope Honorius III. These laypeople are commonly referred to as the Third Order of Franciscans.

As the order continued to expand at a rapid rate, further clarification and explanation of the rule was needed. While the "long rule" containing twenty-three chapters was issued in 1221, the pope accepted a shortened version (twelve chapters) in 1223. The rule mandated both corporate and individual poverty, as well as both an active and contemplative life (a rather revolutionary idea for the time).

Since the Church had always strongly encouraged foreign missionary work, Francis made certain that the rule included this aspect of evangelization. It was the first such declaration for any religious order. Serving as an example for others, Francis set out on several missionary trips. Within a few short centuries, the Franciscans found themselves in such diverse and distant places as China and Africa. During the sixteenth century, the Franciscans would play a major role in the evangelization of the New World.

With the continuing rapid expansion of the order, the Franciscans soon experienced growing pains. Members differed in their opinions about whether the original rule was too severe and impractical. This would become the central crisis facing the order: it was even present before Francis' death in 1226. One of the two differing groups of Friars called themselves the Spirituals; they wanted a precise adherence to the letter of the rule (and the spirit of their saintly founder), but the majority of friars favored a more moderate interpretation. Neither side would temper their position.

In 1310, under the leadership of Saint Bonaventure, who had been superior general of the order from 1257–1274, the Franciscans brought the matter before the Holy See. After many years of discussion and prayer, Pope John XXII decided against the Spirituals. Subsequent to this decision, in 1322, he reversed the rule concerning corporate poverty. Not happy with the decision, many Spirituals left to establish the schismatic body known as the Fraticelli. Within the order, the elimination of the law against personal ownership caused some problems because some members began accumulating wealth, becoming lukewarm in their practice of the rule.

As more reforms were introduced, the internal divisions increased. Eventually, a split occurred among the Franciscans. This was formally recognized in 1415 and accepted by the Council of Constance. The two new groups consisted of the Observants, those who preferred the rules of poverty, and the Conventuals, those who wanted the pope's decision to stay as it was. In 1517, the two groups became permanently separated. The Observants became officially known as the Order of Friars Minor of the Regular Observance, while the Conventuals became known as the Order of Friars Minor Conventual.

In the years that followed, the Observants gave birth to new Franciscan groups including the Capuchins, the Discalced, the Reformati, and the Recollects. The Friars Minor (Observants) continued to thrive during the 1500s, but the French Revolution and Napoleonic

Wars provided them with great challenges, as well as destruction. Today, with more than eighteen thousand members, they rank as the second largest religious order in the Church. The Capuchins are listed as the fourth largest, with more than eleven thousand members, while the Conventuals number around four thousand members.

Throughout the centuries, the Franciscans and Poor Clares have produced some of the Church's greatest and most famous saints, notably Saint Francis of Assisi, Saint Clare of Assisi, Saint Bonaventure, Saint Anthony of Padua, Saint Bernardine of Siena, Saint Joseph Cupertino, Pope Sixtus IV, Pope Sixtus V, Pope Clement XIV, and countless others.

PREMONSTRATENSIAN CANONS

Commonly known in the United States as the Norbertines (and as the White Canons in England), the Premonstratensian Canons were founded in 1120, by Saint Norbert, in Prémontré, France. Combining both a contemplative and active life, the Canons were among the first orders in the history of the Church to successfully carry out both charisms. Hence, it was their order which helped foster the beginning of the mendicant orders in the centuries that followed.

Although Saint Norbert initially adopted the Rule of Saint Augustine, he later adopted many of the Cistercian ways of life, including the practice of rigorous asceticism. One of the major influences on his life was the renowned Saint Bernard of Clairvaux, a personal friend, who served as a Cistercian abbot.

In 1125, Pope Honorius II formally approved the Order of the Premonstratensian Canons. Quickly, it began to spread throughout all of Western Europe. After a short while, the Canons found themselves embarking on missionary campaigns to Eastern Europe, where they gained considerable influence, especially in Hungary.

As time wore on, a number of reforms took place in the order as many of the rules were enforced and practiced to a lesser degree. In fact, several independent congregations arose because of conflicting viewpoints about how the order should be run. Like other orders, the Canons had to pay a heavy price during the French Revolution, watching helplessly as their order almost ceased to exist in the years following the Napoleonic Wars (1796–1815). Fortunately, in the past century, the order has once again begun to blossom, due mainly to a major revival in Belgium.

PART 2

Standing On Holy Ground

A "WHO'S WHO" IN MONASTICISM

SAINT ANTHONY OF EGYPT (c. 251–356)

Born around 251, today Saint Anthony of Egypt is recognized as the founder of Christian monasticism. In 269, after giving up all his possessions, he withdrew from society in order to pursue a life of severe asceticism and solitude. Surviving on only bread and water, Anthony spent the next fifteen years praying and meditating while living in a cemetery tomb near his native village. Around 285, he moved to a mountaintop, seeking to gain even greater seclusion and isolation. As word spread about Saint Anthony, more and more people became interested in imitating the hermit's austere lifestyle. Due to his popularity, he left his hermitage in 305 to organize a community of ascetics under a unified rule. Six years later, Anthony left the area to travel to Alexandria where he labored on behalf of the Church, providing moral support to Christian believers who were suffering persecution at the hands of the Roman government. Later, after returning to the desert, he settled on Mount Kolzim (near the Red Sea) with his disciple Macarius, where he remained until around 355, when he left to assist Saint Athanasius in defending the Church against the heresy of Arianism. Once this job was finished, he returned one last time to Mount Kozim, where he remained until the end of his life, providing advice and counsel to his numerous followers. Saint Anthony died in 356, and his feast day is celebrated today throughout the Church on January 17.

SAINT ATHANASIUS (920–1003)

A Byzantine monk, Saint Athanasius is best known for being the founder of the renowned monastic site of Mount Athos. Originally from the Greek Empire of Trebizond, Saint Athanasius founded the monastery of Laura on Mount Athos in 961. It was the first settlement of anchorites on the mountain. Although the hermits who already lived there fiercely opposed him, Athanasius quickly gathered the support of Emperors Nicephorus II Phokas and John I Tzimiskes. Around 972, the emperors named Athanasius the abbot general of Mount Athos, thus putting him in charge of almost sixty monasteries. Today, he is revered as a major figure in Byzantine monasticism. (He is also commonly referred to as *Athanasius the Athonite*.) His feast day is July 5.

SAINT BASIL THE GREAT (c. 329–379)

Recognized as one of the greatest doctors of the Church, Saint Basil the Great is honored as one of the eminent Cappadocian Fathers (along with his brother Saint Gregory of Nyssa). After obtaining an excellent education at Caesarea during his youth, Basil underwent a spiritual conversion in 357, as he embarked on a journey to the monasteries of Egypt, Palestine, and Mesopotamia. Upon his return, he established a monastic community near Annesi. His innovations, and specifically his Rule, later earned him the title "Father of Eastern (or Oriental) Monasticism." In 360, he left his hermitage to take part in the general church council at Constantinople. In the years that followed, he fought unceasingly against the heresies of the day, especially Arianism. On January 1, 379, the great Saint Basil died. Because he was so beloved, his funeral was attended by not only many Christians, but also by Jews and non-Christians alike. Today, the Rule of Saint Basil is still followed by the members of the religious life of the Orthodox Churches. Basil is ranked as one of the greatest saints in the Church because of his spiritual achievements and extensive contributions to Christianity during the fourth century. His feast day is January 2.

SAINT BENEDICT OF ANIANE (c. 750–821)

Saint Benedict of Aniane is recognized as being one of the leading monastic reformers in France. Serving under both Pepin II the Short and later his son Charlemagne, he became a monk in 773 at Saint-Seine. In 779, he established his own monastery at Aniane hoping to reform French monasticism. In 817, the Synod of Aachen granted official approval to his systematization of the Benedictine Rule under the title, *Capitulare Monasticum.* In later years, he introduced reforms for all monasteries, which subsequently became official policy. His feast day is February 11.

SAINT BENEDICT OF NURSIA (c. 480–c. 550)

Saint Benedict of Nursia, the founder of the monastery of Monte Cassino, is recognized as the Father of Western Monasticism. Born in Nursia and educated at Rome, Saint Benedict left society around 500 in order to pursue a strict ascetic life and to escape the wickedness and immortality of the world of the day. Settling inside a cave at Subiaco, it was not long before he attracted a number of followers from the surrounding area, who sought to imitate his lifestyle. However, because of local problems, Benedict and a few of his brethren left Subiaco in 525 for Monte Cassino. After founding a new monastery there, he devoted his efforts to reforming monastic institutions throughout Christendom, as well as composing his famous Rule. Although Benedict never intended to found a religious order, his holy life and the example he set led to the founding of the Benedictines. His influence was far-reaching, as his Rule has had a major impact on both Christianity and Western Monasticism. Saint Benedict died around 550 and was buried in Monte Cassino in the same grave as his sister, Saint Scholastica. His feast day is July 11.

SAINT BERNARD OF CLAIRVAUX (1090–1153)

Saint Bernard of Clairvaux is considered to be one of the greatest monastic figures in the medieval Church. Born in France to a noble family, he entered the monastery of Cîteaux at the age of twenty-three and immediately began living a very rigorous and austere life. At Cîteaux, Bernard came under the teaching of the exceptional abbot (later saint), Stephen Harding, who asked him in 1115 to select a site for a new monastery. After choosing Clairvaux, Pope Callistus II granted its charter, and within a short time, the new monastery gained widespread attention since it had become the center of the Cistercian Order. Saint Bernard quickly earned the respect of many throughout Christendom as a brilliant abbot and mystic. In the years that followed, he preached ceaselessly against the heresies of his day and gathered support for the Second Crusade. Canonized in 1174, Pope Pius VIII named him a doctor of the Church in 1830. His feast day is August 20.

SAINT BRUNO (c. 1030–1101)

Saint Bruno, along with Saint Robert of Molesmes, was the founder of the Carthusian Order. Born of wealthy parents in Cologne, Germany, Saint Bruno studied at the renowned Cathedral School of Rheims. A brilliant scholar, he served as director of studies at the school for eighteen years and was later appointed chancellor of his diocese. In the years that followed, Bruno faced many trials because of his challenges against the corrupt archbishop. Bruno finally returned to Reims, but despite his popularity and the expressed wishes of the public that he be named archbishop, he set out with Saint Robert of Molesmes to found a monastic community near Grenoble. Only six years after settling at Chartreuse, Bruno left for Rome, responding to the orders of one of his former students, Pope Urban II. Since the pope needed his counsel, he was not allowed to return to Chartreuse, but was permitted to settle as a hermit at La Torre, Italy near Rome. As a result, La Torre became the second Charterhouse (house of Chartreuse). Saint Bruno remained there until his death in 1101. His feast day is October 6.

SAINT JOHN CASSIAN (365–435)

Saint John Cassian, a monk and ascetic writer, is usually recognized as the first monk to introduce the Eastern style of monasticism into the West. Although he spent his early days living in Bethlehem, John departed for Egypt, where he received eremitical instruction from the Egyptian ascetics in the desert. In 399, he left for Constantinople, where he studied under the patronage of Saint John Chrysostom. Following his ordination in 405, Saint John Cassian founded the monastery of Saint Victor (at Marseilles, France) and served as its abbot for the remainder of his life. While at Saint Victor (c. 420–429), he wrote two very important works: *Institutes* and *Conferences*. *Institutes* (full title: *Institutes of the Monastic Life*) presented the basic rules for the monastic life and was an important source for Saint Benedict in the creation of his own rule; *Conferences* (full title: *Conferences of the Egyptian Monks or Collations of the Fathers*) presented conversations of the foremost figures of Eastern Monasticism, the Fathers of the Desert. Although never canonized a saint in the West, today he is still venerated as a saint in the Eastern Church. His feast day is celebrated in southern France on July 23.

SAINT COLUMBANUS (c. 543–615)

Saint Columbanus, also known as Saint Columban, is best known for his promotion of monasticism throughout much of Western Europe. Born and educated in Ireland, he left his country around 590 to establish new monasteries on the European continent. Upon reaching Gaul (France), he founded his first two monasteries in the mountains of Vosges. Despite facing many trials and tribulations along the way, he persevered in his quest. Eventually, he was forced to escape to Italy where he founded the monastery of Bobbio (c. 612). By the end of his life, not only had he helped spread monasticism throughout the continent, but he had also instituted a rule for all monasteries to follow. Even though the rule became known for its rigid authority and austerity, it spread quickly throughout France, Germany, and elsewhere in Europe, until it was eventually replaced by the less severe Rule of Saint Benedict. His feast day is November 23.

DOM PROSPER GUÉRANGER (1805–1875)

Dom Prosper Guéranger was a French Benedictine monk who played an extremely important role in reestablishing the Benedictine Order in France, as well as bringing Gregorian chant back to the Church. Ordained in 1827, he purchased the priory of Solesmes in 1833, and worked unceasingly over the next few years to reopen it as a formal Benedictine monastery. In 1837, Pope Gregory XVI named him the first abbot of Solesmes. As abbot, he became a prominent clergyman in France, working in all of the French dioceses to have the many local variations of the rite replaced by the Roman rite. Among his most famous writings were those about liturgical matters, which included *Liturgical Institutions* (3 vols., 1840–1851) and *The Liturgical Year* (9 vols., 1841–1866).

SAINT MACARIUS (c. a. 300– c. a. 390)

Saint Macarius the Egyptian, also known as Saint Macarius the Great, is credited with being one of the most important Desert Fathers who helped foster monasticism in Christianity. Born in upper Egypt, he retired, at the age of thirty, to the desert of Scete, seeking a life of solitude. As Macarius's reputation for sanctity, wisdom, and miraculous powers grew, so did the number of his followers. Before long, a colony of hermits was established at the site. It later became a renowned place for monastic pilgrimages. Ordained a priest around 340, Saint Macarius was regarded by writers of his era as being particularly gifted in spiritual leadership and guidance. A strong supporter of Saint Athanasius and a very outspoken leader against the heresy of Arianism, Saint Macarius was banished to an island in the Nile in 374. In his later years, he returned to the desert where he spent his final days. His feast day is January 15.

SAINT MARTIN OF TOURS (c. 316–397)

Declared a patron saint of France, Saint Martin of Tours is recognized as being one of the major figures in the evolution and expansion of Western Monasticism. The son of a pagan soldier, he was coerced into entering the Roman imperial army at a rather young age. However, after sharing his cloak with a beggar, he was struck with a vision where Christ told him to abandon the military and pursue the spiritual life. Following his request, Saint Martin left the army and, in 360, founded the first monastery in Gaul. Eleven years later, Hilary of Poitiers consecrated him bishop of Tours. Saint Martin never ceased to promote the spread of monasticism, and in time, became known for the numerous conversions that took place within his territory. Revered as a miracle worker during his lifetime, he was one of the earliest non-martyrs to be venerated by the Church. His feast day is November 11.

SAINT ODO OF CLUNY (879–942)

Serving as the second abbot of Cluny, Saint Odo played a major role in the promotion and expansion of the Cluniac monastic reform. Born in Tours, he entered the monastery in 909 as a result of the influence of Saint Berno. Twenty years later, he became the abbot of Cluny and eventually played a major role in the reformation of monasteries throughout France, Italy, and the remainder of Christendom. Pope John XI respected Saint Odo greatly and entrusted further responsibilities of monastic reform to him. His feast day is November 18.

SAINT PACHOMIUS (c. a. 290–c. a. 347)

An Egyptian saint, Saint Pachomius is recognized as the founder of Christian cenobitic (or communal) monasticism. Born near Thebes, Egypt, he converted to Christianity in 313 after serving in the Roman legion. Withdrawing into the desert to seek seclusion, Saint Pachomius served as a disciple under the famed hermit, Palemon. A short while later, he founded a community of monks and created a rule for them that called for a balanced life consisting of prayer and work: it was the first such rule in the history of monasticism. Since the rule proved to be so extraordinary and adaptable, Pachomius was able to institute it in all of the ten monasteries he founded, which included both men and women. In the centuries that followed, his rules and teachings exerted great influence on monastic giants such as Saint Basil, Saint Benedict, and Saint John Cassian. Saint Pachomius is venerated by both the Eastern and Western Churches, as well as the Coptic Church. His feast day is May 14.

SAINT PAUL THE HERMIT (d. c. 347)

Saint Paul the Hermit, also known as Paul of Thebes, is traditionally accepted as the first Christian hermit. According to early sources, Saint Paul is said to have escaped to the desert during the Decian persecutions of 249–251. There he spent the remainder of his life in a cave, passing his days in prayer and penance. The famed Saint Anthony of Egypt visited him on one occasion, seeking instruction about humility. After Paul's death, Anthony buried him in the cloak that had been provided by the great Saint Athanasius. According to legend, two lions were said to have helped dig his grave. His feast day is January 15.

SAINT ROBERT OF MOLESMES (1027–1110)

Saint Robert of Molesmes is honored as one of the founders of the Cistercian Order. Born of noble parents in northeastern France, he entered the Benedictine Order at the age of fifteen. Named an abbot at a very young age, Saint Robert left for Molesmes in 1075, to help a group of hermits institute the Benedictine Rule. Although the new monastery initially prospered, the hermits soon lost their pious spirit. Saint Robert subsequently left to begin a new hermitage in a nearby forest. When the bishop learned of this, he ordered Robert to return to Molesmes. However, as his efforts for reform again failed, Robert was granted permission, in 1098, to leave the monastery and retire to the forest of Cîteaux. Here, accompanied by six of his monks, he laid the foundations of Cistercian life. However, one year later, responding to the request of the Molesmes monks and a papal legate order, Saint Robert returned to Molesmes. This time, his prayers and leadership succeeded in restoring a true religious spirit to the house. He remained at Molesmes for the remainder of his life. His feast day is April 29.

SAINT ROMUALD (c. 952–1027)

Saint Romuald, the founder of the Camaldolese Order, is best known for instituting one of the strictest monastic reforms in the tenth century. Elected superior of his abbey in 996, Saint Romuald immediately sought to reform the undisciplined life of his monks. After three years, meeting with little success, he left to live in various monasteries and preach the spirit of penance and prayer. Eventually, he assembled a few men who were willing to live the monastic rule of Saint Benedict according to its original requirements. As a gesture of gratitude for land that was donated by the Count Maldolus to build a monastery, Romuald named his new order Camaldolese. The premise of the new order was to blend the eremitic life of eastern monks with the community life of Western Monasticism. Much of the monks' time would be spent in solitude, except when they would join the others for community prayers. Saint Romuald, the founder and abbot, died in his monastery at Val Castro, Italy, in 1027. His feast day is June 19.

SAINT SCHOLASTICA (c. a. 480—c. a. 543)

Saint Scholastica is the natural sister of the famed Saint Benedict of Nursia. Although little is known about her life, she is said to have consecrated herself to God at an early age, moving into a hermitage near her brother at Monte Cassino. According to early records, Saint Scholastica and Saint Benedict would meet once a year at a house close to Monte Cassino to discuss various aspects of their spiritual lives. Three days after their last meeting, she died. Four years after his sister's death, Saint Benedict died and was laid to rest in the same grave. Her feast day is February 10.

SAINT STEPHEN HARDING (d. 1134)

Saint Stephen Harding is considered to be one of the most important English monastic reformers and is often called the "second founder" of the Cistercians. Born in England, he left his country to study in Paris and Rome. After joining the monastery of Molesmes, he was sent to become a monk at Cîteaux. Elected abbot in 1109, Stephen insisted that the community continue its strict observance of the rule, despite its declining numbers. In 1112, when all seemed hopeless, Saint Bernard of Clairvaux arrived at Cîteaux with thirty monks. This led to a new spirit within the monastery, as the abbey again began to prosper. As a result of an increasing number of monks, new monasteries had to be established. By the time of Saint Stephen's death in 1134, thirteen new houses had been founded under Cîteaux. In 1119, Pope Callistus II approved the *Charter of Love* (the order's constitution), which stipulated the rules covering the government of the monasteries tied to Cîteaux. His feast day is April 17.

LEARNING MONASTIC LINGO

Abbess   If you know what an abbot is, then you know what an abbess is. An abbess is the female spiritual and temporal leader (or superior) of a community of nuns. *Interesting fact:* To have an abbess, a community must have twelve or more nuns.

Abbey   A religious house comprised of monks or nuns, presided over by an abbot or abbess. *Interesting fact:* To be an abbey, a community must have no fewer than twelve religious.

Abbot   This is the title given to the leader (or superior) of a community of twelve or more monks. Characteristics of this title or position include the following: An abbot is elected for life by the community members, and his duties or responsibilities include the administration of property, upholding and preserving the rules and constitutions of the community, as well as implementing and enforcing discipline. In some communities the title has been changed to guardian (Franciscans), prior (Dominicans), and rector (Jesuits). *Interesting fact:* The title "abbot" comes from the word *abba* meaning father.

Abbot General   An abbot who oversees a collection of independent abbeys is called the "abbot general," or "abbot president." Usually the independent abbeys that fall under the abbot general are located in the same province, district, or country and comprise a congregation. The abbot general acts somewhat as a superior general albeit with limited powers. The ultimate purpose of this role is to promote the general interest of the order. *Interesting fact:* The abbot general usually serves as a representative to the Holy See (Vatican).

Abbot, Titular   Another kind of abbot is a "titular abbot." In short, this abbot represents an abbey that has either been destroyed or suppressed. *Interesting fact:* A titular abbot exercises none of the functions of an abbot.

Active Orders   An "active order" refers to those communities or religious institutes that engage in some form of activity such as teaching, serving the poor, missionary work, and so on. These orders can be comprised of priests, brothers, or sisters, and probably are the ones you are familiar with and have seen in your own respective cities. *Interesting fact:* The order which Mother Teresa founded (Missionaries of Charity) is considered an active order.

Asceticism   Simply put, asceticism is the practice of denying oneself pleasures while also living out disciplinary practices such as fasting, limited sleep and talking, and so on. The purpose of asceticism is to acquire the habits of virtue. *Interesting fact:* The word *asceticism* comes from the Greek *askesis*, which means practice, bodily exercise, and athletic training.

Ambrosian Chant   With similar roots to Gregorian chant, Ambrosian chant is said to have been developed and composed by Saint Ambrose and implemented into the liturgies of his archdiocese in Milan, Italy. *Interesting fact:* Saint Ambrose lived in the fourth century, hence, that was the beginning of Ambrosian chant.

Anchorite   A very unique calling or form of living in the Christian tradition, an anchorite (anchoress is the female version) is a person who withdraws from society in order to live a life of asceticism, prayer, and solitude. Present from almost the earliest days of the

Church, many of the early anchorites settled down or resided in the deserts of Egypt. These "vocations" and style of living later led to the founding of monastic life and institutions. *Interesting fact:* Carthusians and Camaldolese monks are examples of anchoritic monasticism.

Learning some basic monastic history and terms before your travels can enrich your visits to Europe's abbeys and convents a great deal.

KEVIN J. WRIGHT

Augustinian Rule   In short, the Augustinian Rule is the collection of rules or laws established by Saint Augustine and later implemented by different religious communities, including the Augustinian Canons. Much of the rule focuses on aspects of living out charity, poverty, obedience, detachment from the world, labor duties, celibacy, mutual duties of superiors and community members, fraternal charity, prayer in common, fasting, care of the sick, silence, reading during meals, and so on. *Interesting fact:* Although used by communities in the early fifth century, it was later almost forgotten but then revived in the eleventh century.

Barefoot Friars   A term commonly used for Discalced monks. *Interesting fact:* The word *discalced* comes from the Latin *dis*, which means "without," and *calceus*, which means "shoe."

Basilians   Monastic communities of the Byzantine rite who follow the Rule of Saint Basil (Basilians take their name from Saint Basil the Great). *Interesting fact:* Basilians are part of the non-Latin rite of the Catholic Church.

Basilian Rule   Saint Basil the Great (329–379) established a way or rule of life, which today serves as the foundation of monasticism in the Eastern Church. Two forms of the rule exist: The first one consists of fifty-five prescriptions/instructions, and the second or longer one consists of three hundred thirteen. *Interesting fact:* In the eighth century, Saint Theodore revised the rule, and it is this revised rule which is carried out today.

Bible Reading   Commonly referred to as *Lectio Divina* within monastic or contemplative circles, "Bible reading" refers to the reading of Scripture. The purpose is to gain insights into the truths of faith while aiding one's prayer and meditation. *Interesting fact:* If a person attends daily Mass for a period of three years, he or she will hear virtually the entire reading of the Bible.

Black Fast   One of the most austere and ardent forms of fasting in the history of the Church, the Black Fast is a form of penance and consists of the following: Only one meal is permitted, in the evening, and meat, dairy products, and alcohol are not allowed. *Interesting fact:* This form of fasting is primarily only still found in the Eastern rite and among select monastic orders.

Black Monks   The name commonly used is in reference to the Benedictine monks. The title developed from their black religious habits. *Interesting fact:* The term was used in the Middle Ages and is seldom used today.

Black Canons   Similar to the above title of Black Monks, Black Canons was a term used in the Middle Ages in reference to members of the Augustinian Canons. *Interesting fact:* This term was also used for the Benedictine monks, albeit the title of Black Monks was the more common term for them.

Breviary   Simply put, the breviary is a book comprised of the Liturgy of the Hours (or Divine Office). It is essentially an abridgement of the monastic offices. *Interesting fact:* The term *breviary* comes from the Latin word for abridgement *(Brevarium)*.

Calefactory   A term with several different meanings. It once referred to the heated room in a monastery where monks could warm themselves. Today, the term is often used to designate the recreation room. It is also the name ascribed to the vaselike utensil that a priest uses to warm his hands during liturgical functions. *Interesting fact:* The term comes from the Latin word for "to warm."

Canonical Hours   A term referring to the section of the Liturgy of the Hours, which the Church designates to be recited at different hours throughout the day. This fixed portion includes the following: office of readings, lauds, prime (now suppressed), terce, sext, nones, vespers, and compline. *Interesting fact:* The office of readings is commonly referred to as vigils, or matins.

Canons Regular   Communities of clergy who follow the rule of Saint Augustine and live the monastic life. *Interesting fact:* The largest order of this community today is the Order of Premonstratensians (also called the Norbertines).

Cappadocian Fathers   A term ascribed to three renowned fourth-century Christian theologians: Gregory of Nazianzus, Gregory of Nyssa, and Basil the Great. *Interesting fact:* The name was coined from the fact that each of them were from Cappadocia (present-day Turkey).

Cell   A term used for any of the following: (1) The small living quarters where a monk, hermit, or other religious resides. (2) A small group of monks who live in community but separate from their home monastery. (3) Small memorial chapels built in Christian cemeteries over a tomb. *Interesting fact:* Cell comes from the Latin word for small room *(cella)*.

Cellarer   An older term once used in reference to the monk or person responsible for the temporal goods of a community. *Interesting fact:* The title used for this person today is "procurator."

Chant   A form of sacred singing comprised of either of the following: recitative in nature with a short two to six tones for an accentus, or melodic in one of three styles: syllabic, neumatic, or melismatic. *Interesting fact:* There are many different forms of chant, including Gregorian chant and Ambrosian chant.

Cenobite   The name given to a hermit or anchorite that resides in a community. Cenobites were ancestors of the monastic orders. *Interesting fact*: Communities or orders such as the Benedictines and Cistercians are considered cenobitic.

Cloister   A popular term heard often in reference to monasteries or convents. The name is used in reference to select monastic or religious communities that adopt a contemplative lifestyle and withdraw from the world. Not only do the residents or members of a cloister rarely leave their property, outsiders are seldom invited in as well. The term cloister can also refer to the physical enclosure or area of a particular community. *Interesting fact:* Cloister comes from the Latin words for "to bar" or "to bolt" *(claustrum)* and "to close" *(claudere)*.

Cluny   One of the most influential abbeys in the history of the Church, Cluny was a Benedictine abbey founded in 910. It is where one of the largest reforms of Western Monasticism took place. It was known for its strict adherence to the Rule of Saint Benedict, especially through prayer and spiritual renewal. *Interesting fact:* The abbey's influence lasted for almost three centuries, and it was in existence until the end of the eighteenth century.

Coenobium (also Coenobites)   A name used to describe a group of monks who live in community. Individually each member is called a cenobite (see page 34). One of the most famous cenobites is Saint Pachomius (d. 346), as he wrote the first rule for cenobites and is honored as the "Founder of Monasticism." *Interesting fact:* Coenobium can also refer to the monastery church.

Convent   One of the most recognizable terms by people of all faiths, a convent refers to the building (or group of buildings) where a religious community lives. *Interesting fact:* Today the term is usually reserved to describe the dwelling place of nuns, but it can also be used to describe the dwelling place for religious men.

Cowl   One the most identifiable traits of a monk, the cowl is the hood worn by religious orders (especially monks). *Interesting fact:* It can also refer to the long-hooded robe worn by monastic men and women during the recitation/singing of the Liturgy of the Hours.

Day Hours   The phrase or term "Day Hours" is primarily used in reference to what is also called "Daytime Prayer." This is the daily cycle of prayer of the Liturgy of the Hours that includes the following: midmorning (officially, *terce*, or the "third" hour, about 9:00 AM); midday (*sext*, the "sixth" hour, noon); and mid-afternoon (*none*, the "ninth" hour, about 3:00 PM). *Interesting fact:* Although contemplatives are expected to recite all of these Hours, priests and religious engaged in active apostolates are expected to recite only one of these Hours.

Dissolution of the Monasteries   This phrase is ascribed to the disbanding, sacking, and liquidation of the monasteries and religious houses in England by King Henry VIII (1509–1547). Much of this action derived from King Henry's commitment to furthering his claims and supremacy over the Church of England, as well as strengthening his treasury. In 1536, the Act of Dissolution of Smaller Monasteries was passed, which forced the closure of those monasteries with an annual value below £250. After seizing the goods and riches of approximately two hundred fifty monasteries, King Henry then pursued the larger and more wealthy monasteries with the passing of the Act for the Dissolution of Greater Monasteries in 1539. By 1540, virtually every monastery had been closed. Subsequently many of the clergy and religious joined the Church of England. *Interesting fact:* In the midst of all the monastery and religious house closings, many valuable manuscripts, works of art, treasure, and buildings were destroyed; thus in many cases, precious documents that dated over one thousand years were forever lost.

Divine Office   For centuries, the term used to describe the official, public daily liturgical prayer of the Church. Today, it is called the Liturgy of the Hours. Although it is the public daily prayer of the Church, the prayers are often recited privately by religious and laity alike. *Interesting fact:* The purpose of the Liturgy of the Hours is for the Church to sanctify all hours of the day.

Dom   When visiting monasteries, you will see the title "Dom" very often. It is the title used before the names of monks in select monasteries. *Interesting fact:* Just as we use "Mr.," "Ms.," or "Mrs." as titles in society, monks use "Dom."

Eastern Monasticism   In the Church there are essentially two major forms of monasticism—Western Monasticism and Eastern Monasticism. Taken together, Christian monasticism began in the deserts of Egypt by Saint Anthony (251–356) in the third century. As more followers joined him, Saint Anthony formed the first community of hermits. From this evolved Western Monasticism, which was especially shaped by Saint Benedict. Eastern Monasticism was shaped largely by the Cappadocian Fathers, especially Saint Basil the Great (fourth century). In subsequent centuries, monasticism reached as far as Russia and the Slavic countries. *Interesting fact:* In Eastern Europe, monasticism continued throughout the Communist years, and today serves as an important component of Christian renewal in this part of the world in the post-Communist era.

Familiar   The term ascribed to a layperson who works within a monastic community or setting but has taken no religious vows. *Interesting fact:* A "familiar" shares in the spiritual benefits of the prayers and good works of the religious community in which he or she lives.

Friar   Simply put, a friar is a member of one of the mendicant orders. Some of the most recognized mendicant orders are the Franciscans, Dominicans, Carmelites, and Augustinians. *Interesting fact:* The term *friar* comes from the Latin word for brother *(frater).*

Graduale Romanum   The *Graduale Romanum* is the liturgical book containing the Latin text of the proper chants sung at Mass, complete with the Gregorian chant notation. This book differs from the *Liber Usualis* which contains all the chants of the Mass (and musical notation), as well as the Liturgy of the Hours. *Interesting fact:* A smaller version of the *Graduale Romanum* is called the *Graduale Ximplex* and is for use in smaller churches.

Gregorian Chant   Gregorian chant is often synonymous with plain chant, but with more individuality and characteristic expression. In addition, it comprises not only the church music of the early Middle Ages, but also later compositions written in a similar style right up to modern times. Pope Saint Gregory the Great (540–604) is often the person credited for compiling and arranging the chant during his time—hence, the name "Gregorian chant." *Interesting fact:* Although Gregorian chant is seldom heard these days in most Catholic churches, a 1974 publication by the Vatican entitled "Letter to Bishops on the Minimum Repertoire of Plain Chant" was sent to bishops and religious community leaders around the world, instructing that basic chants should be taught to all the faithful.

Gregorian Modes   Gregorian Modes refers to the eight musical scales used in Gregorian chant (divided into authentic and plagal groups). *Interesting fact:* Only one accidental occurs in the Gregorian modes, the half-tone lowering of the seventh note of the scale to "B-flat."

Gyrovagi   A term ascribed to monks who are not part of a monastic community and/or reside in their community. In short, they are wandering monks acting like "nomads." *Interesting fact:* Hopefully during your travels of visiting monasteries and meeting monks and religious community members, you will never come across a Gyrovagi. This type of living is—and always has been—considered an abuse by the Church of monastic and communal living.

Hermit   Most people are familiar with this term in one way or another. In short, it refers to a person who completely withdraws from society in order to contemplate and pursue God through silence, prayer, and penance. Hermits first began in the Church in the third century and are credited with essentially being the forerunners of monasticism. The Christian origin and understanding of hermits springs from Elijah in the Old Testament and Saint John the Baptist in the New Testament. Interesting fact: Hermit comes from the Greek term for one who dwells in the desert (*eremites*).

Hieromonk   A monk of the Eastern Church who is also a priest. *Interesting fact:* The Western Church roots lie in the Roman Empire and the Eastern Church in the Eastern Empire at Constantinople.

Hood   Similar to the cowl, the hood is one of the most recognizable pieces of a religious order. It can either be part of a religious person's entire garment/cloak or separate from it. *Interesting fact:* Today the hood is primarily worn by contemplative orders, including monks, nuns, and some mendicant orders.

Hours, Little   Also called Daytime Prayer (see Day Hours on page 33). *Interesting fact:* If you are interested in learning or reciting these prayers, there are many books available on the topic of praying the Little Hours.

Liber Usualis   The *Liber Usualis* is like the "encyclopedia" or "bible" of Gregorian chant. This book contains the chants for the following: (1) ordinary and propers of Masses, (2) rites and special Masses, and (3) Liturgy of the Hours. *Interesting fact:* The Benedictine monks of Solesmes are the original editors of this book.

Little Office of the Blessed Virgin Mary   The Little Office of the Blessed Virgin Mary is a liturgical devotion to the Blessed Virgin Mary comprised of hymns, antiphons, psalms, and collects. It is designed in a similar fashion to the Liturgy of the Hours. It is often prayed on Saturdays, the day dedicated to the Blessed Virgin Mary according to the Church. This office is prayed in addition to the regular Liturgy of the Hours. *Interesting fact:* A new edition of the Little Office was published in 1988 in the United States, and this edition is primarily intended for those who may find the regular Liturgy of the Hours book too expensive or too confusing to use.

Liturgy of the Hours   As previously discussed in other entries, the Liturgy of the Hours is the official cycle of the Church's daily prayer life. Through the centuries, it was called the Divine Office (and is still sometimes referred to as this); however, since Vatican II, the proper name is Liturgy of the Hours. In short, the Liturgy of the Hours are designated prayers and readings that are to be recited (or sung) at fixed hours of the day by all religious, including priests, brothers, monks, sisters, and nuns—and anyone else whose vocation requires it. The prayers and readings are primarily taken from Scripture as well as the writings of the Church fathers and saints. Standard Catholic prayers and other commentaries are also included. It is arranged according to a one-week cycle called a Psalter. A daily cycle of the Liturgy of the Hours includes the following: morning prayer (*lauds*), midday prayer (*terce, sext,* or *none*), evening prayer (*vespers*), night prayer (*compline*), and the Office of Readings. Anyone can pray the Liturgy of the Hours, and it is available for purchase at most Catholic stores (or on the Internet); it consists of a four-volume set, or you can purchase the abbreviated edition which is one volume. *Interesting fact:* There is another hour that is called the "first hour" (*prime*); however, this is no longer used nor required for the universal Church. Contemplative monastic communities though still observe and pray it.

Mandyas Found primarily in the Byzantine Church, the mandyas is a monk's full-length vesture. *Interesting fact:* A monk's mandyas can range from a simple black cloak to an ornate and very colorful one with much symbolism.

Matins Originally, the morning hours of *lauds*. Later on, it referred to the preceding hour of *vigils*, sung around midnight. These vigils eventually were incorporated into monastic practice and evolved into the hour of the Liturgy of the Hours known as *matins*. Matins has the following structure: Psalm 95/94 (the invitatory); hymn; psalms; readings from sacred Scripture; commentaries on sacred Scripture (or, on feast days, an appropriate reading); responsories; canticle on solemn feasts. *Interesting fact:* Matins comes from the Latin for morning hours *(tempora matutina)*.

Maurists Maurists are a community of monks within the French Congregation of Benedictines. Founded in 1618 by Saint Maur, they were later disbanded during the French Revolution. *Interesting fact:* The Maurists become well known and respected for the research with the lives of the saints.

Monastery   A term used in the title of this book, a monastery in simple terms is the dwelling house or residence of a religious community. More precisely in modern times, it primarily refers to the dwelling hours or residence of a contemplative religious community that includes monks or nuns. What does a typical monastery consist of? It is oftentimes built around a quadrangle and includes a church or chapel, a refectory, chapter hall, common room, work rooms, and individual rooms (cells) for the residents. *Interesting fact:* Normally either the entire property, or at least a portion of the property of a monastery, is closed to the public. This portion is usually called the enclosure.

Monasticism   Simply put, monasticism within the Christian tradition refers to those individuals who withdraw themselves from society to completely dedicate themselves to God through prayer, silence, and penance. The two main forms of monasticism are anchoritic (hermits and those who essentially live alone) and cenobitic (those who live in community). *Interesting fact:* Examples of anchoritic monasticism are Carthusians and Camaldolese; cenobitic monasticism includes orders such as the Benedictines and Cistericians.

Monk   One of the most common religious terms in the world, within the Christian tradition a monk refers to a person who withdraws from society in order to pursue God completely and solely through prayer, silence, and penance. The primary difference between a monk and other religious (that is, parish priest, friar, and so on) is that the latter usually performs some type of "active apostolate" which engages the world or society (that is, feeding or taking care of the poor, teaching, and so on). *Interesting fact:* The word *monk* can refer to both men and women monastic religious, albeit typically in the English-speaking world it refers solely to the men, while the word *nun* refers to the women.

Nocturn   A much older term referring to "night offices." *Interesting fact:* The term comes from the Latin word meaning "of the night" *(Nocturus).*

Nun   A woman who is a member of a religious community and has professed solemn vows. *Interesting fact:* Today the word is commonly used by people to describe any woman who belongs to a religious community—whether the woman is professed or not.

Oblate   An oblate is a term used to describe a layperson who is specially united to a particular religious order by simple vows. *Interesting fact:* The word once referred to children who were sent to a monastery by their parents for the purpose of studying there and being raised by the monks.

Office   A shortened way of referring to the Divine Office, or more properly in this post-Vatican II era, the Liturgy of the Hours. *Interesting fact:* It can also refer to a section of the Liturgy of the Hours that might be recited.

Office of the Dead   One of the offices of the Liturgy of the Hours, sung or recited for the purpose of praying for the dead. *Interesting fact:* This special office is prayed on All Souls' Day (November 2), as well as after the death of a person.

Plainchant   Commonly also referred to as plainsong, plainchant was the music of the Church in the early Middle Ages (prior to the beginning of polyphony). In fact, it was the exclusive music of the Church until the ninth century. Plainchant is essentially a monophonic (single melodic line), liturgical chant usually sung with Latin texts and without accompaniment. *Interesting fact:* The word plainchant comes from the Latin words for flat/level and cantus/song.

Prime   The Liturgy of the Hours referred to as "prime" is no longer used today in the Church, except primarily within monastic circles. *Interesting fact:* Prime was recited before the morning work period and consisted of the following: reading of a saint, part of the monastic rule, and a prayer that referenced "prospering by the work of one's hands."

Priory   The term ascribed to the dwelling place or residence of a monastic order that is governed by a prior (men's community) or prioress (women's community). *Interesting fact:* There are different kinds of priories: "conventual" priories are autonomous (but not officially an abbey), while "simple" or "obedientiary" priories are dependent upon or subject to another abbey.

Prior   The name or title sometimes given to the leader of a particular monastic community. At a convent or women's monastery, the title is prioress. *Interesting fact:* The prior can sometimes refer to the main assistant to an abbot.

Prioress   See previous entry for prior.

Rule   In short, the word *rule* refers to the summarized rules and regulations of a religious community, touching on all aspects from daily duties to penance to discipline to apostolate (that is, caring for the sick, providing hospitality, and so on). *Interesting fact:* There are many different "Rules" within the Catholic Church and monastic communities; for example, there is the Rule of Saint Benedict, the Rule of Saint Augustine, the Basilian Rule, and so on.

Rule of Saint Benedict   One of the most popular monastic communities in the world is the Benedictine Order, which was founded in sort by Saint Benedict of Nursia (c. 480–543). The Rule of Saint Benedict refers to the rules and regulations that Saint Benedict set forth to govern the life of his religious community members. Its emphasis is on the balance between living the spiritual life and carrying on with the daily activities of residing in a monastic community. *Interesting fact:* As the Rule of Saint Benedict is seen as being one of the most practical and balanced, it has been the most influential and widely used monastic rule in the West.

Sext   The midday prayers of the Liturgy of the Hours. *Interesting fact:* Sext is often said or sung right before lunch.

Sister   This is a term most people are familiar with—whether they belong to the Catholic Church or not. In short, a woman is considered a sister if she belongs to a religious community or institute whose members never profess solemn vows. *Interesting fact:* So what's the difference between a sister and a nun? A nun is a woman who belongs to a religious community or institute and professes solemn vows.

Solesmes   The French town which is home to one of the most influential monasteries in the Catholic Church: The Abbey of Saint Peter. The monks are known for their tremendous work and research in regards to restoring Gregorian chant to its original and pure form. The founder of the Solesmes monastery is Abbot Prosper Gueranger, who was primarily responsible for producing the *Liber Usualis* (see dictionary entry for this term/book). *Interesting fact:* You can visit this monastery and hear the monks sing their renowned and beautiful Gregorian chant. To learn more about this famed monastery visit www.solesmes.com.

The Great Chartreuse   The Great Chartreuse translated means "The Great Charter House." This is the name given to the original foundation house of the Carthusian monks, which was founded in 1084 by Saint Bruno in France. *Interesting fact:* If you've ever drank a liqueur called Chartreuse, then you've drank the liqueur originally made by the monks at The Great Charter House.

Tones   Tones is a method of eight standard melodies with variations for plainchant. *Interesting fact:* Tones is primarily only used in the Eastern churches.

Tonsure   A tonsure is a type of haircut used by monks or religious communities from the fourth or fifth centuries up until the last century, ending with Vatican II (1960s). It is seldom used in today's religious or monastic communities. It is essentially the shaving of most of one's hair on the head (usually just leaving a "ring of hair" around the middle part of the head). *Interesting fact:* The tonsure had been used primarily as a symbol of one's admission to the clerical state.

Votive Office   A votive office is essentially a special or unique office that can be substituted for the prescribed office (Liturgy of the Hours) of the day. For example, a votive office can be celebrated for a special pilgrimage, local feast, or other special devotion/occasion. A votive office is not part of the general calendar. *Interesting fact:* A votive office cannot be said on a solemnity day, or on select feast days of the Church. An example of a votive office is the Office for the Dead, which can be said in conjunction with the death of one's fellow religious community member.

GREGORIAN CHANT: MUSIC OF THE ANGELS

WHEN ONE THINKS OF MONASTERIES, the sounds of Gregorian chant often come to mind. Although this form of music is heard less and less in the churches of today, its popularity, nevertheless, continues to grow at an accelerating rate. One example of this may be the fact that the recordings of Gregorian chant by the monks of Santo Domingo de Silos "hit number one" on the European pop charts and made a major splash in the United States in the mid 1990s—and its influence and effects have remained.

What exactly is Gregorian chant? It is the name given to the form of plainchant that was traditionally believed to have been organized and arranged by Pope Saint Gregory I in the fifth and sixth centuries (hence, the name Gregorian chant). Believed to have originated from Jewish sources, the chant is a vocal form of music which uses a conventional scale of eight notes. Since the time of Pope Gregory, the chant has continued to evolve and change, mostly due to its adaptation to different regions. Unfortunately however, by the eleventh century, since the music had become increasingly very complex and ornate, it could only be mastered by extensively trained choirs. As a result, general interest and appeal in chant began a steady decline in the years that followed, in spite of the small revival it enjoyed after the Council of Trent (1545–1563).

In the 1800s, however, the Benedictine Abbey of Solesmes sparked a renewed appreciation for this form of music. Then, in the twentieth century, many of the popes, including Pope Saint Pius X (reigned 1903–1914), Pope Pius XI (reigned 1922–1939), and Pope Pius XII (reigned 1939–1958), helped further the cause of Gregorian chant. The Second Vatican Council promoted Gregorian chant through its document *Sacrosanctum Concilium* (Constitution on the Sacred Liturgy), which stated that this form of sacred music was to "be given pride of place in liturgical services."

However, in the past forty years, despite calls for its continued application, Gregorian chant has essentially been relegated to the monasteries. Ironically, in recent years, Gregorian chant has enjoyed a renaissance in secular music. Many professional choirs and schola cantorums have taken up this music with vigor. Fortunately, with the advent of CDs, MP3 players, and other music devices, today it is possible to bring the ancient sounds of the monks into one's own home and daily life.

GREGORIAN CHANT WEB SITE(S)

There are literally hundreds of excellent Gregorian chant Web sites on the Internet which feature everything from chant resources to choirs to recordings to publications. Simply perform a search for "Gregorian chant."

GREGORIAN CHANT RESOURCES

An Overview of Gregorian Chant by Dom Jacques Hourlier (Paraclete Press, 1996); *Reflections on the Spirituality of Gregorian Chant* by Dom Eugène Cardine (Paraclete Press, 1995).

Learning About Gregorian Chant (CD) by the Monks of The Abbey of Solesmes; directed by Dom Jean; text by Dom Daniel Saulnier; read by Sarah Moule (Paraclete Press, 2004).

BENEDICTINE CONGREGATION OF SOLESMES

IN THE PAST TWO CENTURIES, no other branch of the Church has made an impact on monasticism as much as the Benedictine Congregation of Solesmes. Since the early 1800s, they have served as leaders in the liturgical renewal and restoration of Gregorian chant, while at the same time, also

Serving as one of the most renowned and influential monasteries in the world, the Benedictine Congregation of Solesmes welcomes visitors and travelers from around the world who wish to experience the monastic life.

influencing and founding numerous other monasteries throughout Europe, as well as other parts of the world. Likened to the legendary monastery of Cluny during the Middle Ages, the congregation of Solesmes owes its prominence principally to one man and to one abbey—Dom Guéranger and the Abbey of Saint Peter.

Located in the countryside of western France, the Abbey of Saint Peter (along with the women's Abbey of Cecilia) today flourishes as a worldwide center of Gregorian chant spirituality and performance. Approximately eighty monks belong to the Solesmes community of men, and about sixty nuns to the Solesmes community of women. Both have achieved worldwide recognition for their contributions to restoring the ancient and authentic Gregorian chant of the Church.

For more than a century, the Benedictine monks and nuns of Solesmes have been heavily involved in the research of Gregorian chant. One of their aims is to assimilate the spiritual riches it contains into the life of prayer within the Church. Many people throughout the world are familiar with the Benedictine monks of Solesmes through their recordings and publications. As well as chant, the monks do extensive research and writing about monastic traditions and papal teachings.

The men's monastery was founded at Solesmes in 1010, but it was closed during the devastating time of the French Revolution. In 1833, a young priest from the local diocese, Father Guéranger, purchased the deserted building. Within five years, he had not only received the Vatican's recognition for his newly established Benedictine community, but also had the status of his priory raised to the dignity of an abbey. Furthermore, the abbey would serve as the head of the newly established Congregation of Solesmes, the successor to the Congregations of Saint Maurus and Saint Vanne, as well as the more venerable and ancient family monasteries belonging to Cluny.

Initiating a rediscovery of Christian tradition, the soon-to-be first abbot of Solesmes extensively researched Church history, liturgy, Gregorian chant, and Scripture. Wanting to reinstate it as "a center for prayer and studies in service to the Church," Dom Guéranger underscored both the primacy of the Divine Office and the liturgy with his monks, as well as the pursuit of the intellectual life. He knew that a persistent search for the truth was a prerequisite for an authentic spiritual life for monks.

In his most famous work, *The Liturgical Year*, Dom Guéranger not only taught his monks but also the entire world to live by and in the Church, and to pray with her and as she does. Believing the Church's chant to be the most perfect expression of her liturgical prayer, with his monks, he undertook the task of the restoration of Gregorian (chant) melodies which centuries of neglect and change had left virtually unrecognizable. After his death in 1875, the monks continued his work, and today they remain in the forefront of papal, monastic, and Gregorian chant research.

In 1866, with the help of Mother Cecilia Bruyère, Dom Guéranger also founded the women's monastery of Saint Cecilia in 1866. In large part due to the growth of Solesmes, several other monasteries were also either revived or established under his jurisdiction. In the years following his death, the monks of Solesmes founded more than two dozen abbeys and houses. Among these are the renowned monasteries of Fontgambault, Clervaux, Liguge, Saint-Wandrille, Wisques, Ganagobie, and Santo Domingo de Silos (the home of the world-famous monks whose recordings of Gregorian chant "hit number one" on the European pop charts in the mid 1990s). In 1981, they opened their first monastery in the United States, a women's abbey in Westfield, Vermont. To learn more about the Monastery of the Immaculate Heart of Mary, visit www. ihmwestfield.com.

To this day, they continue to expand; in the last several years, Solesmes has founded the priory of Palendriai in Lithuania, and Fontgombault, a daughter house, has founded the priory in Clear Creek, Oklahoma. To learn more about the men's Clear Creek Monastery, visit www.clearcreekmonks.org.

What distinguishes the Solesmes Congregation from all others in the Benedictine Order is that all the monasteries are wholly contemplative, foregoing any pastoral or outside responsibilities. Their vocation is truly the splendor with which they celebrate the liturgy of the Church. Every day, they spend four or more hours in community prayer, one hour in personal prayer, and the remainder of their time doing manual labor, studying, or in recreation. At the heart of each abbey's community life are the Mass and the Liturgy of the Hours.

In accordance with Vatican II and the Constitution on the Sacred Liturgy, the monks and nuns of Solesmes have "preserved the use of the Latin language and given prominent place to Gregorian chant" in their liturgies. They also give special attention to the visual aspects of the Mass with their vestments, ceremonial practices, and incense. The result is Solesmes' world-renowned role in the liturgical renewal and restoration of Gregorian chant today.

SOLESMES WEB SITE
To learn more about the Benedictine Congregation of Solesmes, visit their Web site at: www.solesmes.com.

CONTACT INFORMATION
Abbaye Saint-Pierre
1 Place Dom Guéranger
72300 Solesmes (France)
Tel: (0243) 95-03-08
Fax: (0243) 95-03-28
Abbey email: abbaye@solesmes.com
Guesthouse email: hospes@solesmes.com

PLACES TO STAY
Within monastery walls
Since the guesthouse is located within the monastic enclosure, only men (either individuals or small groups) may be accommodated for spiritual retreats in silence. Monks can provide counsel if it is desired, and the maximum stay is one week. All guesthouse visitors are expected to assist at the offices. Meals are taken with the monks. During free time, individuals can stroll around certain parts of the monastic grounds, as well as visit the library. All rooms are single occupancy, with sheets and towels provided. Contact the guestmaster prior to your proposed arrival date.

On monastery property but not within walls
Two accommodation facilities located on the monastic property, but not within the monastic enclosure, include St. Clement and La Marbrerie. The first building can accommodate groups up to twenty people, while the latter dormitory facility can accommodate up to forty people (especially geared toward young people and youth groups). Many amenities are available including kitchen facilities and restrooms. Groups are expected to assist at most offices. All guesthouses, including St. Clement and La Marbrerie, are reserved only for groups with genuine religious motivation and interest in experiencing the monastic life of Solesmes. (Reservations must be made months in advance due to high demand.) The cost is decided on a case by case basis by the guestmaster.

Other Accommodations
Although not operated by the monks, there is a hotel located in front of the Abbey of Saint Peter, which is open to all people.

For more information, contact them at:
Grand Hotel de Solesmes
Tel: (0243) 95-45-10
Fax: (0243) 95-22-26
Web site: http://grandhotelsolesmes.com

DAILY SCHEDULE

10:00 am: Sung Conventual Mass (one hour, fifteen minutes)
            (*Note: Office of Tierce integrated with the Mass)
 1:00 pm: Sext (fifteen minutes)
 1:45 pm: None (fifteen minutes)
 5:00 pm: Vespers (thirty minutes)
            (*Note: On Thursdays at 4:00 PM in summer,
            5:30 PM in winter)
 8:30 pm: Compline (twenty minutes)

The abbey church is open from 9:00 AM to 6:00 PM and for compline. On Sundays and feast days, it is open from 11:30 AM to 6:00 PM. A bookstore and an exhibit about the abbey are open—except during religious services—from 11:00 AM to 7:00 PM daily, and from 11:30 AM to 7:00 PM on Sundays and feast days. Groups wishing to visit the abbey are asked to contact the guestmaster prior to their arrival.

HOW TO REACH SOLESMES

Situated in the western part of France, about one hundred fifty miles from Paris, the abbey of Solesmes stands above the valley of the Sarthe River, almost two miles from the city of Sablé-sur-Sarthe, midway between Le Mans and Angers.

By Road

From Paris, take autoroute A11 West (Paris-Nantes route), exit at Sablé-rur-Sarthe (between Le Mans and Angers), and follow the signs to Solesmes. Another option is to take autoroute A81 (Paris-Rennes route), exit at Brûlon (between Le Mans and Laval), and follow the signs to Solesmes.

By Train

From Paris, take either the TGV or conventional train from the Montparnasse train station to Le Mans. Change trains at Le Mans (you must purchase a separate ticket) and continue on the train from Le Mans to Sablé-sur-Sarthe. From here, you must either take a taxi or walk to Solesmes, a distance of two miles along the Sarthe River.

From London (Waterloo Station), take the TGV direct to Le Mans (stopping at Lille and Charles de Gaulle Airport but bypassing the city of Paris). Change trains at Le Mans (you must purchase a separate ticket) and continue on the train from Le Mans to Sablé-sur-Sarthe. From here, you must either take a taxi or walk to Solesmes, a distance of two miles along the Sarthe River.

SOLESMES CHANT RECORDINGS & PUBLICATIONS
Chant recordings available from the Abbey of Saint Peter of Solesmes include:

Apostles and Martyrs
Bishops and Doctors
Chants of Easter
Christ in Gethsemane
Christmas
Christmas Night
Christmas: The Night Office
Easter
Eastertide
Epiphany & Presentation
Feasts of Our Lady
Gregorian Chant Rediscovered
Gregorian Chant: The Monks and Their Music (video)
Gregorian Requiem
Gregorian Sampler
Maundy Thursday
Requiem Mass
Saint Benedict
Solesmes & Dom Guéranger 1805ñ1875 (book; by Dom Louis Soltner)
Tenebrae of Good Friday
Tenebrae of Holy Thursday
Tenebrae of Holy Saturday
The Church Sings Her Saints I and II
Vespers and Compline

CONTACTING THE MONASTERIES, CONVENTS, AND PLACES OF RETREAT

SINCE IT IS VERY IMPORTANT to make reservations before your arrival with most of the monasteries and convents listed in this book (if you plan to stay overnight), I have provided the necessary information about how to contact and correspond with these various places.

Although every effort has been made to ensure the accuracy of all the information contained in this book, I ask you to please keep in mind that telephone and fax numbers (as well as email and Web site addresses) in Europe change quickly and often. Much of this is due to the rapid development of their communication technologies, but there are several ways to overcome this situation.

If you experience any problems dialing either to telephone or fax numbers, contact the operator and ask to be connected to international dialing assistance. With the name and address of the place you want to contact in hand, an international operator can usually track down the newest city codes and telephone numbers.

Another option, one that continues to become more effective over time, is to search the Internet for the monastery or convent's name or Web site. As more and more monasteries and convents are joining the World Wide Web with each passing day, it is becoming easier to locate up-to-date information on the Internet.

However, if you are unable to locate a particular monastery or convent's Web site on the Internet, the next best option is to visit the Web site for the monastic order to which they belong. For example, if I wanted some information about a particular Benedictine abbey in Spain, I would first visit the Benedictine Order Web site (www.osb.org) to see if that monastery is listed. If so, there will usually be a direct link to their Web site. If they are not listed, I would then perform a search on the Internet for that particular abbey.

If all else fails, as a last resort, you can contact the national tourist office of the country where it is located. Since the tourist offices usually can be easily found on the Internet, you can either phone, email, or fax them directly with your questions.

When telephoning or faxing a monastery or convent in Europe, here are a few extra things to remember:

- Dial the code number to exit your country.
- Dial the code number of the country you are calling.
- Dial the city code of the place you are calling.
- Dial the local phone number of the place you are calling.
- Keep in mind that to dial a number from outside a particular country, you may need to drop the first number (it is usually a zero) of the particular city code. These numbers are used if dialing only from *within the country or area.*
- If writing a letter overseas, always remember to include the country in the mailing address.

But what should you include in a letter to a monastery or convent—especially if you are hoping to make a reservation? I recommend including the following:

- The monastery/convent contact information, including name, mailing address, telephone/fax number, and email address. (Whenever possible, address the letter to the Guestmaster.)
- Your contact information, including name, mailing address, telephone/fax number, and email address.
- The purpose of your visit (that is, personal spiritual retreat, group spiritual retreat, vocational purposes, and so on).
- The number of people in your group, or whether you will be traveling alone.
- Desired dates of arrival and the proposed length of stay.
- Gender and ages of the members of your group. (Note: some monasteries/convents accept only men or women and/or individuals above a certain age.)
- Where applicable, include an official letter from your priest, minister, or rabbi stating your intention to stay overnight at a monastery/convent for spiritual purposes. Although these letters are required only at a very small minority of places, they can come in handy. (If possible, have the letter translated into the language spoken in the country—or countries—you will be visiting.)
- Always be very respectful, polite, and understanding in your letters. Remember, you are asking to be invited into their homes!

MAKING THE BEST OF YOUR MONASTIC TRAVELS

TO MAKE THE BEST of one's monastic travels, keep in mind the following four ideas:

1. Good Planning
2. Good Research
3. Experiencing the Monastic Life
4. Trusting in Divine Providence

Without a doubt, a fruitful trip always begins with good planning. This includes everything from designing an engaging itinerary, obtaining the necessary travel documents, to buying the right walking shoes and breaking them in several months in advance. A good thing also to keep in mind when mapping out a trip is never to oblige yourself to see everything—or every monastery. Select the places you might like to visit within your allotted time, and then just follow that plan (but do allow for divine Providence to take you elsewhere at times).

How can you make the most of your monastic travels? Engage yourself fully in the experience, hospitality, and daily life of each monastery you visit. KEVIN J. WRIGHT

Otherwise, if you try to visit too many places too quickly, frustration can often set in; you cannot completely absorb each place fully. In fact, the best advice I have ever heard is this: visit just as many places as you are able, and plan on coming back at another time to do the rest (not a bad idea!).

Another vital component of making it a great trip is to do the necessary research beforehand. Especially if you are embarking on a trip to the great monasteries of Europe, it will be to your advantage to learn, in advance, as much as you can about the history of the sites or about the monastic orders you will be visiting. The more you know about a subject, the more you can derive and profit from it. This book, along with others about the same topic, can provide you with the necessary preliminary groundwork. Of course, as I have previously mentioned, the Internet can also be a valuable tool. It is amazing to see just how much information can be found about monasticism on the World Wide Web. In fact, hundreds of monasteries are joining the Internet with their own Web sites. To help you with this part of your research, I have provided a comprehensive list of monastic-related Web sites in the appendix of this book, as well as general trip planning tools and resources.

"Experiencing the monastic life" is another key ingredient for a successful and enjoyable trip. No matter how much you plan and research before a trip, if you don't "experience the monastic life" during your travels, everything else can be futile. By "experiencing the monastic life," I mean taking advantage of what each monastery has to offer. By attending the services, walking the grounds, speaking with the monks (if and when appropriate), enjoying the silence, participating in the schedule of the abbey, and praying or reflecting, you can then begin to get a true sense of what monastic life is all about. By doing this, you can gain a much deeper appreciation of the places you will be visiting, and the people you will meet. And of course, above all, simply take time to enjoy the personal hospitality of each monastery or convent you are visiting.

The most important element, however, of any monastic trip, is handing over the reigns of your life to God and trusting in divine Providence. Although this may sometimes be the most difficult part of the journey, it is always the most rewarding. By abandoning yourself to divine Providence, you open yourself up to the unknown, yet exciting, plans of God. It is because of divine Providence that many apparent travel "mishaps," such as missed or rerouted trains, can turn into incredible blessings. At every bend and turn, there are new friends to meet, new places to see, and new experiences to behold. During my travels of backpacking through countless European countries, it was amazing just how many times "detoured plans" turned into unexpected highlights. That's how I learned about places such as Solesmes, Santo Domingo de Silos, Montserrat, Fontgombault, Klosterneuburg, Heiligenkreuz, and Kalwaria Zebrzydowska—all monasteries and abbeys listed in this book. Trusting in God's divine Providence during our travels is not always easy, but it does allow us to advance in our faith— and that is the purpose of a monastic pilgrimage.

PART 3

Europe's Monastery and Convent Guesthouses

*(includes maps of countries
and monasteries)*

AUSTRIA

BENEDIKTINERABTEI ALTENBURG

Abt Placidus Much-Str. 1
3591 Altenburg (Bez Horn)
Tel: (02982) 34-51, 34-51-14 (guest shop)
Fax: (02982) 34-51-13
Email: kultur.tourismus@stift-altenburg.at,
info@stift-altenburg.at
Web site: www.stift-altenburg.at

Founded in 1144, today the Altenburg Abbey is home to a community
of Benedictine monks. Visitors can tour the imposing abbey church,
which features a number of beautiful frescoes, sculptures, and other
religious artwork. All are invited to participate in the daily prayer life
of the monks, as well as attend the many summer concerts. The most
popular sites to visit include the abbey's restaurant, special exhibitions,
courtyards, wine cellar, gift shop, and especially the ancient abbey with
its cloister dating from the 14th century. To learn more about the abbey's winery, you can email: gutsverwaltung@stift-altenburg.at.

Where to stay? Accommodations in the guesthouse are available for
men only. Participation in religious services and community life are
expected. Meals are included and shared with monks. Contact the abbey to make a reservation.

How to get there? Altenburg is about fifty-five miles northwest of Vienna. By car from Vienna travel on the B303 to Horn, then head in the direction of Zwettl for about 3.5 miles to Altenburg. From Krems (valley of the Danube), travel to Altenburg via Kamptal Bundesstraße. Altenburg is accessible by train; other nearby rail stations lie in Horn and Rosenburg. Taxi service is available (on request) from Horn/ Rosenburg to Altenburg.

BENEDIKTINERABTEI SAINT GEORGENBERG-FIECHT

6130 Fiecht (Schwaz)
Tel: (05242) 632-76-0/37 • Fax: (05242) 632-76-33
Email: info@st-georgenberg.at
Web site: www.stift-fiecht.at; www.st-georgenberg.at

Founded in 1138, today the Abbey of Saint Georgenberg is home to a community of Benedictine monks. Mass is celebrated daily, with the March 19 feast day of Saint Joseph (the patron of the abbey church) receiving the largest number of visitors annually.

Where to stay? The monastery operates a large guesthouse for both men and women, with approximately seventy beds available. The monastery offers housing for groups or individuals in single, double, and multi-bed rooms. In addition, the monastery offers wonderful facilities for meetings and gatherings.

How to get there? Fiecht is about twenty miles northeast of Innsbruck. Take A12 and A13 toward Salzburg and Schwarz. Exit toward Vomp/Benediktiner-Abtei Fiecht and follow the signs. Fiecht is accessible by train.

STIFT GÖTTWEIG

3511 Göttweig (Krems)
Tel: (02732) 855-81-0, 85581-231 • Fax: (02732) 855-81-244/266
Email: info@goettweig.at; goettweig@kloesterreich.at
Web site: www.stiftgoettweig.at

Among the many monasteries of Austria, the Benedictine Abbey of Göttweig remains one of the most famous. Dating from 1065, the abbey has long served as a major place of pilgrimage because of its reputation as a hub for culture, art, religion, architecture, and warm hospitality. Perched above a hill with breathtaking views of the world-famous

Danube valley below, Göttweig continues to welcome visitors from all over the world who come to tour its abbey, cloister, crypt, museum, art collections, wine cellar, exhibitions, and the local interpretative forest trail to the mammoth trees, "Adalbert-Rast." The monastery also operates a restaurant serving specialties from the regional cuisine (reservations are required for lunch and dinner). The abbey restaurant offers panoramic views of the valley below; for more information about the restaurant, email restaurant@stiftgoettweig.at.

Where to stay? The abbey is open for both men and women who are interested in participating in spiritual exercises and primarily a silent retreat (referred to as "Holidays in the Abbey"). The guesthouse is called St. Altmann and is located across from the abbey church. To book a room reservation, contact: Mr. Sven Hofmann, A-3511 Stift Göttweig, Pforte-Reception, Tel: 02732/85581-332; Fax: 02732/85581-244. Email: urlaub@stiftgoettweig.at.

How to get there? By road take the Autobahn A1 from Vienna (35 miles) or Salzburg (130 miles) to St. Pölten; exit at Krems (12 miles) and from there follow signs to Stift Göttweig. By train, travel to St. Pölten, connecting to Göttweig, Paudorf, or Furth. Upon arrival take the bus or taxi to the abbey.

SAINT HEMMA GUESTHOUSE
DOMKUSTODIE SALVATORIANERKOLLEG
Domplatz 11
9342 Gurk
Tel: (04266) 8236-0/14, (04266) 8557-0 • Fax: (04266) 8236-16
Email: dom.info@dom-zu-gurk.at; gaestehaus.sds@dom-zu-gurk.at
Web site: www.dom-zu-gurk.at

Founded in 1043 by Saint Hemma, this monastery is home to a community of Salvatorian fathers and brothers. Attracting visitors from throughout Europe and abroad, this pilgrimage site features the tomb of Saint Hemma, as well as a number of beautiful religious artworks housed in the Episcopal chapel. Guided tours of the sanctuary are available, and key sites to view include the crypt, frescoes of the Bishop's Chapel, Gurker Lenten cloth, and arcaded courtyard of Propsthof.

Where to stay? The Salvatorians operate a comfortable guesthouse, which is open to both men and women. A variety of accommodations are available for individuals and groups including several rooms perfectly suited for receiving youth groups.

How to get there? Gurk is located on highway 93, about one hundred forty miles southwest of Vienna and fourteen miles from Friesach. From Klagenfurt, take Route 83 north, turning left on highway 93 and heading west to Gurk (eleven miles). Gurk is not accessible by train; the nearest railway station is at Treibach-Althofen (ten miles).

ZISTERZIENSERABTEI HEILIGENKREUZ

2532 Heiligenkreuz im Wienerwald
Tel: (02258) 87-03/102 • Fax: (02258) 87-03-114
Email: information@stift-heiligenkreuz.at,
tourismus@stift-heiligenkreuz.at, pkw@stift-heiligenkreuz.at
Web site: www.stift-heiligenkreuz.at

Founded in 1133, the Heiligenkreuz Abbey is home to a community of about fifty Cistercian monks. The abbey is well known for its beautiful Liturgy of the Hours and Mass, both of which are sung in Gregorian chant. Guided tours of the abbey are available with prior arrangemens and sometimes by a monk (monastic life permitting). All guided tours must be booked in advance. You can also shop in the abbey guest store or eat in the abbey restaurant (fax: 02258/8703-114).

Where to stay? The monastery guesthouse provides different types of accommodations with approximately thirty-eight beds for independent travelers and three youth hostels (dormitory-style rooms) with another fifty beds. To make reservations, email gastmeister@stift-heiligenkreuz.at. For student groups, email pkw@stift-heiligenkreuz.at or fax (02258) 8703-327.

How to get there? Heiliegenkreuz is about fifteen miles southwest of Vienna. By road head west on A21, following the signs to Salzburg and Linz, exiting at the signs indicating Heiligenkreuz. Heiligenkruz is not accessible by train, only bus (from Vienna and other nearby cities). The nearest rail station: Baden OEBB.

AUGUSTINER CHORHERRENSTIFT

3130 Herzogenburg (Sankt Pölten)
Tel: (02782) 831-13/12 • Fax: (02782) 831-12-28
Email: stift@herzogenburg.at; stift-fuehrungen@herzogenburg.at; fuehrungen@stift-herzogenburg.at; od.pfarre@herzogenburg.at
Web site: www.herzogenburg.at/stift

Founded in 1244, today the Abbey of Augustiner Chorherrenstift is home to a community of Augustinian monks. Mass is celebrated daily in the abbey church and special guided tours are available with prior request. Be sure to view the Late-baroque abbey church, frescoes, treasury, collections of Gothic and baroque works of art, choir chapel, library, art gallery, hall for festivities, and the Chamber of Rarities and Coins.

Where to stay? Guestrooms are available; however, one must reserve them in advance by writing or sending a fax directly to the abbey.

How to get there? Herzogenburg is located about forty-five miles west of Vienna. By road, take A1 west from Vienna for almost thirty miles and then merge on to S33 toward Krems/St. Polten-Ost/Landhaus. Herzogenburg lies on the main train line between St. Polten and Krems, and the town is also accessible by bus from St. Polten or Krems (bus line "Wien-Hütteldorf - Herzogenburg").

BILDUNGSHAUS MARIA LUGGAU
ServitenKloster
Maria Luggau
9655 Maria Luggau
Tel: (04716) 601 • Fax: (04716) 601-17
Email: bildungshaus.luggau@aon.at
Web site: www.lesachtal.com/bildungshaus

A place of pilgrimage since 1513, Maria Luggau receives several thousand visitors each year who come to pray before a miraculous image of the Virgin Mary. In the nineteenth century, the Servite Fathers built a monastery here near the shrine to take care of the pilgrims' needs.

Where to stay? Today the Servites continue their role of providing hospitality by operating a very large and comfortable guesthouse which accommodates approximately sixty-five people (five singles, thirty doubles).

How to get there? Maria Luggau is located about one hundred eight miles southeast from Innsbruck. Nearest rail station: Abfaltersbach or Oberdrauburg.

BENEDIKTINERSTIFT MELK
Abt-Berthold-Dietmayr Straße 1
3390 Melk
Tel: (02752) 555-225, 523-12 • Fax: (02752) 5555-226, 52312-52
Email: kultur.tourismus@stiftmelk.at; marketing@stiftmelk.at
Web site: www.stiftmelk.at

Founded more than nine hundred years ago, throughout the centuries the Melk Abbey has served as one of Austria's most important spiritual and cultural centers. Home to a community of Benedictine monks, the monastery welcomes thousands of visitors annually who come to tour its immense complex whether on vacation or pilgrimage. Guided tours of the abbey's church, library, and grounds are available. To make a group tour reservation, email tours@stiftmelk.at. Dining at the restaurant is one of the most popular activities for guests. For more information or to make reservations at the restaurant, Tel: (02752) 52555; Fax: (02752) 54444; Email: stiftsrestaurant@stiftmelk.at.

Where to stay? A guesthouse is available; however, reservations can be very difficult to obtain. Only "temporary monastic retreats" are available. For more information contact the guestmaster by email at gastpater@stiftmelk.at or Tel: (02752) 52312-460.

How to get there? Melk is about fifty-five miles west of Vienna. From Vienna, take A1 west, exiting at the signs for Melk. The town is also easily accessible by train and bus from throughout Austria (although train service is much more efficient). If you arrive by river cruise, you can easily reach the abbey by walking or taking a taxi.

STIFT SCHLÄGL
4160 Schlägl 1
Tel: (07281) 8801-0/344/332 • Fax: (07281) 8801-227
Email: zv@stift-schlaegl.at; guesthouse holzschlag@stift-schlaegl.at
Web site www.stift-schlaegl.at

Founded in 1218, the Abbey Schlägl is a monastery of the Order of Premonstratensians, also known as the Norbertine Fathers. The monks are devoted to a number of apostolic activities including parish work, catechesis and teaching, education, science, culture, and economic involvement.

Where to stay? The abbey runs a large seminar center, which is used as a place for meditation, meetings, and educational classes. For its participants, the center offers forty-beds, seminar rooms, a meditation room, and a number of other facilities.

How to get there? Schlägl is located about one hundred fifty miles northwest of Vienna along A1 and B1. From Linz, head north along B127 for about thirty miles. Schlägl is accessible by train.

STIFT SCHLIERBACH

KlosterstraBe 1
4533 Schlierbach (Inzersdorf)
Tel: (07582) 83-013-0 • Fax: (07582) 83-013-176
Email: office@stift-schlierbach.at
Web site: www.stift-schlierbach.at

Founded in 1355, today the Schlierbach Abbey is home to a community of Cistercian monks. Visitors can take guided tours of the monastery, as well as attend daily Mass with the monks. Visitors and guests can dine in the abbey restaurant (Stiftskeller) and purchase the delicious "monastery-made" cheeses in the gift shop. A number of concerts and art exhibitions take place at the abbey each year.

Where to stay? A comfortable guesthouse is available for those individuals and groups seeking a place for prayer and silence.

How to get there? Schlierbach is located about one hundred miles west of Vienna along A1 and A9. Schlierbach is accessible by bus and train.

BENEDIKTINERABTEI SECKAU

Abteiverwaltung
8732 Seckau 1
Tel: (03514) 52-34-0, 5234-101 • Fax: (03514) 52-34-105
Email: verwaltung@abtei-seckau.at
Web site: www.abtei-seckau.at

Founded in 1140, the Abbey of Seckau is home to a community of Benedictine monks. A very prominent monastery throughout the ages, visitors are welcome to tour the immense abbey grounds and church—both of which feature numerous works of art and grand architecture. A restaurant and shop are also on the premises.

Where to stay? Even though only men can be accommodated in the guesthouse (which is located within the monastic enclosure), other individuals and couples can be accommodated in the Hotel Hofwirt which is located on the abbey grounds. Reservations should be made in advance.

How to get there? Seckau is located about one hundred miles southwest of Vienna along the A2 and S36. By train travel to Knittelfeld and then continue by bus from Knittelfeld to Seckau.

STIFT SEITENSTETTEN

Am Klosterberg 1
3353 Seitenstetten
Tel: (07477) 423-00, 423-00-38 • Fax: (07477) 423-00-50/250
Email: stift@stift-seitenstetten.at, wirtschaftskanzlei@stift-seitenstetten.at, kultur@stift-seitenstetten.at
Web site: www.stift-seitenstetten.at

Founded in 1112, the Abbey of Seitenstetten is home to a community of Benedictine monks. Guided tours of the monastery grounds, church, cloister, library, and museum are available (be sure to see the knights' chapel). Throughout the year, a number of seminars, conferences, and retreats take place at the abbey. There is a gift shop on the premises which sells religious books, CDs, tapes, liquor, and other products of the abbey.

Where to stay? The monastery operates a small guesthouse of seven rooms with thirteen beds. There is also a guesthouse located on the exterior of the monastery, which can provide accommodations for up to twenty-six people. The monastery warmly welcomes groups for seminars and conferences. For reservations, Tel: (07477) 42300-38; Fax: 07477/42300-50; Email: papepi@stift-seitenstetten.at; gastpater@stift-seitenstetten.at.

How to get there? Seitenstetten is located about ninety miles west of Vienna along A1 (exit Haag). By train arrive at St. Peter-Seitenstetten and take a taxi the remainder of approximately one to two miles.

SCHOTTEN STIFT

Freyung 6
1010 Vienna
Tel: (1) 534-98-0 • Fax: (1) 534-98-105
Email: schotten@schottenstift.at; benediktushaus@schottenstift.at
Web site: www.schottenstift.at

Founded almost eight centuries ago, the Abbey of Schotten is home to a community of Benedictine monks. Located in the heart of Vienna, visitors are welcome to attend religious services with the monks and tour their museum.

Where to stay? The monks operate a very comfortable guesthouse called Saint Benediktushaus (Saint Benedict House), located in the middle of Vienna—yet protected from the noise of the city. Conference room facilities are available for twenty to thirty people. To make reservations for individuals or groups (up to fifteen people) with the single, double, and triple bedrooms, contact: Saint Benediktushaus, Freyung 6a, 1010 Vienna, Guesthouse Tel: (1) 534-98-900; Guesthouse Fax: (1) 534-98-12, (1) 534-98-905.

How to get there? The abbey is located in the center of the Freyung Square (in Vienna), near Schottenngasse.

CHORHERREN STIFT VORAU
8250 Vorau (Graz)
Tel: (03337) 2351/0, 281-54
Email: office@stift-vorau.at
Web site: www.stift-vorau.at

Originally founded in 1237, today the Abbey of Chorherren Vorau is home to a community of Augustinian monks. Mass is celebrated daily, and all visitors are welcome to participate in religious services with the monks in the abbey church.

Where to stay? Sixteen comfortable guestrooms are available for those visitors who seek a place for personal prayer and retreat. Many seminars and conferences take place at the abbey throughout the year.

How to get there? Vorau is located about halfway between Graz and Vienna; it takes about seventy-five minutes by car to reach Vorau from either of these two cities. A train station is located at Rohrback/Vorau and you can reach the monastery by bus or taxi.

ZISTERZIENSERSTIFT STIFT ZWETTL
Stift Zwettl 1
3910 Zwettl
Tel: (02822) 20202-17, 550-0 • Fax: (02822) 20202-40, 550-50
Email(abbey information):
abtei@stift-zwettl.at; info@stift-zwettl.co.at
Web site: www.stift-zwettl.co.at

Founded in the twelfth century, the Abbey of Zwettl is home to a community of Cistercian monks. Located in the countryside of the northern region of Austria, the monastery has long attracted visitors because of its rich history and tradition, and for its magnificent church—often referred to as "a royal cathedral in Cistercian Guise." Pilgrims and tourists can visit the abbey, pray in the church, and take contemplative walks in the nearby fields. The abbey operates both a large guesthouse and restaurant. (Be sure to visit the abbey Web site which features a live video-cam!).

Where to stay? The abbey operates a well-established guesthouse for individuals and groups. To make reservations contact the guestmaster by email: gastpater@stift-zwettl.at or bildungshaus@stift-zwettl.co.at.

How to get there? Zwettl is located at about seventy miles northwest of Vienna and about three miles from the abbey itself (Stift Zwettl). By road from Vienna take 4 north, go east on 38 to Rastenfeld and follow the directions to Zwettl. If traveling by train or bus to Zwettl, you will need to switch and take a local bus to the abbey.

BELGIUM

ABBAYE NOTRE-DAME-DU-VAL-DIEU
Rue Val-Dieu 227
4880 Aubel
Tel: (087) 68-73-81, 68-74-02, 69-28-28 • Fax: (087) 68-69-83, 69-28-23
Email: abbaye@val-dieu.net; infotourist@val-dieu.net
Web site: www.val-dieu.net

Founded in 1216, the Abbey of Notre-Dame-du-Val-Dieu is home to a community of Cistercian monks. Guided tours for groups are possible, but reservations must be made in advance. One of the highlights is visiting the abbey brewery. To make group tour reservations of the brewery, including beer tasting, contact infotourist@val-dieu.net or casse-croute@val-dieu.net). Abbey cheeses, religious artwork, and music tapes can be purchased at the gift shop. Concerts and conferences, which take place throughout the year at the monastery, are open to the public.

Where to stay? With more than twenty guestrooms available, both individuals and groups are welcome to stay for several days of prayer and reflection. Young people traveling together are invited to participate in the prayer life of the monastery, as special accommodations are available for them. Conference facilities are also available for groups from ten to one hundred people. To make reservations, contact hotellerie@val-dieu.net.

How to get there? Aubel is located almost eighty miles east of Brussels along E40 towards Masstricht/Liege. Aubel is accessible only by both bus. The nearest train stations: Welkenraedt or Verviers.

ABBAYE DES PRÉMONTRÉS
2, rue A. De Moor
1421 Bois-Seigneur-Isaac
Tel: (067) 21-24-73, (067) 89-24-20 • Fax: (067) 21-43-22, (067) 89-24-29
Email: abbayebsi@hotmail.com

In 1413, the Order of Regular Canons of Saint Augustine built a monastery here to welcome the thousands of pilgrims who would come annually to venerate a Eucharistic Miracle dating back to 1405. In 1903, the members of the Order of the Premonstratensians from Mondaye (Calvados, France) took over the abbey. They gave it to their Belgian counterparts in 1921, as well as a gift shop which sells many items related to the eucharistic miracle. French, Dutch, English, and Italian are spoken by the monks. The central highlight of the abbey is the Chapel of the Holy Blood and the maginificent reliquary housing the miraculous eucharistic cloth.

Where to stay? Today, the monks operate a guesthouse with eleven rooms, with reservations required three weeks in advance.

How to get there? Bois-Seigneur-Isaac is located about fifteen miles south of Brussels. Only bus service is available to Bois-Seigneur-Isaac; if traveling by train, the nearest rail station is fifteen minutes away by bus/taxi at Braine l'Alleud.

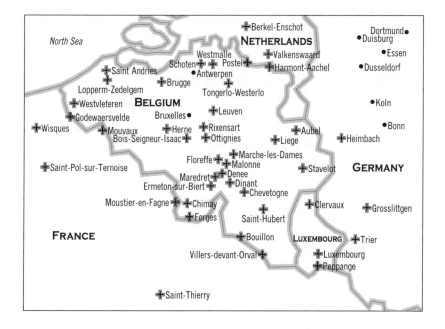

Map showing locations across North Sea, Netherlands, Belgium, Germany, France, and Luxembourg:

Berkel-Enschot, NETHERLANDS, Dortmund, Duisburg, North Sea, Westmalle, Valkenswaard, Essen, Schoten, Postel, Saint Andries, Harmont-Aachel, Dusseldorf, Antwerpen, Lopperm-Zedelgem, Brugge, Tongerlo-Westerlo, Westvleteren, BELGIUM, Koln, Godewaersvelde, Bruxelles, Leuven, Wisques, Mouvaux, Herne, Rixensart, Bonn, Bois-Seigneur-Isaac, Ottignies, Aubel, Heimbach, Liege, Marche-les-Dames, Floreffe, Malonne, Saint-Pol-sur-Ternoise, Maredret, Denee, Stavelot, GERMANY, Ermeton-sur-Biert, Dinant, Moustier-en-Fagne, Chimay, Chevetogne, Clervaux, Grosslittgen, Forges, Saint-Hubert, FRANCE, Bouillon, LUXEMBOURG, Trier, Villers-devant-Orval, Luxembourg, Peppange, Saint-Thierry

ABBAYE NOTRE-DAME-DE-CLAIREFONTAINE
Cordemois
6830 Bouillon
Tel: (061) 229-080, 46-61-59 • Fax: (061) 229-081, 46-63-76
Email: accueil@abbaye-clairefontaine.be; abbesse@abbaye-clairefontaine.be
Web site: www.abbaye-clairefontaine.be

Founded in 1845, today the Abbey of Notre-Dame-de-Clairfontaine is home to a community of Trappist monks. Visitors are welcome to attend religious services with the monks, which include Mass and the Liturgy of the Hours (both of which are sung or said in French). With a bakery on the premises, visitors can purchase the abbey's own breads and cookies.

Where to stay? Twenty guestrooms are available for those individuals who seek a personal or group retreat in a monastic setting of prayer and silence.

How to get there? Bouillon is located about one hundred miles south of Brussels. From Brussels, Dinant, or Beuraing, travel E411 and exit 25 in Libramont and continue along N89 to Bouillon. By train travel, one option is to travel to Libramont and then continue by bus to Bouillon. Nearest rail station: Sedan or Charleulle-Mezieres.

MONASTERIUM DE WIJNGAARD
Monastery of the Vineyard
Begijnhof 24-30
8000 Brugge
Tel: (050) 33-00-11 • Fax: (050) 33-18-81
Email: secretariaat@dewijngaard.org
Web site: www.dewijngaard.org

Founded in 1927, the Monastery of the Vineyard is home to a community of Benedictine nuns. Central to the life of the sisters are the Mass and Liturgy of the Hours, both of which are sung in Gregorian chant. Another attraction at the monastery is the Beguine museum; for more information about the museum visit www.museumsite.be.

Where to stay? The priory has a guesthouse where women, girls, and married couples can come to rest, pray, relax, or study (for a minimum of three days).

How to get there? The monastery is accessible by foot from downtown Brugges (about a ten-minute walk), or take a taxi.

MONASTÈRE DE CHEVETOGNE
Rue du monastere 65
5590 Chevetogne
Tel: (083) 21-17-63 • Fax: (083) 21-60-45
Email: abbaye@monasterechevetogne.com
Web site: www.monasterechevetogne.com

Founded in the 1920s, the Monastery of Chevetogne is comprised of a community of Benedictine monks who are organized into two liturgical groups, and celebrate according to both the Latin and the Byzantine Rites. Since there is both a Latin and Byzantine church, guests are encouraged to join the monks for the daily Divine Office in both rites. The abbey's CDs of Slavonic liturgical chants are available for purchase, along with their many icons and books.

Where to stay? The monastery has three separate guesthouses which are open to receive individuals and groups who want to make a retreat and share in the prayer life of the monks. (Each guesthouse is designated to receive either men, women, or groups.) Twelve rooms in the monastery building are available for men; the second guesthouse, Bethanie, is available for women and families; the third guesthouse, Emmaus, is available for groups.

How to get there? Chevetogne is located about sixty-five miles southeast of Brussels and twenty-five miles from Namur. By road travel along E411 (Brussels-Luxemburg), taking Exit #1 "Custinne-Leignon" and then following the signs for Chevetogne and Leignon; at the village of Chevetogne, continue to follow the signs for the monastery (Eglise Orientale). By train travel to Ciney, located about 6 miles from Chevetogne, along the line Brussels-Luxembourg. Take the bus "#43 Dinant-Ciney-Mont Gautheir" in the direction of Mont-Gautheir and stop at "Rue du Monastere." If the bus is not available, take a taxi.

ABBAYE NOTRE-DAME-DE-LA-PAIX
Chaussée de Trélon, 1
6460 Chimay
Tel: (060) 21-11-64 • Fax: (060) 21-49-36
Email: vdbrosa@biz.tiscali.be

Founded in 1207, today the Abbey of Notre-Dame-de-la-Paix is home to a community of Trappist monks. Visitors are welcome to participate in the prayer life of the monks, which includes Mass and the Liturgy of the Hours. Religious vestments, hosts, and the abbey's beer may be purchased at the gift shop. The monastery is located near the Abbey of Scourmont, which is known for its famous Trappist Beer production.

Where to stay? About twelve guestrooms are available to those individuals and groups who wish to experience the monastic life more fully.

How to get there? Chimay is located about seventy miles south of Brussels and thirty-five miles from Charleroi. Nearest rail station: Fourmies.

ABBAYE DE MAREDSOUS

Rue de Maredsous, 11
5537 Denée
Tel: (082) 69-82-11 • Fax: (082) 69-83-21, (082) 69-82-09/69-82-21
Email: info@maredsous.com
Web site: www.maredsous.com

Founded in 1872, the Benedictine Abbey of Maredsous was the first monastery constructed in Belgium after the French Revolution. Among the sites to be explored or visited on the grounds include a library, chapel, garden, walking paths, sports grounds (for youth groups) and a cafeteria. Among the most popular items sold at the abbey gift shop are the cheeses and beers produced by the monks.

Where to stay? The monks operate a guesthouse with seventeen double bedrooms and thirty-one single bedrooms, which is open to both men and women who seek a time of spiritual renewal and prayer. A lecture room is available with video capabilities for a group of forty people, along with two smaller lecture rooms for groups of fifteen people. It is possible to have retreats led by a monk. For more information email: hotellerie@maredsous.com.

How to get there? Denee is located about fifty-five miles southeast of Brussels via A54/E19. By train, arrive at Namur and then switch to the bus line 21 "Namur Maredsous" for Maredsous.

ABBAYE NOTRE-DAME-DE-LEFFE

Place de líAbbaye 1
5500 Dinant
Tel: (082) 22-23-77 • Fax: (082) 21-37-28
Web site: www.abbaye-de-leffe.be

Founded in 1152, the Abbey of Notre-Dame-de-Leffe is home to a community of Premonstratensians (Norbertine Fathers). When visiting the monastery, individuals can ask to take a tour of the abbey and its grounds (only certain parts of the cloister, however, are open to the public). All are welcome to attend religious services with the monks, which include Mass, the Liturgy of the Hours, and Eucharistic Adoration.

Where to stay? Groups seeking a spiritual retreat may be accommodated in the abbey guesthouse.

How to get there? Dinant is located about sixty-three miles southeast of Brussels and twenty-five miles from Namur. Take E411 to Brussels, exit at 20 (Achene) and follow signs to Dinant-centre. From Namur take A92. Direct trains are available from Brussels via Namur.

MONASTÈRE NOTRE-DAME
Rue du Monastère
5644 Ermeton-sur-Biert
Tel: (071) 72-00-40, 72-73-92, 72-00-48 • Fax: (071) 72-73-92, 72-00-48
Email: monastere.ermeton@skynet.be; ermeton@skynet.be
Web site: www.ermeton.be

Founded in 1917, the Monastery of Notre-Dame is home to a women's community of Benedictine monks. As well as visiting the ancient chapel and castle, the faithful can participate in the prayer life of the monks, which includes Mass and the Divine Office (in French).

Where to stay? The abbey operates a guesthouse, which features more than twenty-eight rooms, receiving both men and women. (Families with infants can also be accommodated.) All are welcome regardless of age including families, children, individuals, and groups.

How to get there? Ermeton-sur-Biert is about fifteen miles from Namur and ten miles from Dinant. Ermeton-sur-Biert is accessible by both train and bus.

CARMEL DE SAINTE-THÉRÈSE DE JÉSUS
5, rue du Carmel
5150 Floreffe
Tel: (081) 44-43-64 • Fax: (081) 44-61-64

Founded in 1860, the Convent of Sainte-Thérèse de Jésus is home to a community of Carmelite nuns. Mass is celebrated daily, along with the Divine Office, both of which are open to all visitors.

Where to stay? Individuals seeking a time of personal retreat may be accommodated in the convent guestrooms.

How to get there? Floreffe is located about forty-five miles southeast of Brussels.

ABBAYE NOTRE-DAME-DE-SCOURMOUNT
6464 Forges
Tel: (060) 21-30-63, 21-05-11 • Fax: (060) 21-40-18, 21-36-96
Email: abbaye@scourmont.be
Web site: www.scourmont.be

Founded in 1850, today the Abbey of Notre-Dame-de-Scourmount is home to a community of about twenty Trappist monks. The monks of Chimay are probably best known for their own beer "Chimay," which is brewed within the monastery and under the responsibility of the monks themselves. Only six beers in Belgium can carry the appellation "Trappist" and Chimay is one of them. In addition, Chimay is famous for the four cheeses this monastic community produces. Although the abbey of Scourmont is not accessible to the public, one can visit the gardens, the cemetery, and the church.

Where to stay? Even though there are a small number of guestrooms available, individuals seeking a time of prayer, solitude, and silence may be accommodated. Small groups can also stay at the guesthouse. To make reservations, you can email hotellerie@chimay.be.

How to get there? Forges is located about seventy-five miles south of Brussels via N5, A54, and E19. Forges is accessible by train, but you will need to take a local bus or taxi to the abbey.

SAINT BENEDICTUS ABDIJ DE ACHELSE KLUIS
De Kluis 1
3930 Hamont-Aachel
Tel (abbey): (011) 800-760, 800-766 • Tel (guesthouse): (011) 800-766
Fax: (011) 648-130
Email: gastenhuis@achelsekluis.org
Web site: www.achelsekluis.org

Founded in 1686, the Abbey of Achelse Kluis is home to a community of Cistercian monks. Serving as a place of prayer and contemplation, the monastery invites all visitors to join them in the chapel for Mass and the singing of the Divine Office.

Where to stay? The monastery guesthouse receives men, women, and groups, and provides an opportunity for individuals to join the monks in their prayerful rhythm of life. Retreats are not organized by the monks, but groups are allowed to have their own group retreats.

How to get there? Hamont-Aachel is about seventy miles northeast of Brussels via N74 and E314. By rail, take the train to Neerpelt and then switch to the bus line 18A to Achel, or take the train to Hassel and switch to bus line 18A. From here you will need to take the local bus or taxi.

MONASTÈRE DE MARIE-MÉDIATRICE
Heilige Geeststraat 24
1540 Herne, Belgium
Tel: (02) 396-17-43 • Fax: (02) 396-07-99
Email: dominicaines.herne@skynet.be

Founded in 1926, today the Monastery of Mary Mediatrix is home to a community of Dominican nuns of the rosary. Visitors are welcome to attend religious services with the monks, which include Mass and the Liturgy of the Hours (in French). The way of life of the nuns is that they see contemplation as the foundation of all apostolate.

Where to stay? The monks operate a guesthouse called the "House of Prayer" which can receive both men and women who seek a time of prayer and silence. The House of Prayer Guesthouse is open for spiritual retreats, Bible study, meetings, personal retreats, and those who wish to experience the monastic life.

How to get there? Herne is located about twenty-five miles southwest of Brussels and about one mile from the Enghien rail station.

ABDIJ KEIZERSBERG (ABBAYE DU MONT-CÉSAR)
Mechelsestraat 202
3000 Leuven
Tel: (016) 310-060 • Fax: (016) 310-066
Web site: www.keizersberg.be

Founded in 1899, the Abbey of Keizersberg is home to a community of Benedictine monks. Every day visitors can attend the religious services of the monastery, which include Mass and the Liturgy of the Hours (both are sung in Dutch and Gregorian chant). Beer and cheese are two of the major products produced by the abbey, both of which can be purchased at the gift shop.

Where to stay? Guest-room accommodations are available for those individuals or groups (maximum twenty) who wish to partake in the monastic prayer life of the abbey. Retreatants are expected to participate in the daily services of the monks.

How to get there? Leuven is twenty miles east of Brussels via E40. Leuven is accessible by train and bus. The abbey can be reached by the local bus 4, 5, or 6.

ABBAYE-DE-LA-PAIX-NOTRE-DAME-D'AVERBODE
Boulevard d'Avroy, 54
4000 Liège
Tel: (04) 223-77-20 • Fax: (04) 223-35-80
Web site: www.abdijaverbode.be/nl

Founded in 1627, the Abbey of Paix-Notre-Dame is home to a community of Benedictine monks. While visiting, the faithful can participate in the prayer life of the monks (Mass and the Liturgy of the Hours are said/sung in French). Specialists in painting, the monks sell some of their creations—including jewelry, china dishes, scarves, clothing, and religious icons—at the gift shop.

Where to stay? Many conferences and organized retreats are held at the guesthouse throughout the year. Both individuals and groups can be accommodated in the abbey guesthouse.

How to get there? Liege is located about sixty miles east of Brussels via E40. Liege is accessible by train and bus.

MONASTÈRE NOTRE-DAME-DE-BÉTHANIE
8, Sysen
8210 Loppem-Zedelgem
Tel: (050) 38-31-71 • Fax: (050) 38-82-74

Founded in 1921, the Monastery of Notre-Dame-de-Béthanie is home to a women's community of Benedictine monks. Visitors are invited to attend the daily recitation of the Divine Office (sung in Dutch), as well as Mass on Sundays.

Where to stay? Guestrooms are available for those individuals and groups who wish to embark on a personal or group retreat in a prayerful atmosphere.

How to get there? Loppem-Zedelgem is located about fifty-five miles northwest of Brussels. Loppem-Zedelgem is accessible by regional bus on line 61 Brugge-Loppem-Zedelgem-Merkemveld.

MONASTÈRE CLARTÉ NOTRE-DAME
41, rue des Monastères
5020 Malonne
Tel: (081) 44-47-40 • Fax: (081) 45-02-67
Email: clarissesmalonne@swing.be

Founded in 1903, the Monastery of Clarté Notre-Dame is home to a community of Poor Clare nuns. The Liturgy of the Hours is celebrated daily in French.

Where to stay? The monastery operates a guesthouse for those individuals or groups who wish to spend a few days in a monastic retreat (thirteen guestrooms are available). Visitors who stay overnight in the guesthouse may be asked to help work in the garden.

How to get there? Malonee is located about fifty miles southeast of Brussels via E411. You can travel to Malonee by bus from Namur.

MONASTÈRE DE BETHLÉEM
Notre-Dame-des-Sources-Vives
5024, Marche-les-Dames
Tel: (081) 58-99-07

Originally founded as a Cistercian abbey in the thirteenth century, today the Monastery of Bethléem is home to a community of Bethlehem monks. Visitors can attend religious services with the monks in the abbey church (Mass and the Liturgy of the Hours are said in French). Religious articles and products made by the monks may be purchased.

Where to stay? Individuals wishing to partake in the monastic life may be accommodated in the guesthouse, but they must strictly adhere to the silent and prayerful atmosphere of the abbey.

How to get there? Marche-les-Dames is located about forty miles southeast of Brussels. Marche-les-Dames is accessible by train.

ABBAYE DE MAREDRET

Rue des Laidmonts, 9
5537 Maredret
Tel: (082) 69-91-34, 69-91-45, 69-90-63 • Fax: (082) 69-90-89
Web site: www.maredret.be/abbayedemaredret

Founded in 1893, the Abbey of Maredret is home to a women's community of Benedictine monks. Visitors can attend the Divine Office and Mass with the monks, both of which are sung in French and Gregorian chant. A guided tour of the abbey church is available upon request.

Where to stay? Guesthouse accommodations are available for those individuals and small groups who wish to undertake a monastic retreat.

How to get there? Maredret is located 60 miles south/southeast of Brussels. Take the train to Namur, switching to local bus to arrive at Maredret.

ABBEY DE POSTEL

Norbertijnenabdij Postel (Abbaye Norbertine)
Abdijlaan, 16
2400 Mol-Postel
Tel: (014) 37-81-21, 37-81-23 • Fax: (014) 37-81-23
Email: info@abdijpostel.be
Web site: www.abdijpostel.be

Founded in 1140, the Abbey of Postel is home to a community of Canons Regular of Premonstratensians (Norbertine Fathers). As well as exploring the twelfth-century church, visitors can participate in the prayer life of the monks by attending Mass and the Liturgy of the Hours. Dutch, French, German, and English are spoken at the abbey. The monks operate a large farm and a famous dairy.

Where to stay? Thirty guestrooms (nine of which are double rooms) are available at the "Kontaktcentrum" for those individuals who wish to embark on a personal or group retreat in a monastic setting. There are also three conference rooms for groups including a recreation room. To make reservations contact the guestmaster at gastenkwartier@abdijpostel.be.

How to get there? Postel (Mol-Postel) is located about sixty miles northeast of Brussels. Postel is accessible by bus and the abbey by taxi.

MONASTÈRE SAINT-ANDRÉ-DE-CLERLANDE

1, Allée de Clerlande
1340 Ottignies
Tel: (010) 41-74-63, 43-56-52 • Fax: (010) 41-80-27
Web site: www.clerlande.com

Founded in 1971, the Monastery of Saint-André-de-Clerlande is home to a community of Benedictine monks. One of the major apostolates of the monks is the making of religious icons.

Where to stay? Individuals, couples, and groups (no larger than ten people) are welcome to stay in the guesthouse which has seven double rooms, five rooms for youth, several meeting rooms, and an oratory.

How to get there? Ottignies is located about twenty miles southeast of Brussels. By car take E411 "Brussels-Namur-Luxembourg" and exit at #6 (Wavre). Take the train to Ottignies and then switch to local bus or taxi.

MONASTÈRE DE L'ALLIANCE

Rue du Monastere, 82
1330 Rixensart
Tel: (02) 652-06-01 • Fax: (02) 652-06-46
Email: monastere@benedictinesrixensart.be

Founded in 1968, the Monastery of the Alliance is home to a community of Benedictine monks. The Liturgy of the Hours is recited in the abbey church (in French), and all visitors are welcome to attend.

Where to stay? A guesthouse with twenty-four rooms is available to those individuals who wish to participate more fully in the prayer life of the monastery.

How to get there? Rixensart is twenty miles southeast of Brussels via E411; exit at #4. Rixensart is accessible by train and bus.

SINT ANDRIESABDIJ VAN ZEVENKERKEN
Abbaye de Saint-André
Zevenkerken 4
8200 Saint Andries (Brugge 2)
Tel: (050) 40-61-80, 38-01-36 • Fax: (050) 40-61-92, 38-79-60
Email: abt@zevenkerken.org, info@zevenkerken.org
Web site: www.sint-andriesabdij.org, www.zevenkerken.org

Founded in 1902, the Abbey of Saint André is home to a community of Benedictine monks. Visitors are welcome to attend Mass (recited in Dutch) in the chapel. Ceramics and religious icons made by the monks may be purchased in the abbey gift shop.

Where to stay? Individuals or groups who seek a time for personal prayer and contemplation can ask to stay in one of the thirty guestrooms. Rooms are available for group gatherings and retreats; meals are often taken in silence. To make reservations email the guestmaster at gastenpater@sint-andriesabdij.org.

How to get there? Saint Andries is located about sixty miles northwest of Brussels via E40 (near Brugge). If traveling by rail, take the train to Brugge then transfer by bus to arrive at Sint Andries.

NOTRE-DAME-D'HURTEBISE
2, rue du Monastère
6870 Saint-Hubert
Tel: (061) 61-11-27 • Fax: (061) 61-32-76

Founded in 1938, the Abbey of Notre-Dame-d'Hurtebise is home to a community of Benedictine monks. While visiting the monastery, the faithful can participate in religious services with the monks, which include the Liturgy of the Hours and Mass (recited in French).

Where to stay? Individuals or groups seeking a few days of retreat can ask to be accommodated in the abbey guesthouse which features thirty-seven rooms (single or double), as well as an oratory and meeting rooms. Hermitages are available for those seeking a sabbatical.

How to get there? Saint-Hubert is located ninety miles southeast of Brussels via E411 and N89. You can reach nearby Libramont by train and then continue by local bus to the monastery.

PRIORIJ REGINA PACIS
Sint-Amelbergalei 35
2900 Schoten
Tel: (03) 658-44-68 • Fax: (03) 658-83-01
Email: benedictinessen.schoten@skynet.be
Web site: www.benedictinessen-schoten.be

Founded in 1879, today the Priory of Regina Pacis is home to a women's community of Benedictine monks. Visitors can attend the daily Mass and Liturgy of the Hours, both of which are celebrated in the abbey church. Once a month, a Byzantine Rite Mass is also celebrated, which is open to all.

Where to stay? Guestrooms are available for those individuals who wish to participate more fully in the prayer life of the monastery.

How to get there? Schoten is located about forty-five miles north of Brussels via A12 and just northeast of Antwerpen. Schoten is accessible by bus from Antwerpen (six miles).

MONASTÈRE SAINT-REMACLE
Wavreumont
4970 Stavelot
Tel: (080) 86-23-18 • Fax: (080) 88-01-82
Email: wavreumont@belgacom.net

Founded in 1950, the Monastery of Saint-Remacle is home to a community of Benedictine monks. Mass and the Liturgy of the Hours are celebrated daily (in French); all visitors are welcome to participate.

Where to stay? The monastery operates a guesthouse, which provides accommodations for individuals and groups seeking a time of prayer and silence. A series of retreats are also offered during the year complete with the monastic liturgy, presentations, and meetings. The contact information for hospitality and the guestrooms is hôtellerie: (080) 28-03-71.

How to get there? Stavelot is located about one hundred miles southeast of Brussels. The monastery is located between Verviers and St. Vith along the highway A 27 (E42). Exit #11 (Malmedy). Take the Liege-Luxembourg train to Trois-Ponts, switch to the Bus Line 45a-37 "Liege-Cologne" and stop at Verviers (bus #395). Exit at the road

"Wavreumont" and the monastery is located about half a mile from here.

ABBAYE D'ORVAL
6823 Villers-devant-Orval
Tel (guesthouse): (061) 32-51-10 • Tel (switchboard): (061) 31-10-60
Fax (guesthouse): (061) 32-51-36 • Fax (abbey): (061) 31-55-95
Email (abbey): econome@orval.be
Web site: www.orval.be

First founded by Benedictine monks in 1070, Orval Abbey was later refounded by the Trappist Cistercian monks in the twelfth century. Although the monks are involved in a number of economic activities to support their livelihood, they have become best known for their beer and cheese throughout the world. In fact, Orval is only one of six breweries in the world that is allowed to have their beer designated a "Trappist" product—a strictly controlled mark of quality. Visitors can tour parts of the ruins of the old abbey (12th-13th century), enter its underground museum, and view an audiovisual presentation about the monastery.

Where to stay? Individuals and groups who are looking for a time of spiritual renewal, as well as personal and community prayer, are invited to spend time on retreat in the monastic guesthouse (for periods from two to seven days).

How to get there? Villers-devant-Orval is located about one hundred twenty miles south of Brussels and forty-five miles from Luxembourg. Take the train to Florenville and then transfer to the local bus (line 24) from Florenville to Villers-devant-Orval.

NORBERTIJNENABDIJ TONGERLO
(ABBAYE NORBERTINE DE TONGERLO)
Abdijstraat 40
2260 Tongerlo-Westerlo
Tel: (014) 53-99-00 • Fax: (014) 53-99-08
Email: abdij@tongerlo.org
Web site: www.tongerlo.org

Originally founded in 1130, today the Abbey of Tongerlo is home to a community of Canons Regular of Premonstratensians (Norbertine

Fathers). Visitors can tour the abbey church, museum, and attend the Divine Office and Mass with the monks (sung in Dutch). Dutch and French are spoken at the abbey. Bread, cheese, butter, and beer produced by the monks may be purchased at the gift shop. Every year, on November 14, a large pilgrimage to the monastery takes place in honor of Saint Siard.

Where to stay? Individuals, families, or small groups interested in participating more fully in the life of the monastery can be accommodated in the abbey's guestrooms. Guests are expected to join the monks at the services.

How to get there? Tongerlo-Westerlo is located about forty miles northeast of Brussels via E314. Take the train to Herentals, switching to the local bus to Westerlo Village.

ABBAYE DE WESTMALLE
Abdij der Trappisten
Antwerpsesteenweg 496
2390 Westmalle
Tel: (033) 12-92-00, 12-92-22 • Fax: (033) 12-92-09, 12-92-28, 12-92-20
Email: info@trappistwestmalle.be
Web site: www.trappistwestmalle.be

Founded in 1794, the Abbey of Notre-Dame du Sacré Coeur is home to a community of Trappist monks. World famous for their cheese and beer, people from all over the globe come to visit the abbey. All are welcome to attend the Liturgy of the Monks and Mass, both of which are sung in Dutch.

Where to stay? Since guestrooms are limited, only those individuals who wish to undertake a personal retreat of prayer and silence can be accommodated. The guest facilities and schedule focus on contemplation. Groups are occasionally accepted and there are no guided retreats by the monks.

How to get there? The abbey is located along the N12 Antwerp-Turnhout road, between Westmalle and Sint-Antonius-Zoersel. From Antwerp there is regular bus service (Antwerp-Turnhout) to Westmalle with a stop at the abbey.

SAINT SIXTUS-ABDIJ

Abbaye Notre-Dame-de-Saint-Sixte
Donkerstraat 12
8640 Westvleteren
Tel: (057) 40-03-76 • Tel (guesthouse): (057) 40-19-70
Fax: (057) 40-14-20
Email: gastenhuis@sintsixtus.be
Web site: www.sintsixtus.be

Originally founded in 1260 (or even possibly as early as 806), today the Abbey of Notre-Dame-de-Saint-Sixte is home to a community of Trappist monks. Along with monasteries such as those at Orval, West-malle, and Chival, the Abbey of Notre Dame de Saint-Sixte is one of only six breweries who have the right to produce "Trappist" beer.

Where to stay? Although the abbey guesthouse will be closed for renovations until the year 2010, you can still visit the abbey during the day.

How to get there? Westvleteren is located about eighty-five miles west of Brussels. Westvleteren is not accessible by train or bus. From Brussels travel to Diksmuide and then take a taxi for the last twenty miles to Westvleteren.

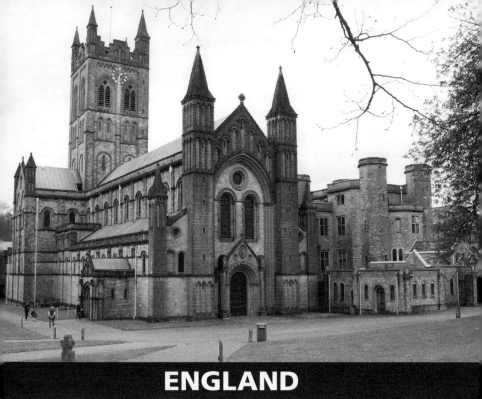

ENGLAND

THE RECEPTION OFFICE
The Friars
Aylesford, Kent ME20 7BX
Tel: (01622) 71-72-72 • Fax: (01622) 71-55-75
Email: friarsreception@hotmail.com, friarsevents@hotmail.com
Web site: www.carmelite.org/aylesford

Founded in 1242, Ayles-ford Priory is home to a community of Carmelite friars. According to tradition, this is where the Blessed Virgin Mary revealed the famous Brown Scapular to Saint Simon Stock (the prior general of the order at that time). A very popular place of pilgrimage, Aylesford welcomes pilgrims from all over the world who come to explore the abbey grounds and engage in either personal or group retreats.

Where to stay? Very well equipped to receive large numbers of people, the priory has extensive conference facilities for religious groups, educational courses, and business groups. There is a program of retreats arranged by the Carmelite community, and everyone is welcome to join in the prayer life of the friars. The abbey guesthouse can accommodate up to one hundred people in single or double rooms. Anyone wishing to bring a group should contact the pilgrimage secretary prior to their arrival.

How to get there? Aylesford is located about thirty-five miles southeast of London. Aylesford is accessible by train and bus.

BELMONT ABBEY
Belmont, Hereford HR2 9RZ
Tel: (01432) 277-388, 374710 • Fax: (01432) 277-597
Email: procoffice@aol.com, procurator@belmontabbey.org.uk
Web site: www.belmontabbey.org.uk

Founded in 1859, the Belmont Abbey is a member of the English Benedictine Congregation, which is currently the oldest of the twenty-one Benedictine congregations throughout the world, claiming continuity with the congregations established in the thirteenth century by the Holy See. As well as operating the guesthouse and its Common Novitiate (House of Studies), the Belmont monks serve in most of the Catholic parishes in the surrounding area.

Where to stay? Recognized as the second largest English Benedictine House in England, the abbey operates a very comfortable and well-established guesthouse (Hedley Lodge), which accommodates up to forty people with seventeen guestrooms. Conference rooms are available. Both private and guided retreats are available for either individuals and/or groups. For reservations contact hedley@belmontabbey.org. uk or retreats@belmontabbey.org.uk. Hedley Lodge telephone: (01432) 37-47-47; (07799) 811-646; Hedley Lodge fax: (01432) 374-754; (01432) 277-597; Retreats office: (01432) 374-712.

How to get there? Belmont is located about one hundred fifty miles west/northwest of London and about 2.5 miles southwest of Hereford on the A465 Abergavenny Road; Hedley Lodge is only two miles from the City Centre. Hereford is accessible by train and bus from London.

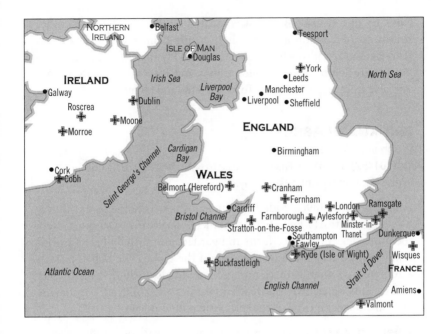

BUCKFAST ABBEY

Buckfastleigh, Devon TQ11 0EE
Tel: (01364) 643-301, 642-519, 645-550 • Fax: (01364) 643-891
Email: enquiries@buckfast.org.uk
Web site: www.buckfast.org.uk

Originally founded in 1018 by the Cistercians, Buckfast Abbey was later refounded in 1882 by a community of Benedictine monks. Renowned for its history and architecture, the monastery provides a wealth of activities to do and sites to see for the visitor: the abbey church, Medieval Guest Hall, gardens, video presentations, and a gift and monastic produce shop.

Where to stay? Southgate is the monastic retreat house which can accommodate up to twenty people for individual or group retreats. In addition to Southgate, there are some guestrooms in the monastery itself which are available to men who come on their own: apply to the guestmaster to stay in one of them. The abbey does not usually offer guided retreats. Groups of up to eight, fifteen, and fifty-six people can be accommodated in three different houses.

How to get there? Buckfast is located almost two hundred miles southwest of London and only half a mile from the A38 dual road (carriageway), midway between Exeter and Plymouth. The nearest rail stations are South Devon, Newton Abbot, and Totnes; local bus service is available from Newton Abbot, Totnes, Exeter, and Plymouth.

PRINKNASH ABBEY

Cranham, Gloucestershire GL4 8EX
Tel: (01452) 812-455 • Fax: (01452) 814-420, 812-529, 812-066
Web site: www.prinknashabbey.org

Founded in the 1890s, today Prinknash Abbey is home to a community of about thirty Benedictine monks. As a means to support itself, the monastery operates a farm and garden, and distributes its world-renowned pottery and incense around the globe. The abbey farm is a zoolike park that features numerous animals, including birds, deer and various waterfowl—perfect for families and children. Visitors are welcome to spend time in the monastic retreat house.

Where to stay? Currently no guesthouse is available as the abbey is developing a new hospitality center and guesthouse for men, women, and groups. However, check the abbey's Web site for updates and the launch of its new guesthouse.

How to get there? Cranham is located about one hundred five miles west of London via the M4; head towards Stroud, pass the "Cross Hands" junction, and drive up the hill. Prinknash is on the right. Gloucester is accessible by train; take a taxi to arrive at the abbey.

SAINT MARY'S PRIORY

Fernham
Faringdon, Oxfordshire SN7 7PP
Email: fernhampriory@btinternet.com
Web site: www.btinternet.com/~fernhampriory/index.htm

Although the earliest days of the Benedictine community date back to the sixth century, the actual founding of Saint Mary's Priory was in the eighteenth century. All are invited to join the sisters in the Liturgy of the Hours. It is interesting to note that Saint Mary's Priory has never aspired to the status of abbey, and has accepted the Virgin Mary as their Abbess.

Where to stay? In 1991, the nuns opened Saint Gabriel's Retreat House, which receives both men and women who wish to spend time in silence and prayer.

How to get there? Fernham is located about eighty miles west of London via M40/A40. Fernham is accessible by bus.

SAINT MICHAEL'S ABBEY
280 Farnborough Road
Farnborough, Hampshire GU14 7NQ
Tel: (01252) 546-105 • Fax: (01252) 372-822
Email: info@farnboroughabbey.org
Web site: www.farnboroughabbey.org

Founded in 1887, Saint Michael's Abbey is home to a community of Benedictine monks. As well as attending religious services in the monastery, visitors can spend time touring the spectacular abbey church. Among the monks' main apostolic works is the restoration of ancient books and the production of vestments and religious icons.

Where to stay? Ten guestrooms (nine singles, one double) are available, but are only open to men and/or young people who desire to partake in the prayer life of the community. The South Lodge offers accommodations for women. To make reservations, contact guestmaster@farnboroughabbey.org.

How to get there? Farnborough is located about forty miles southwest of London and can be reached by road via the M3, A325, and A30. Farnborough is accessible by train and bus.

EALING ABBEY
Charlbury Grove
London, W5 2DY
Tel: (20) 8862-2100, (0181) 862-2100 • Fax: (20) 8862-2206, (0181) 862-2199
Email: ealingmonk@aol.com
Web site: http://members.aol.com/ealingmonk

Founded in 1897, Ealing Abbey is located in the heart of west London and is home to a community of Benedictine monks. As well as prayer, the main apostolic duties of the monks include parish work, running a school, and offering spiritual retreats and courses.

Where to stay? Visitors may join the monastic community in their daily prayers, for a meal, or even stay overnight in one of their guestrooms. Visitors can stay as little as a day.

How to get there? Ealing Abbey is located in London about quarter mile north of Ealing Broadway Station and is served by local buses via Eaton Rise. It's twenty minutes from Earls Court and thirty-five minutes from Oxford Circus.

SAINT MILDRED'S ABBEY
Minster-in-Thanet
Near Ramsgate
Kent CT12 4HF
Tel: (01843) 821-254
Web site: www.minsterabbeynuns.org

Founded in 1050, Saint Mildred's Abbey is home to a community of Benedictine monks. Visitors are invited to attend religious services with the monks and pray before the relics of Saint Mildred in the monastery church. The monks also operate an excellent restaurant, which is open to all visitors.

Where to stay? A guesthouse, which is open during the spring and summer, is available to those individuals and groups who wish to participate more fully in the prayer life of the abbey. The Guesthouse is located on the grounds of the ancient monastery of St. Mildred in Minster near Ramsgate in Kent. Hospitality is offered to groups for conferences or retreats of all ages. Men are welcome only as part of a group or family.

How to get there? Minster near Ramsgate is located about seventy-five miles east of London. Trains leave Charing Cross each hour for Minster/Ramsgate. The monastery is only a three minute walk from the rail station.

SAINT AUGUSTINE'S ABBEY
Saint Augustine's Road
Ramsgate
Kent CT11 9PA
Tel: (01227) 767-345 • Fax: (01843) 582-732

Founded in 1856, Saint Augustine's Abbey is home to a community of Benedictine monks. All visitors are welcome to participate in religious services with the monks, which include Mass and the Liturgy of the Hours. The monks' apostolic work includes the production of liturgical vestments and ornaments.

Where to stay? Six guestrooms are available for those men who come with a desire to spend time in prayer and silence.

How to get there? Ramsgate is located about seventy-five miles east of London. Ramsgate is accessible by train.

SAINT CECILIA'S ABBEY

Ryde, Isle of Wight PO33 1LH
Tel/Fax: (01983) 562-602
Email: info@stceciliasabbey.org.uk
Web site: www.stceciliasabbey.org.uk

Founded in 1882, the women's monastery of Saint Cecilia became a part of the Solesmes Congregation in 1950. Services are sung daily in Gregorian chant by the Benedictine nuns, and guests can follow along using the Liturgy of the Hours books which are provided (translations are in English). The gift shop features religious books, cards, icons, crafts, as well as CDs and cassettes of Gregorian chant.

Where to stay? Adjacent to the abbey is the Garth Retreat House, which provides accommodation for men and women who wish to spend several days in a monastic atmosphere of prayer and recollection.

How to get there? Take the train to Portsmouth Harbour and then cross by ferry or catamaran to the Isle of Wight and Ryde Pier Head or Ryde Esplanade. Take a taxi or bus to the abbey (nearest bus stop is at East Hill Road).

DOWNSIDE ABBEY

Stratton-on-the-Fosse
Bath BA3 4RH
Tel: (01761) 235-161, 235-100 • Fax: (01761) 235-105, 235-124
Email: monks@downside.co.uk
Web site: www.downside.co.uk

Founded in 1854, today Downside Abbey is home to a community of Benedictine monks. As well as touring the vast and beautiful church, visitors can spend time attending religious services with the monks, which includes the singing of the Divine Office and Mass in Gregorian chant. Classical music concerts, which are open to all visitors, are held throughout the year at the abbey.

Where to stay? The monastery operates an excellent guesthouse available for men only. "The Bainesbury House" features eleven rooms, a garden, library, restaurant, and several meeting rooms. To make reservations, email the guestmaster at dommartin@downside. co.uk; Tel: (01761) 235-153; Fax: (01761) 235-124.

How to get there? Bath is located one hundred fifteen miles west of London. Downside Abbey is located in Stratton-on-the-Fosse, twelve miles south of Bath. The Abbey is about two and a half hours drive from London. The most convenient railway station for visitors from London is Bath, from where you can take a taxi or bus to the abbey. Visitors arriving by train from the North, Midlands and West should use Bristol's Temple Meads station, which is about half an hour from Downside.

AMPLEFORTH ABBEY

York, YO6 4EN
Tel: (01439) 766-889, 766-000, 766-714
Fax: (01439) 766-755, 766-724, 788-770
Email: monks@ampleforth.org.uk, pastoral@ampleforth.org.uk
Web site: www.ampleforth.org.uk

Founded in 1802, today Ampleforth Abbey is home to a Benedictine community of about one hundred monks. More than ten thousand people visit the monastery annually for a time of recollection and quiet prayer, or to participate in the various retreats and courses offered.

Where to stay? The abbey has several sites for accommodating guests with fifty-five beds in total including the Guesthouse, Archway, Central Building, and the Grange. Visit the Hospitality Web site at www. ampleforth-hpo.org.uk.

How to get there? Ampleforth Abbey is located on the southern edge of the North Yorkshire Moors, about twenty-two miles north of the City of York. By road take A1(M) as far as the A168. Alternatively you take the A19 south (towards York). York is easily accessible by rail and bus.

FRANCE

MONASTÈRE NOTRE-DAME-DE-LA-PAIX-DIEU

1064 chemin de Cabanoule
30140 Anduze
Tel: (04) 66-61-73-44 • Fax: (04) 66-61-87-94, 66-61-87-94
Email: communaute@cabanoule.org

Founded in 1970, the Monastery of Notre-Dame-de-la-Paix-Dieu is home to a women's community of Cistercian-Trappist monks. Mass and the Liturgy of the Hours are celebrated daily in French. Both are open to the public.

Where to stay? Twelve guestrooms (including one which is equipped for those with physical challenges) are available for those individuals who wish to participate in a personal retreat in a monastic environment.

How to get there? Anduze is located thirty miles from Nimes. The nearest train station is in Ales. Anduze and is accessible by bus; once you arrive in Anduze, take a taxi for the remaining two or three miles to the abbey.

MONASTÈRE DE LA THÉOPHANIE
Monastère Grec Catholique
Le Ladeix
19190 Aubazine
Tel/Fax: (05) 55-25-75-67

Founded in 1965, the Monastery of Théophanie is home to a small monastic community of nuns who belong to the Greek Melkite Catholic Church (a Byzantine Rite church in communion with Rome). Nestled in the foothills of southwestern France, the monastery's function is to make the richness of Eastern Christian Liturgy and Spirituality known to the western world. The religious services are sung in French, with some traditional Greek and Arabic melodies. For their apostolic ministry, the sisters create incense, translate religious works, make rugs, and perform agricultural duties. Some items available in their gift shop include incense, icons, oriental prayer beads, prayer rugs (pure wool), walnuts, and medicinal herbs. English, French, and Dutch are spoken at the monastery.

Where to stay? Eleven single guestrooms and three double guestrooms are available for women, priests, religious, couples, and families. Men may be accommodated, but they must present proper references (for example, a letter from their parish priest).

How to get there? Aubazine is ten miles from Brive-La-Gaillarde.

PRIEURÉ SAINTE-MARIE
La Cotellerie
53170 Bazougers
Tel: (02) 4366-43-66 • Fax: (02) 4366-43-67
Email: la.cotellerie@wanadoo.fr
Web site: http://www.la-cotellerie.com

Founded in 1971, the Priory of Sainte-Marie is home to a community of Canons Regular. Visitors are invited to participate in the religious services, which include Mass and the Liturgy of the Hours (both of which are sung in French). The priory gift shop sells honey, fruits, fresh apple cider, icons, medals, and religious books.

Where to stay? Three guesthouse buildings are available for individuals, couples, and families. A dormitory is available for groups of young people. To make a reservation, email: hotelier@la-cotellerie.com.

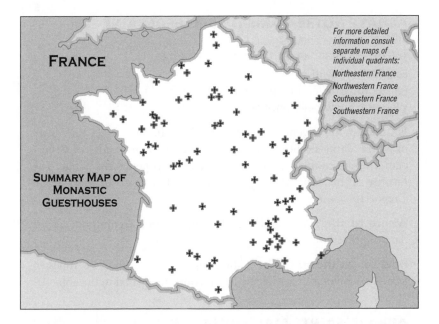

How to get there? Bazougers is only eleven miles from Laval. Laval is accessible by train; you can then switch to a taxi for the remaining short distance to the priory.

ABBAYE NOTRE-DAME-DU-BEC
27800 Le Bec-Hellouin
Tel: (02) 32-43-72-60, 32-44-86-09 • Fax: (02) 32-44-96-69
Email: accueil@abbayedubec.com
Web site: www.abbayedubec.com

Founded in 1034, the world famous Abbey of Notre-Dame-du-Bec was once home to the great Saint Anselm, and today is home to a community of Benedictine-Olivetan monks. Visitors to the monastery can not only join in the Liturgy of the Hours and Mass of the monks (sung in Gregorian chant and French), but can also take a guided tour of the historic abbey and church.

Where to stay? The monastery has two separate guesthouses. One is located within the abbey complex; the other is on the exterior. Reservations are required at least one month in advance. To make reservations, email or call the abbey guesthouse at Tel: (02) 32-43-72-62.

How to get there? Le Bec-Hellouin is seventeen miles from Elbeuf.

ABBAYE NOTRE-DAME-DE-BELLEFONTAINE

49122 Bégrolles en Mauges
Tel: (02) 41-75-60-40, 41-75-60-41, 41-75-60-45
Fax: (02) 41-75-60-49
Email: info@bellefontaine-abbaye.com
Web site: www.bellefontaine-abbaye.com

Founded in the eleventh century by the Benedictines, today the Abbey of Notre-Dame-de-Bellefontaine is home to a community of Cistercian-Trappist monks. All religious services are open to the public. The Liturgy of the Hours is sung in French, and parts of the Mass are in Gregorian chant.

Where to stay? Men and mixed groups can be accommodated for days of prayer and retreat.

How to get there? Cholet is about eight miles south of Bégrolles en Mauges. Cholet is accessible by train; continue by taxi to the abbey.

ABBAYE SAINTE-MARIE-DU-DÉSERT

31530 Bellegarde-Sainte-Marie
Tel: (05) 62-13-45-45 • Fax: (05) 62-13-45-35
Email: abstemarie@inTel:com.fr; abstemariedesert@wanadoo.fr
Web site: http://abbayedudesert.com

Founded in 1852, the Abbey of Sainte-Marie-du-Désert is home to a community of Cistercian monks. Offices are sung in French, and all visitors are welcome to join the monks in their daily life of prayer. Gift shop items include the abbey's candies, honey, books, and religious objects.

Where to stay? A guesthouse with twenty-five rooms (thirty beds in total) is available for individuals and small groups seeking a time of prayer and silence. Meeting rooms are available for groups. The abbey also can accommodate individuals and groups at the nearby Notre Dame house, especially groups of young people. The house features dormitories with a capacity of thirty people.

How to get there? Bellegarde is located about twenty miles west of Toulouse, the latter of which is accessible by train and bus. To reach the abbey from Toulouse, take a taxi. Nearest rail station: Bellegarde.

MONASTÈRE NOTRE-DAME-DES-SEPT-DOULEURS

60, avenue Général-Compans
31700 Blagnac
Tel: (05) 34-60-53-90 • Fax: (05) 61-30-46-34

Founded in 1852, today the Monastery of Notre-Dame-des-Sept-Douleurs is home to a women's community of Dominican monks. Mass, eucharistic adoration, and other religious services in the chapel are open to the public.

Where to stay? A family "pension" connected to the monastery offers comfortable guestrooms for visitors seeking a spiritual retreat. A park and garden are nearby.

How to get there? Blagnac is about thirty miles from Toulouse. Nearest rail station: Toulouse Matabia.

ABBAYE NOTRE-DAME-DE-BON-SECOURS

îLa Trappeî
84570 Blauvac
Tel: (04) 90-61-81-17 • Fax: (04) 90-61-98-07
Email: hoteliere@abbaye-blauvac.com
Web site: www.abbaye-blauvac.com

Founded in 1820, Our Lady of Bon Secours Abbey is home to a community of Cistercian-Trappist nuns. All visitors are encouraged to join the monks in the Liturgy of the Hours and Mass (sung in both French and Gregorian chant). The abbey gift shop features beehive produce, lavender essence, olive wood crosses, rosaries, and hosts.

Where to stay? Guestrooms are available for those individuals who come for a time of prayer and silence. Meeting rooms are available along with a dining room that accommodates almost fifty people. Two to three days is recommended as the maximum duration of your stay, if it's the first time visiting.

How to get there? Blauvac is located about ten miles east of Carpentras. The nearest train station is at Avignon; then switch to bus service heading to Carpentras. You can take a taxi from Carpentas to the abbey.

▼ FRANCE NORTHEAST

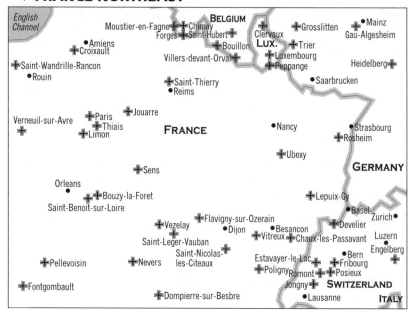

BELGIUM

English Channel

Moustier-en-Fagne ✠✠ Chimay
Forges ✠✠ Saint-Hubert ✠
✠ Grosslitten
● Mainz
Gau-Algesheim

● Amiens
✠ Croixault
Clervaux
LUX.
● Bouillon
✠ Trier
✠ Luxembourg

✠ Saint-Wandrille-Rancon
Villers-devant-Orval ✠
✠ Peppange
Heidelberg ✠

● Rouin
✠ Saint-Thierry
● Saarbrucken

● Reims

✠ Jouarre

Verneuil-sur-Avre
✠
✠ Paris
✠ Thiais
✠ Limon
FRANCE
● Nancy
● Strasbourg
✠ Rosheim

✠ Ubexy

✠ Sens
GERMANY

Orleans
●
✠✠ Bouzy-la-Foret
✠ Lepuix-Gy

Saint-Benoit-sur-Loire
● Basel
Zurich ●

✠ Vezelay
✠ Flavigny-sur-Ozerain
✠ Develier
Luzern

● Dijon
● Besancon
✠ Vitreux ✠ Chaux-les-Passavant
Engelberg
●

Saint-Leger-Vauban
Saint-Nicolas-
les-Citeaux
Estavayer-le-Lac ✠
● Bern
✠ Fribourg

✠ Pellevoisin
✠ Nevers
✠ Poligny
Romont ✠✠ Posieux

✠ Fontgombault
Jongny ✠
SWITZERLAND

✠ Dompierre-sur-Besbre
● Lausanne
ITALY

FRANCE NORTHWEST ▼

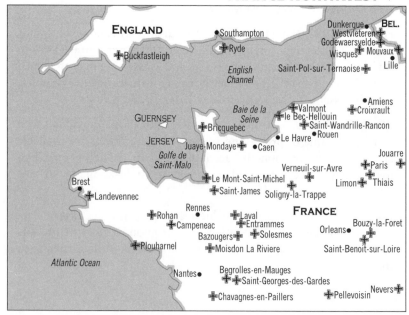

ENGLAND
● Southampton
Dunkerque ● **BEL.**
Westvleteren
Godewaersvelde ✠

✠ Ryde
Wisques ✠ ✠ Mouvaux

✠ Buckfastleigh
Saint-Pol-sur-Ternaoise ✠
Lille

English Channel
● Amiens
✠ Croixrault

Baie de la
Seine
✠ Valmont
✠ le Bec-Hellouin

GUERNSEY ◁
✠ Bricquebec
✠ Saint-Wandrille-Rancon

JERSEY ◁ Juaye-Mondaye ✠
● Caen
Le Havre ● Rouen

Golfe de
Saint-Malo
Jouarre

Brest
✠ Le Mont-Saint-Michel
Verneuil-sur-Avre ✠
✠ Paris ✠

✠ Landevennec
✠ Saint-James
Soligny-la-Trappe
Limon ✠ ✠ Thiais

Rennes
●
✠ Laval
FRANCE

✠ Rohan
✠ Campeneac
✠ Entrammes
Orleans ●
Bouzy-la-Foret ✠

Bazougers ● ✠ Solesmes

✠ Plouharnel
✠ Moisdon La Riviere
Saint-Benoit-sur-Loire

Atlantic Ocean
Nantes ●
Begrolles-en-Mauges
✠✠ Saint-Georges-des-Gardes

✠ Chavagnes-en-Paillers
✠ Pellevoisin
Nevers ✠

▼ FRANCE SOUTHEAST

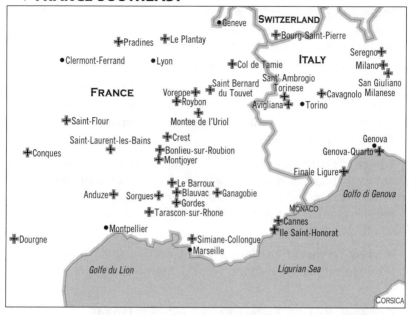

FRANCE SOUTHWEST ▼

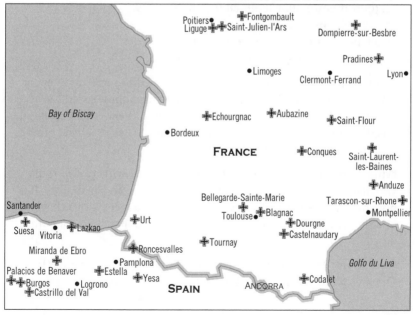

MONASTÈRE SAINTE-ANNE

26260 Bonlieu-sur-Roubion (Drôme)
Tel: (04) 75-53-92-23 • Fax: (04) 75-53-86-50
Email: sainte-anne.de.bonlieu@mondaye.com

Founded in 1171 by the Cistercians, today the Monastery of Sainte-Anne is home to a community of Premonstratensian Canons Regular (Norbertine Fathers). Visitors are welcome to join the monks in their daily life of prayer in the abbey church.

Where to stay? A guesthouse is available with eight rooms and a dormitory that can accommodate forty people, but reservations should be made in advance of your arrival by either sending a fax or a letter to the guestmaster. Two meeting rooms with fifteen and sixty seats respectively is available.

How to get there? Bonlieu-sur-Roubion is located about eight miles from Montelimar. Nearest train station: Montelimar (eight miles).

COMMUNAUTÉ MONASTÈRE NOTRE-DAME

73, route de Mi-Feuillage
45460 Bouzy-la-Foret
Tel (guesthouse): (02) 38-46-88-96, 38-46-88-99
Fax: (02) 38-46-88-97
Email: bouzy.accueil@orange.fr; ndcalee@aol.com
Web site: www.benedictines-bouzy.com

Founded in 1617, the monastery is home to a community of Benedictine nuns. As well as devoting their lives to prayer, these sisters are best known for their production of "Emerald Water." Very rich in essential oils, this lotion has many different uses, but it is especially soothing for minor cuts and burns.

Where to stay? The sisters offer a guesthouse with twelve rooms, two meeting rooms, three dining rooms, a library, and an oratory. It is possible for guests to seek spiritual guidance and meet with a chaplain or sister. A maximum of twenty people in a group can be accommodated.

How to get there? Bouzy-la-Foret is located twenty-eight miles from Orleans. Nearest train station: Gien (sixteen miles).

ABBAYE NOTRE-DAME-DE-GRÂCE

50260 Bricquebec
Tel: (02) 33-87-56-10, 33-52-20-01
Fax: (02) 33-87-56-13, 33-87-56-16, 33-52-56-51
Tel/Fax: (02) 33-52-29-69
Email: ocso.bricquebec@wanadoo.fr
Web site: http://catholique-coutances.cef.fr/communautes/
bricquebec/

Founded in 1824, Our Lady of Grace Abbey is home to a community of Cistercian-Trappist monks. Offices are chanted in French, and all visitors are encouraged to join the monks in prayer. You may purchase CDs and cassette recordings of Gregorian chant, as well as liturgical chants in both French and Japanese, at the abbey gift shop.

Where to stay? Guestrooms are available only for men (for a maximum of seven days), who must be there for spiritual purposes.

How to get there? Bricquebec is fifteen miles from Cherbourg-Octeville. Nearest train station: Valognes (eight miles) and Cherbourg (eleven miles).

ABBAYE LA-JOIE-NOTRE-DAME

56800 Campénéac
Tel: (02) 97-93-42-07, 97-93-10-41
Fax: (02) 97-93-11-23, 97-93-13-27, 97-93-11-45
Email: abbaye.joie.nd@wanadoo.fr, atelierlajoie@wanadoo.fr

Founded in 1921, the Abbey of La-Joie-Notre-Dame is home to a community of Cistercian monks. All visitors are encouraged to join the monks in their daily life of prayer, which includes Mass and the Liturgy of the Hours. Chocolate, cheese, fruit, and biscuits are just some of the abbey's products that may be purchased in their gift shop.

Where to stay? Guestrooms are available for individuals and groups seeking a place of retreat.

How to get there? Ploermel is six miles from Campénéac. Nearest train station: La Brohiniere (nineteen miles).

ABBAYE NOTRE-DAME-DE-LÉRINS

Île Saint-Honorat, B.P. 157
06406 Cannes Cedex
Tel: (04) 92-99-54-00, 92-99-54-10
Fax: (04) 92-99-54-01, 92-99-54-11
Email (guesthouse): hotellerie@abbayedelerins.com;
(abbey): info@abbayedelerins.com
Web site: www.abbayedelerins.com

Founded in 1869, today the Abbey of Notre-Dame-de-Lérins is home to the Congregation of the Immaculate Conception of Sénanque and Lérins. The offices are sung in French and Byzantine chant, and everyone is invited to join the monks in their life of prayer. Among the products available for purchase are the abbey's various liqueurs (La Lérina and La Sénancole), wines, and a variety of different kinds of honey.

Where to stay? Guestrooms are available for those individuals seeking spiritual refreshment and peace. Groups are welcome with a maximum of thirty people. Maximum stay is one week with the guesthouse closed in November. Reservations must be made two months in advance. To make a reservation, Tel: (04) 92-99-54-20; Fax: (04)- 92-99-54-21; Email: hotellerie@abbayedelerins.com.

How to get there? Cannes is accessible by train and bus. The best way to reach the abbey is by taxi.

COMMUNAUTÉ DES SOEURS DOMINICAINES DE SAINTE-CATHERINE-DE-RICCI

16, avenue Isola-Bella
06400 Cannes
Tel: (04) 93-38-06-09 • Fax: (04) 93-39-71-40

Home to a community of contemplative Dominican nuns, the Monastery of Sainte-Catherine-de-Ricci welcomes visitors to their guesthouse for prayer and personal retreats. All individuals are invited to participate in their religious services.

Where to stay? Twelve guestrooms are available.

How to get there? Cannes is accessible by train and bus. The best way to reach the abbey is by taxi.

MONASTÈRE NOTRE-DAME-DE-L'ACTION-DE-GRÂCES

10-12, rue Pasteur
11400 Castelnaudary
Tel: (04) 68-23-12-92 • Fax: (04) 68-23-69-46

Founded in 1854, the Monastery of Notre-Dame-de-l'Action-de-Grâces is home to a community of Poor Clares of Perpetual Adoration. All visitors are welcome to join religious services in the chapel, which include Mass and the Liturgy of the Hours.

Where to stay? A guesthouse, located on the exterior of the monastery, provides accommodation for up to thirty visitors. Guestrooms located within the monastic enclosure are available for consecrated religious and young women who are considering a vocation.

How to get there? Castelnaudary is located about thirty miles southeast of Toulouse, which is accessible by train and bus. Take a taxi to reach the abbey in Castelnaudary.

ABBAYE NOTRE-DAME-DE-LA-GRÂCE-DIEU

25530 Chaux-les-Passavant
Tel: (03) 81-60-44-45 • Fax: (03) 81-60-44-18
Web site: www.la-grace-dieu.org

Founded in 1139, the Abbey of Notre-Dame-de-la-Grâce-Dieu is home to a community of Cistercian monks. Visitors are welcome to attend the monks' Mass and Divine Office (held in the abbey chapel), both of which are sung in French and Gregorian chant. A film about the history of the abbey can be viewed upon request.

Where to stay? In their guesthouse, the monks can receive priests, consecrated religious, women, couples, and young people. All visitors are expected to respect the monastic atmosphere of prayer and silence.

How to get there? Chaux-les-Passavant and the abbey are located about twenty-five miles east of Besancon. Nearest train station: Le Valdahon (six miles).

CARMEL
Chavagnes-en-Paillers
85250 Saint-Fulgent
Tel: (02) 5-42-21-80

Founded in 1617, the convent is home to a community of Carmelite monks. Both the Liturgy of the Hours and Mass are open to the public, and everyone is encouraged to participate. Annually, on the last Sunday in August, there is a great pilgrimage to the convent where celebrations are held in honor of the Blessed Virgin Mary.

Where to stay? Those individuals who wish to pursue a personal retreat in a cloistered environment may request accommodations in their guesthouse.

How to get there? Cholet is located about thirty-five miles from Saint-Fulgent. Nearest train station: L'hebergement les Brouzils (ten miles).

ABBAYE SAINT-MICHEL-DE-CUXA
66500 Codalet
Tel/Fax: (04) 68-96-02-40

Founded in 878, the Abbey of Saint Michael of Cuxa is home to a community of Benedictine monks. Guided tours of the tenth-century church and crypt are available, and visitors are welcome to attend Mass and vespers. Wine, cheese, and ceramics are all available at the abbey gift shop.

Where to stay? Guestrooms are available for those who wish to participate in the life of the monks and spend a few days in retreat.

How to get there? Perpignan is located about thirty miles from Codalet. Nearest train station: Prades Molitg les bains (one mile).

ABBAYE SAINTE-FOY
12320 Conques
Tel: (05) 65-69-85-12 • Fax: (05) 65-72-81-01

Founded in 1120, the Abbey of Sainte-Foy is home to a community of Premonstratensian Canons (Norbertine Fathers). Both the Liturgy of the Hours and Mass are open to the public, and everyone is invited to attend.

Where to stay? The abbey operates a guesthouse and dormitory, which provides accommodation for those who seek either a personal or group retreat.

How to get there? Conques is located about ninety-five miles from Brive-La-Gaillarde. Nearest train station: Crausac (eight miles).

MONASTÈRE SAINTE-CLAIRE
53, rue des Auberts
26400 Crest
Tel: (04) 75-25-49-13 • Fax: (04) 75-25-28-80

Founded in 1826, the Monastery of Sainte-Claire is home to a community of Poor Clare nuns. Visitors are invited to attend both the Mass and vespers in the abbey.

Where to stay? The monastery provides several types of accommodation, making it suitable for individuals, families, or groups.

How to get there? Valence is about twenty-three miles from Crest, the latter of which is accessible by train.

PRIEURÉ NOTRE-DAME-D'ESPÉRANCE
4, rue Pétrie
Croixault
80290 Poix de Picardie
Tel: (03) 22-90-01-27 • Fax: (03) 22-90-64-33

Founded in 1966, Our Lady of Hope Priory is recognized as the first member of the "Our Lady of Hope" Congregation. All Offices are in French.

Where to stay? The priory's guestrooms can accommodate up to thirty people.

How to get there? Amiens is located about twenty-seven miles from Croixault. Nearest train station: Poix de Picardie (one mile).

ABBAYE DE NOTRE-DAME-DE-SEPT-FONS

03290 Dompierre-sur-Besbre
Tel: (04) 70-48-14-90 • Fax: (04) 70-48-14-93, 04-70-48-14-87
Email: septfons@septfons.com
Web site: www.abbayedeseptfons.com

Founded in 1132, the Abbey of Notre-Dame-de-Sept-Fons is home to a community of Trappist monks. All visitors are invited to attend Mass in the abbey chapel. An excellent thirty-minute film about the life and history of the abbey is available upon request.

Where to stay? Those individuals who wish to embark on a monastic retreat of prayer and silence can be accommodated in one of the abbey's twenty-seven guestrooms.

How to get there? Moulins is located about twenty miles from Dompierre-sur-Besbre. Nearest train station: Dompierre Sept Fons.

ABBAYE SAINT-BENOÎT-D'EN-CALCAT

81110 Dourgne
Tel: (05) 63-50-32-37, 63-50-84-10 • Fax: (05) 63-50-34-90
Email: communaute@encalcat.com
Web site: www.encalcat.com

Founded in 1890, the Abbey of Saint-Benoît-d'En-Calcat is home to a community of Benedictine monks. As well as touring the abbey church, visitors can participate in religious services with the monks, which are sung in both French and Gregorian chant. Among the many items available at the gift shop are the abbey's religious artwork, ceramics, and music tapes and CDs.

Where to stay? With excellent guesthouse facilities, the abbey provides three types of accommodation: (1) Fifteen rooms for men inside the monastic enclosure; (2) twenty-three rooms for women or families; (3) two dormitories with twenty-five beds for young people. Maximum stay of one week. Meeting with a monk for spiritual guidance is possible.

To make reservations at the guesthouse within the monastery, Tel: (05) 63-50-71-57; Fax: (05) 63-50-34-90; Email: hotellerie@encalcat.com.

To make reservations at the guesthouse hotel "La Grange" with twenty beds, living room, kitchen, showers, and accommodations for youth groups, contact La Grange, Tel: (05) 63-50-32-37; Fax: (05) 63-50-34-90; Email: lagrange@encalcat.com.

How to get there? Dourgne is located about ten miles from the Castres (Tarn) train station and eighteen miles from the Castelnaudary (Aude) train station. Dourgne is located about eight miles from the Revel bus station.

ABBAYE SAINTE-SCHOLASTIQUE
81110 Dourgne
Tel: (05) 63-50-31-32 • Fax: (05) 63-50-12-18
Email: sasco81@aol.com; communaute@benedictines-dourgne.org;
econome@benedictines-dourgne.org
Web site: http://benedictinesdourgne.free.fr

Founded in 1890, the Abbey of Saint Scholastica is home to a community of Benedictine monks. Everyone is encouraged to join the monks in the Liturgy of the Hours and Mass, both of which are sung in French and Gregorian chant. Some of the items that may be purchased at the abbey are ceramics, beehive products, paintings, tapestries, icons, religious books, and stained glass.

Where to stay? The abbey features two types of accommodations: regular bedrooms for individuals and couples and dormitory-style rooms for groups of young people. To make reservations, contact Soeur Hoteliere-Abbaye Sainte Scholastique, 81110 Dourgne; Tel: (05) 63 50 75 70; Fax: (05) 63 50 12 18; Email: hotellerie@benedictines-dourgne.org.

How to get there? Dourgne is located about ten miles from the Castres (Tarn) train station and eighteen miles from the Castelnaudary (Aude) train station. Dourgne is located about eight miles from the Revel bus station.

ABBAYE NOTRE-DAME-DE-BONNE-ESPÉRANCE
24410 Echourgnac
Tel: (05) 53-80-82-50 • Fax: (05) 53-80-08-36
Email: communaute@abbaye-echourgnac.org;
abbesse@abbaye-echourgnac.org;
retraitants@abbaye-echourgnac.org
Web site: www.abbaye-echourgnac.org

Founded in 1868, the Abbey of Notre-Dame-de-Bonne-Espérance is home to a community of Cistercians monks. All visitors are welcome to attend religious services with the monks, which are sung in both French and Gregorian chant. Since cheese-making is one of the major activities of the monks, visitors may purchase some of these cheeses at the abbey gift shop.

Where to stay? The abbey guesthouse is open (except during the month of January) to all individuals who seek a place of prayer and silence. Maximum stay is ten days.

How to get there? Echourgnac is located about fifty-five miles northeast of Bordeaux. Nearest train station: Montpon-Menesterol (nine miles).

ABBAYE NOTRE-DAME-DE-PORT-DU-SALUT
53260 Entrammes
Tel: (02) 43-64-18-64, 43-64-18-60 • Fax: (02) 43-64-18-63
Web site: www.portdusalut.com

Founded in 1815, Our Lady of Port du Salut Abbey is home to a community of Cistercian-Trappist monks. The offices are chanted in French, with some Latin Gregorian chant. All visitors can purchase some of the monastery's homegrown produce at the abbey store.

Where to stay? Guestrooms are available to those people who wish to participate in a monastic retreat.

How to get there? Entrammes is seven miles from Laval, the latter of which is accessible by train. Entrammes is accessible by bus from Laval. Nearest train station: Laval (six miles).

ABBAYE SAINT-JOSEPH-DE-CLAIRVAL
21150 Flavigny-sur-Ozerain
Tel: (03) 80-96-22-31 • Fax: (03) 80-96-25-29
Email: englishspoken@clairval.com
Web site: www.clairval.com

Founded in 1972, the Benedictine abbey of Saint Joseph of Clairval provides a very authentic monastic experience for all visitors. The Mass and Divine Office are sung in Latin and Gregorian chant, which all are invited to attend. If you are unable to visit the abbey, you can still stay in touch with them by receiving their excellent monthly newsletter, which includes inspirational stories that provide spiritual comfort and strength. To become a subscriber, simply contact the abbey at the above email or mailing address and ask to be put on the mailing list. You can purchase Gregorian chant CDs and cassettes, as well as exceptionally beautiful religious images and icons, from the abbey by mail.

Where to stay? Men can be accommodated in the monastic guestrooms, but you must write to the guestmaster prior to your visit. There are two types of guest stays: The first are organized retreats by the abbey lasting five days in length and based on the spiritual exercises of St. Ignatius of Loyola. The second consist of individual retreats and participation in the daily life of the abbey.

How to get there? Flavigny-sur-Ozerain is located about forty miles northwest of Dijon and one hundred ninety miles southeast of Paris. If driving along the Paris-Lyon motorway, exist at Bierre-lès-Semur and then continue for another fifteen miles. The nearest train stations are at Les Laumes-Alésia (five miles) and Montbard (seventeen miles). From there you must take a taxi. It is advised to arrive at the train station of Les Laumes-Alésia, in order to have a shorter and less expensive taxi ride.

ABBAYE NOTRE-DAME-DE-FONTGOMBAULT
36220 Fontgombault
Tel: (02) 54-37-12-03 • Fax: (02) 54-37-12-56

Founded in 1091, the Abbey of Notre-Dame-de-Fontgombault is home to a community of Benedictine monks who belong to the Congregation of Solesmes. All visitors are welcome to join the monks in their daily life of prayer, which includes Mass and the singing of the Divine Office in Gregorian chant. At the gift shop, you may purchase many religious products, as well as other items, including the abbey's pottery, farm and garden produce, and their own Gregorian chant CDs and cassettes.

Where to stay? Guestrooms are available to those individuals who wish to spend a few days in a monastic atmosphere of prayer and silence.

How to get there? Poitiers is forty miles from Fontgombault. Nearest train station: Chatellerault (twenty-three miles).

ABBAYE NOTRE-DAME
04310 Ganagobie
Tel: (04) 92-68-00-04 • Fax: (04) 92-68-11-49
Email: ste.madeleine@ndganagobie.com,
monastere@ndganagobie.com
Web site: www.ndganagobie.com

Founded in 950, today the Monastery of Ganagobie is home to a community of Benedictine monks who belong to the Congregation of Solesmes. Daily Mass and the Liturgy of the Hours are sung in Gregorian chant, and all visitors are welcome to join in the prayer life of the monks. Jam, honey, perfume, and Gregorian chant CDs are just some of the items available at the abbey gift shop.

Where to stay? The abbey has fifteen guestrooms for individuals who are seeking a time of retreat and silence. They also have separate housing for groups and young people.

How to get there? Manosque is seventeen miles from Ganagobie. The nearest train stations are at Brillianne-Oraison and ChâteauArnoux-St Auban. Take a taxi to reach the abbey.

ABBAYE SAINTE-MARIE-DU-MONT-DES-CATS
2470 Route du Mont des Cats
59270 Godewaersvelde
Tel (abbey): (03) 28-43-83-60, (03) 28-42-52-50
Tel (guesthouse): (03) 28-42-58-22
Fax: (03) 28-43-83-61, 28-42-54-80, 28-49-14, 28-49-49-79,
    28-49-48-25
Email: montdescats@compuserve.com;
abbe@abbaye-montdescats.com;
econome@abbaye-montdescats.com;
fromagerie@abbaye-montdescats.com
Web site: www.abbaye-montdescats.com

Founded in 1826, the Abbey of Sainte-Marie-du-Mont-des-Cats is home to a community of Trappist monks. All visitors are invited to attend the religious services, which include both Mass and the Liturgy of the Hours. The abbey is very well known for its production of cheese.

Where to stay? A guesthouse is available to those individuals who wish to participate in a monastic retreat of prayer and silence. The guesthouse is closed in January. To make reservations, Tel: (03) 28 43 83 63; Fax (03) 28 43 83 64.

How to get there? Lille is twenty-five miles from Godewaersvelde/ Route du Mont des Cats; take the road between Lille and Dunkirk. By train take Paris-Lille then Lille-Hazebrouck or Lille-Bailleul; another option is Paris-Hazebrouck.

ABBAYE NOTRE-DAME-DE-SÉNANQUE
84220 Gordes
Tel: (04) 90-72-17-92, 90-72-05-72, 90-72-02-05
Fax: (04) 90-72-17 -95, 90-72-15-70, 90-72-07-45
Email: ndsenanque@aol.com; frere.hotelier@senanque.fr
Web site: www.senanque.fr

Founded in 1148, the Abbey of Notre-Dame-de-Sénanque is home to a community of Cistercian monks. Visitors can participate in the prayer life of the monks by attending their religious services, which are sung in French, Byzantine, and Gregorian chant. Tours to designated parts of the twelfth-century monastery are available.

Where to stay? Individuals and groups who wish to embark on a retreat in a traditional monastic environment can ask to be accommodated in one of the abbey's guestrooms. The guesthouse is usually closed January and February. Contact the guesthouse at Tel/Fax: (04) 90-72-17-95; Email: frere.hotelier@senanque.fr.

How to get there? Avignon is twenty-four miles from Sénanque. The nearest train stations are at Avignon or Isle-Fontaine-de-Vaucluse (eight miles). From either train station, take a taxi to reach the abbey.

ABBAYE NOTRE-DAME DE JOUARRE
6, rue Montmorin
77640 Jouarre
Tel: (01) 60-22-06-11 • Fax: (01) 60-22-31-25
Email: communaute@abbayejouarre.org
Web site: www.abbayejouarre.org

Founded in 635, Our Lady of Jouarre Abbey is home to the Benedictine community of Mary's Immaculate Heart. Visitors can join the nuns in their life of prayer in the monastery church (offices are sung in French and Gregorian chant), as well as take a guided tour of the seventh-century crypt. Some of the craft items that may be purchased include the abbey's ceramics, pottery, small statues, and nativity scenes.

Where to stay? Guestrooms are available for families, young people, individuals, and groups. To make a reservation, email: hotes@abbayejouarre.org.

How to get there? Paris is forty-three miles from Jouarre; Jouarre is accessible by train and is about two miles from the abbey.

ABBAYE SAINT-MARTIN DE MONDAYE

14250 Juaye-Mondaye
Tel: (02) 31-92-58-11 • Fax: (02) 31-92-08-05
Email: hotelier@mondaye.com
Web site: www.mondaye.com

Founded in the thirteenth century, the Abbey of Saint-Martin de Monday is home to a community of Premonstratensian Canons (Norbertine Fathers). As well as taking guided tours of the abbey, visitors can attend daily religious services with the monks.

Where to stay? Those individuals or groups who wish to spend several days at the abbey in spiritual retreat should contact the guestmaster prior to their arrival.

How to get there? Juaye-Mondaye is located in Normandy, about seven miles south of Bayeux. Bayeux is accessible by train and is located about seven miles from the abbey; take a taxi to reach the abbey.

ABBAYE SAINT-GUÉNOLÉ

29560 Landévennec
Tel: (02) 98-27-73-34 • Fax: (02) 98-27-79-57
Tel (guesthouse): (02) 98-27-37-53
Email: abbaye.landevennec@orange.fr;
abbaye.landevennec@wanadoo.fr
Web site: http://abbaye-landevennec.cef.fr

Founded in the sixth century, the Abbey of Saint-Guénolé is home to a Benedictine community of monks who belong to the Congregation of Subiaco. Offices are chanted in French, with some pieces in Gregorian chant. Fruit preserves, ceramics, and music cassettes are just some of the articles available at the abbey gift shop.

Where to stay? Guestrooms are available, on a limited basis, to those who wish to participate in the prayer life of the monks.

How to get there? Brest is thirty miles from Landévennec. Nearest train station: Dirinon (six miles).

ABBAYE DE LA COUDRE
Rue Saint-Benoît
53005 Laval
Tel: (02) 43-02-85-85 • Fax: (02) 43-66-90-18
Email: abbcoudre@aol.com; abbessecoudre@wanadoo.fr
Web site: www.abbaye-coudre.com

Founded in 1816, the Abbey of La Coudre is home to a community of Cistercian-Trappist monks. Visitors can participate in religious services, which are sung in both French and Gregorian chant. Well known for its cheese and dairy products, they are sold by the abbey throughout France and Belgium.

Where to stay? Guestrooms are available to those individuals who wish to participate in a monastic retreat. Meals are taken in silence and guests can stay two to eight days. It's often possible to speak with the monks for spiritual guidance.

How to get there? Laval is accessible by train and bus. Take a taxi to reach the abbey.

ABBAYE SAINTE-MADELEINE
84330 Le Barroux
Tel: (04) 90-62-56-05, (04) 90-62-56-31 • Fax: (08) 26-69-93-17

Founded in 1970, the Abbey of Saint Magdalene offers a very authentic experience of traditional monasticism. Guests can participate in the Divine Office and Mass, which are celebrated in the traditional Latin rite and sung in Gregorian chant. Some of the items that may be purchased are the abbey's CDs and cassettes, as well as their special bread and shortbread biscuits. Less than two miles from the monastery is the Abbey of Notre-Dame-de-l'Annonciation (see following entry).

Where to stay? Guestrooms are only available to men and young people who are seeking a quiet time of prayer and seclusion. Please contact the guestmaster before planning to stay overnight in the monastery, since space is limited.

How to get there? Avignon is twenty-four miles from Le Barroux, the latter which is located about seven miles northeast of Carpentras on D938 (direction Vaison-la-Romaine). The nearest train station is at Avignon; you can take bus line #14 to reach Barroux/Carpentras.

ABBAYE DE NOTRE-DAME-DE-L'ANNONCIATION
La Font de Pertus
84330 Le Barroux
Tel: (04) 90-65-29-29 • Fax: (04) 90-65-29-30
Web site: www.barroux.org/monial/monialpres.html

Founded in 1979, the Abbey of Notre-Dame-de-l'Annonciation is home to a community of Benedictine nuns. Visitors are welcome to all the offices, as well as the daily Latin Tridentine Mass, which are sung in Latin and Gregorian chant. The abbey gift shop is open throughout the year, except during its annual retreat (usually in May). Some of the many items that may be purchased are icons, candies, postcards, paintings, jam (made by the sisters with the apricots from their orchard), and recordings of Gregorian chant sung by the nuns in the monastery. Since they have no apostolic duties, the sisters devote themselves to lives of prayer, study, and work. French, English, German, Polish, and Spanish are all spoken at the abbey.

Where to stay? A guesthouse is open all year for men and young people for a maximum of one week.

How to get there? Avignon is twenty-four miles from Le Barroux, the latter which is located about seven miles northeast of Carpentras on D938 (direction Vaison-la-Romaine). The nearest train station is at Avignon; you can take bus line #14 to reach Barroux/Carpentras.

COMMUNAUTÉ DE L'ABBAYE
B.P. 3
50170 Le Mont-Saint-Michel
Tel: (02) 33-60-14-47 • Fax: (02) 33-60-31-02
Web site: http://www.ot-montsaintmichel.com

Founded in the tenth century, the Abbey of Mont-Saint-Michel is an architectural and artistic wonder. To this day, it remains one of the most famous monasteries in all Christendom. Throughout the year, guided tours of the abbey are available (in various languages including English) and provide an insider's glimpse into Medieval Europe.

Where to stay? There are many hotels at Le Mont-Saint-Michel.

How to get there? Mont-Saint-Michel is about one hundred eighty miles west of Paris. The nearest train station is at Pontorson (six miles), where you can switch to bus service to Mont-Saint-Michel.

ABBAYE NOTRE-DAME-DES-DOMBES
01330 Le Plantay
Tel: (04) 74-98-14-40 • Fax: (04) 74-98-16-70
Email: nddombes@Road-neuf.org

Founded in 1863, the Abbey of Notre-Dame-des-Dombes is home to a community of Trappist monks. The Liturgy of the Hours and Mass are sung in French. Among the many items available at the gift shop are the abbey's fruit preserves.

Where to stay? A hostel is available to those individuals who wish to participate in a personal retreat and join the monks in the prayer life of their community.

How to get there? Lyon is twenty-eight miles from Le Plantay. Nearest train station: Villars les Dombes (four miles).

PRIEURÉ SAINT-BENOÎT-DE-CHAUVEROCHE
90200 Lepuix-Gy (Territoire de Belfort)
Tel: (03) 84-29-01-57 • Fax: (03) 84-29-56-80
Email: accueil.chauveroche@orange.fr

Founded in 1980, the Priory of Saint-Beno"t-de-Chauveroche is home to a community of Benedictine monks. All offices are chanted in French, which everyone is invited to attend.

Where to stay? A small guesthouse of seven rooms is available to individuals who want to participate more fully in the prayer life of the community. There is also another guesthouse located not far from the priory which has six rooms and twenty-five beds.

How to get there? Lepuix-Gy is ten miles north of Belfort. Nearest train station: Bas-Evette (six miles).

ABBAYE SAINT-MARTIN

2 Place Lambert
86240 Ligugé
Tel: (05) 49-55-21-12 • Fax: (05) 49-55-10-98
Email: info@abbaye-liguge.com
Web site: www.abbaye-liguge.com

Founded in 361, today the Abbey of Saint Martin is home to a community of Benedictine monks who belong to the Congregation of Solesmes. Visitors are welcome to join the monks in their daily life of prayer, which includes singing the Divine Office and Mass in Gregorian chant. Gregorian chant CDs and cassettes are available at the gift shop, as well as many other religious items including stained-glass creations and reproductions.

Where to stay? The abbey offers several different types of guest housing, each one catering to men, women, young people, and groups. The abbey accommodates more than twelve thousand people each year. You can fill out a form online to make reservations.

How to get there? Ligugé is located about six miles from Poitiers, the latter which is accessible by train (Paris-Poiteers). Take a taxi to reach the abbey.

ABBAYE NOTRE-DAME DE MELLERAY

La Melleraye de Bretagne
44520 Moisdon La Rivière
Tel: (02) 40-55-26-00, 40-55-20-01, 40-55-27-35 • Fax: (02) 40-55-22-43
Email: melleray@wanadoo.fr
Web site: http://pagesperso-orange.fr/abbaye-melleray

Founded in 1142, Our Lady of Melleray Abbey is home to a community of Cistercian-Trappist monks. The abbey features a bookstore and has a number of craft items for sale, including religious graphic arts.

Where to stay? Guestrooms are available for retreat participants, and all visitors are encouraged to join the monks in the Liturgy of the Hours (which is sung in French). To make reservations by phone, Tel: (02) 40-55-27-37.

How to get there? Nantes is located thirty-seven miles south of Moisdon La Rivière, twenty miles from Ancenis, and about fifteen miles from Châteaubriant. The abbey is situated two miles east of La Meilleraye-de-Bretagne on the road to Riaillé. Nearest train station: Chateaubriant (seven miles).

ABBAYE NOTRE-DAME-D'AIGUEBELLE

26230 Montjoyer
Tel: (04) 75-98-64-70, 75-98-64-78 • Fax: (04) 75-98-64-71, 75-98-64-79
Email: contact@abbaye-aiguebelle.com
Web site: www.abbaye-aiguebelle.com

Founded in 1137, the Abbey of Notre-Dame-d'Aiguebelle is home to a Cistercian-Trappist community of monks. All visitors are welcome to join the monks in the Liturgy of the Hours and Mass, which are sung in French, Byzantine and Latin Gregorian chant. Many of the abbey's products are available in the gift shop, including a selection of their syrups, honey, and liqueurs.

Where to stay? A guesthouse with fifty rooms is available to those individuals and groups (maximum twenty-five people) seeking a place of prayer and silence. Reservations are required. To make reservations, contact the guesthouse at Tel: (04) 75-98-64-72; Email: hotellerie.aiguebelle@orange.fr.

How to get there? The abbey and Montjoyer are located about twelve miles from Montélimar and seven miles from Grignan. Nearest rail station: Montelimar (eight miles).

PRIEURÉ SAINT-DODON

18, Grand-rue
59132 Moustier-en-Fagne
Tel: (03) 27-61-81-28 • Fax: (03) 27-61-81-12

Founded in 1968, the Priory of Saint-Dodon is home to a community of Benedictine monks. Visitors are invited to participate in the religious services, which are said in the Byzantine Rite.

Where to stay? A few guestrooms are available for priests, consecrated religious, and laypeople who are seeking a time of prayer and solitude. Individuals or groups are welcome, and there is a meeting room for the latter. A kitchen is at your disposal. **How to get there?** Maubeuge is twenty miles from Moustier-en-Fagne. Nearest train station: Fourmies (eight miles).

MONASTÈRE DE LA VISITATION
192, rue Lorthiois
59420 Mouvaux
Tel: (03) 20-26-94-34

Founded in 1876, the Monastery of the Visitation is home to a community of Visitation monks. The abbey chapel is open throughout the day; all religious services are open to the public (said/sung in French).

Where to stay? Individuals or small groups who want to participate more fully in the prayer life of the monks may be accommodated in the guesthouse. Only young women and consecrated religious, however, can ask to be accommodated in the guestrooms within the monastic enclosure.

How to get there? Lille is six miles from Mouvaux. Nearest train station: Roubaix (one mile).

MONASTÈRE DE LA VISITATION
49, route des Saulaies
58000 Nevers
Tel: (03) 86-57-37-40 • Fax: (03) 86-57-25-98

Founded in 1616, the Monastery of the Visitation is home to a community of Visitation monks. All are welcome to participate in the religious services of the abbey, which includes Mass and the Liturgy of the Hours. The monastery is located in the same town as the shrine and convent of Saint Gildard, which houses the incorrupt body of Saint Bernadette Soubirous (the visionary child from Lourdes).

Where to stay? Nine guestrooms are available to those individuals who want to participate in a monastic retreat of prayer and silence.

How to get there? Nevers is one hundred thirty miles south of Paris. From Paris, take A6 and A77. Nevers is accessible by train and by local bus.

PRIEURÉ SAINT-BENOÎT-SAINTE-SCHOLASTIQUE

3, cité du Sacré-Coeur
75018 Paris
Tel: (0146) 06-14-74 • Fax: (0142) 23-19-33

Founded in 1898, the Priory of Saint-Benoît-Sainte-Scholastique is home to a community of Benedictine monks of Sacré-Coeur-de-Montmarte. All religious services are open to the public and are chanted in French. The monastery is located near the world famous Basilica of Sacré-Coeur.

Where to stay? Individuals, groups, and pilgrims are all welcome to spend several days in retreat at the abbey guesthouse.

How to get there? The Basilica of Sacré-Coeur is located inside the city limits of Paris and situated to the west of the Gare de Nort (Paris' north train station) and north of the Opéra Garnier. The closest Metro stop is Anvers; take the #2 line that runs between Porte Dauphine and Nation. (Anvers is a two or three-minute walk up Rue Steinkerque to the foot of Sacré-Coeur.) The area surrounding the basilica is also accessible by city bus. To reach the basilica itself, you can walk up the long flight of stairs or take the funicular. To reach the guesthouse, walk alongside the basilica until you reach the guesthouse entrance to 3, cité du Sacré-Coeur.

MONASTÈRE DE MARIE, MÈRE DE MISÉRICORDE

3, rue Notre-Dame
36180 Pellevoisin
Tel/Fax: (02) 54-39-0-91

Founded in 1893, the Monastery of Marie, Mère de Miséricorde (Mary, Mother of Mercy) is home to a community of Dominican monks who serve as custodians of the Shrine of Our Lady of Pellevoisin. The Liturgy of the Hours and Mass are chanted in French and are open to the public. To learn more about the shrine and the Church-approved apparitions of the Virgin Mary that took place here in the eighteenth century, please refer to the book: *Catholic Shrines of Western Europe: A Pilgrim's Travel Guide*, Liguori Publications.

Where to stay? With only seven guestrooms available, individuals must come with a desire to participate in the prayer life of the monastery.

How to get there? Pellevoisin is about one hundred thirty miles southwest of Paris. The nearest train stations are at Chateauroux (twenty-two miles) and Tours. You can reach the monastery by taxi, or from Chateauroux and Tours, take a bus to Buzancais and continue by taxi to Pellevoisin (six miles). Another train station is also located at Lucay-le-Male (ten miles).

ABBAYE NOTRE-DAME DE TAMIÉ
Col de Tamié
73200 Tamié (Plancherine)
Tel: (04) 79-31-15-50 • Fax: (04) 79-37-05-24
Email: tamie.abbaye@wanadoo.fr
Web site: www.abbaye-tamie.com

Founded in 1132, Our Lady of Tamié Abbey is home to a community of Cistercian-Trappist monks. Among the many products available at the gift shop is the abbey's famous Tamié cheese.

Where to stay? Guestrooms are available to both men and women who wish to spend up to seven days in silence and prayer.

How to get there? Annecy is twenty-eight miles from Tamié. Nearest rail station: Albertville.

ABBAYE SAINTE-ANNE-DE-KERGONAN
B.P. 11
56340 Plouharnel
Tel: (02) 97-52-30-75 • Fax: (02) 97-52-41-20
Email: economat@abbaye-ste-anne-kergonan.orgeconomat@abbaye-ste-anne-kergonan.org

Founded in 1897, the Abbey of Sainte-Anne-de-Kergonan is home to a community of Benedictine monks who belong to the Congregation of Solesmes. All offices and the Mass are sung in Gregorian chant, which all visitors are welcome to attend. Pottery, ceramics, videocassettes, and Gregorian chant CDs are just some of the items available at the abbey gift shop.

Where to stay? Fifteen guestrooms are available to men who wish to participate in the monastic life of the abbey for a few days.

How to get there? Auray is nine miles from Plouharnel. Nearest rail station: Plouharnel Carnac.

MONASTÈRE DE SAINTE-CLAIRE
13, rue Sainte-Colette
39800 Poligny
Tel: (03) 84-37-11-40 • Fax: (03) 84-37-07-53
Email: monastere.claire.poligny@wanadoo.fr

Founded in 1783, the Monastery of Sainte-Claire is home to a community of Poor Clare nuns. Serving both as an abbey and a shrine, pilgrims can come here and pray before the tomb of Saint Colette. As well as attending religious services with the nuns, visitors can join in the many celebrations that take place throughout the year in honor of Saint Colette. The most popular day of pilgrimage takes place on March 6, the feast day of Saint Colette.

Where to stay? The monastery features eight guestrooms, with preference given to visiting priests and sisters.

How to get there? Chalon-Sur-Saone is seventy-one miles from Poligny. Poligny is accessible by train.

ABBAYE SAINT JOSEPH AND SAINT PETER OF PRADINES
42630 Pradines
Tel: (04) 77-64-80-06 • Fax: (04) 77-64-82-08

Founded in 1818, the Abbey of Saint Joseph and Saint Peter of Pradines is home to the Benedictine community of Mary's Immaculate Heart. All are welcome to join the nuns in their daily life of prayer. The abbey's gift shop features its own woven items and silk scarves, as well as other craft items.

Where to stay? Those who want to spend quiet time in retreat can inquire about staying in one of their guestrooms.

How to get there? Roanne is thirteen miles from Pradines. Nearest rail station: Roanne.

ABBAYE NOTRE-DAME-DE-TIMADEUC

B.P. 17
Bréhan
56580 Rohan
Tel: (02) 97-51-50-29 • Fax: (02) 97-51-59-20
Email: timadeuc.abbaye@wanadoo.fr

Founded in 1841, Our Lady of Timadeuc Abbey is home to a community of Cistercian-Trappist monks. The Liturgy of the Hours is chanted in French, with some Gregorian chant. Among the most popular items that visitors can purchase at the gift shop are the abbey's fruit preserves, cheese, religious icons, CDs, and cassettes.

Where to stay? With more than forty guestrooms available, both men and women are welcome to stay at the monastery for times of prayer and reflection. Two large dormitory-style rooms with twenty-eight beds are available to groups of young people.

How to get there? Vannes is thirty-two miles from Rohan. Nearest rail station: Loudeac.

MONASTÈRE DES BÉNÉDICTINES DU SAINT-SACREMENT

1, rue Saint-Benoît
67560 Rosheim
Tel: (03) 88-50-41-67 • Fax: (03) 88-50-42-71
Email: info@benedictines-rosheim.com
Web site: www.benedictines-rosheim.com

Founded in 1862, the Monastery of Saint-Sacrement is home to a community of Benedictine monks. Visitors are invited to attend religious services, which are sung in Gregorian chant. Private lessons and classes to learn Gregorian chant are available. One of the major duties of the monks is the making of hosts.

Where to stay? The abbey operates a guesthouse which is available to individuals, couples, families, and groups. The guesthouse features a dining room, living room, library, oratory, and meeting rooms for up to sixty people. The guestrooms range from one bed to three beds.

How to get there? Strasbourg is eighteen miles from Rosheim, the latter which is accessible by train and bus. The train station is only about a mile from the monastery.

ABBAYE DE CHAMBARAND

La Trappe
38940 Roybon
Tel: (04) 76-36-22-68 • Fax: (04) 76-36-28-65
Email: ab.chambarand@wanadoo.fr; la.trappe@wanadoo.fr
Web site: www.chambarand.com

Founded in 1931, the Abbey of Chambarand is home to a community of Cistercian-Trappist monks. Mass is celebrated daily in the chapel, with vespers in the evening (both are sung in French and Gregorian chant). The abbey is very renowned for the production of various cheeses, butter, and other dairy products.

Where to stay? The guesthouse is reserved solely for retreat participants and the families of the monks.

How to get there? Grenoble is thirty-nine miles from Roybon. The nearest train stations are at Grenoble and Vienne. The abbey itself is six miles from Royboan (take a taxi to arrive at the abbey).

ABBAYE DE FLEURY

45730 Saint-Benoît-sur-Loire
Tel: (02) 38-35-72-43 • Fax: (02) 38-35-77-82, 38-35-77-71
Email: info@abbaye-fleury.com
Web site: http://abbaye.chez-alice.fr
Abbey of Fleury
45730 Saint Benoît on the Loire
Tel: (02) 38-35-72-43 • Fax: (02) 38-35-77-71

Dating back to the seventh century, the Abbey of Saint Fleury is not only home to a community of Benedictine monks who belong to the Congregation of Subiaco, but is also home to the sacred remains of Saint Benedict —the founder of western monasticism. Each year, thousands of pilgrims and visitors come to pray at his tomb and experience the tranquility of monastic life. Offices are sung in French and Latin, with Gregorian chant at Mass.

Where to stay? Guest accommodations are available to those who wish to join the monks in their daily life of prayer and spend time in a personal or group retreat. To make reservations, contact the hotel facing the basilica at Tel: (02) 38-35-74-38; Fax: (02) 38-35-72-99; Email: accueil@abbaye-fleury.com.

How to get there? Orleans is twenty-four miles from Saint-Benoît-sur-Loire. The nearest train station is at Orleans; then take the bus for Gien or Briare (line #3) from the Orleans bus/coach station.

MONASTÈRE NOTRE-DAME-DES-PETITES-ROCHES

38660 Saint Bernard du Touvet
Tel: (04) 76-08-31-13 • Fax: (04) 76-08-32-17
Email: hotellerie.petitesroches@gmail.com
Web site: www.bernardine.org/touvetf.html

Founded in 1970, the monastery of Notre-Dame-des-Petites-Roches is home to a Cistercian community. All visitors are invited to attend religious services, which include the Liturgy of the Hours and Mass (both of which are sung in French).

Where to stay? A guesthouse with twenty rooms (forty beds) and three dormitories (ten beds each) is available to those individuals or groups who wish to participate in the prayer life of the monastery.

How to get there? Grenoble is twenty miles from Saint Bernard du Touvet via N90 or A41. Take the train to Grenoble, and then bus or taxi to the Saint Bernard du Touvet. Another nearby rail station is at Goncelin.

MONASTÈRE DE LA VISITATION

7, av. du Docteur-Mallet
15100 Saint-Flour
Tel: (04) 71-60-07-82 • Fax: (04) 71-60-43-97

Founded in 1839, the Monastery of the Visitation is home to a community of Carmelite monks. All religious services, which are sung or said in French, are open to the public.

Where to stay? Guestrooms are limited to those individuals seeking a cloistered environment of prayer and silence.

How to get there? Saint-Flour is located about thirty miles from Langeac, which has a train station.

ABBAYE NOTRE-DAME-DES-GARDES
49120 Saint-Georges-des-Gardes
Tel: (02) 41-29-57-10 • Fax: (02) 41-29-57-19
Email: contact@abbayedesgardes.fr
Web site: www.abbayedesgardes.fr

Founded in 1818, the Abbey of Notre-Dame-des-Gardes is home to a community of Trappist monks. All visitors are invited to participate in the prayer life of the monks, which includes Mass and the Liturgy of the Hours (sung in French). Some of the monks' "homemade" products can be purchased at the monastery.

Where to stay? The guesthouse is available to women, couples, consecrated religious, and young people, as well as groups of both men and women for times of personal retreat.

How to get there? Cholet is ten miles from Saint-Georges-des-Gardes, which is about thirty miles south of Angers. Nearest rail station: Chemille.

PRIEURÉ SAINT-JACQUES
50240 Saint-James
Tel: (02) 33-48-31-39 • Fax: (02) 33-48-67-23

Founded in 1930, the Priory of Saint-Jacques is home to a community of Benedictine monks of Jesus Crucified. All visitors are welcome to attend religious services with the monks, including Mass and the Liturgy of the Hours (sung in French).

Where to stay? Those individuals and groups who wish to participate more fully in the prayer life of the monks may ask to be accommodated in the guesthouse.

How to get there? Avranches is thirteen miles from Saint-James. Nearest rail station: Pontorson.

PRIEURÉ NOTRE-DAME-DU-CALVAIRE

11, rue du Parc
86800 Saint-Julien-líArs
Tel: (05) 49-56-71-01• Fax: (05) 49-56-09-77

Founded in 1617, Our Lady of Calvary Priory is home to a community of Benedictine Nuns. The Offices and Mass are sung in French and Gregorian chant; visitors are welcome to join the sisters in religious services.

Where to stay? Guestrooms are available for both individuals and small groups.

How to get there? Poitiers is eleven miles from Saint-Julien Ars, which is accessible by train.

ABBAYE DE NOTRE-DAME-DES-NEIGES

07590 Saint-Laurent-les-Bains
Tel: (04) 66-46-59-00, (04) 66-46-00-38
Fax: (04) 66-46-05-31, (04) 66-46-59-10
Email: info@notredamedesneiges.com
Web site: www.notredamedesneiges.com

Founded in 1850, the Abbey of Notre-Dame-des-Neiges is home to a community of Cistercian monks. All visitors are invited to attend the solemn High Mass with the monks, as well as the Liturgy of the Hours, both of which are celebrated every day.

Where to stay? A guesthouse is available to those individuals and groups who wish to participate in a monastic retreat of prayer and silence. Maximum stay is eight days. Two meeting rooms are available for groups (maximum twenty-two people). To make reservations at the guesthouse, contact Abbaye Notre Dame des Neiges, Maison de Zachée, 07590 Saint Laurent les Bains; Email: maisondezachee@notredamedesneiges.com; Tel: (04) 66-46-59-02; Fax: (04) 66-46-33-06.

How to get there? Saint-Laurent-les-Bains is located about forty-five miles from Puy, fifty-five miles from d'Alès, and forty miles from Mende. Nearest rail station: Langogne or Saint-Laurent-les-Bains/La Bastide. By train travel on the Paris-Marseille line or Paris-Clermont-Ferrand-Nimes; and then taxi from La Bastide (two miles to the monastery).

ABBAYE SAINTE-MARIE-DE-LA-PIERRE-QUI-VIRE
89630 Saint-Léger-Vauban
Tel: (03) 86-33-19-21, 86-33-19-28, 86-33-19-20
Fax: (03) 86-33-19-31, (03) 86-32-22-33
Email: p.abbe@abbaye-pierrequivire.asso.fr
Web site: www.abbaye-pierrequivire.asso.fr

Founded in 1850, the Abbey of Sainte-Marie-de-la-Pierre-qui-Vire is home to a community of about seventy Benedictine monks, which belongs to the Congregation of Subiaco. Both the Mass and the Liturgy of the Hours are sung in French and Gregorian chant, which all visitors are invited to attend. Languages spoken at the abbey include French, English, German, Italian, Spanish, and Swedish.

Where to stay? The monks operate a guesthouse that is open to those men and women who are seeking a place of spiritual refreshment in a monastic environment (it is closed in January). Maximum stay is seven days and minimum is two days. To make reservations, contact the guestmaster at Frère Hôtelier, Abbaye de la Pierre-qui-Vire; 89630 Saint-Léger-Vauban; Fax: (03) 86-32-22-33; Email: accueil@abbaye-pierrequivire.asso.fr.

How to get there? Avallon is about fifteen miles from Saint-Léger-Vauban. The nearest train station is at Avallon; continue by taxi to Rouvray. The next closest train station is Montbard, which is about thirty-five miles from Rouvray.

ABBAYE DE NOTRE-DAME-DE-CÎTEAUX
21700 Saint-Nicolas-les-Cîteaux
Tel: (03) 80-61-31-10, 80-61-11-53 • Fax: (03) 80-61-35-34, 80-62-36-79
Email: visites@citeaux-abbaye.com
Web site: www.citeaux-abbaye.com

Founded in 1098, the world renowned Abbey of Notre-Dame-de-Cîteaux is home to a community of Cistercian-Trappist monks. The Liturgy of the Hours is sung in French, with parts of the Mass and the evening's Salve Regina sung in Gregorian chant. Some of the many items you may purchase include the abbey's cheeses, honey, candy, pottery, CDs, and tape cassettes (which are recorded within the monastery).

Where to stay? Forty guestrooms (usually maximum thirty people) are available to those who wish to join in the prayer life of the monks and spend quiet time in reflection from two to seven days. A dormitory is available for groups of young people (thirty beds). Meeting rooms are available. To make a reservation, you can email the guestmaster at hotelier@citeaux-abbaye.com.

How to get there? Saint-Nicolas-les-Cîteaux is located south of Dijon and ten miles from Nuits-Saint-Georges. The nearest train station is at Dijon (and Nuits-Saint-Georges). From Dijon, continue by local bus "Transco" (bus line #43 Dijon-Seurre—only one departure per day; none on Saturday or Sunday), or taxi to the abbey.

ABBAYE NOTRE-DAME-DE-BELVAL

Troisvaux
62130 Saint-Pol-sur-Ternoise
Tel: (03) 21-04-10-10, 21-03-11-65, 21-04-10-10
Fax: (03) 21-47-18-15
Email: ab@abbaye-belval.com
celleriere@abbaye-belval.com, econome@abbaye-belval.com
Web site: www.abbaye-belval.com

Founded in 1893, the Abbey of Notre-Dame-de-Belval is home to a community of Trappist monks. All religious services are sung in French.

Where to stay? A guesthouse is available solely for those individuals who want to embark on a spiritual retreat in a monastic environment of prayer and silence. For individuals or small groups (twenty-seven rooms), Tel: (03) 21-04-10-14. For groups of twenty to forty people, Tel: (03) 21-04-10-10.

How to get there? Saint-Pol-sur-Ternoise is located about twenty miles west of Arras. Saint-Pol-sur-Ternoise is accessible by train.

MONASTÈRE DES BÉNÉDICTINES

2 place de l'Abbaye
51220 Saint-Thierry
Tel: (03) 26-03-10-72, 26-03-99-37
Fax: (03) 26-03-15-49, 26-03-99-37
Email: communaute.st-thierry@orange.fr

Originally founded in the fifth century, today the monastery is home to a women's community of Benedictine nuns. As well as spending time in the ancient chapel, visitors can attend religious services, which include Mass and the Divine Office.

Where to stay? A guesthouse is available to those individuals and groups who wish to participate more fully in the life of the community, as well as embark on a personal spiritual retreat. Eighteen rooms are available for thirty people. For reservations, email: st-thierry@wanadoo.fr.

How to get there? Saint-Thierry is located about five miles northwest of Reims, which is accessible by train. Continue by taxi to the monastery.

ABBAYE SAINT-WANDRILLE
2, rue Saint Jacques
76490 Saint-Wandrille-Rançon
Tel: (02) 35-96-23-11 • Fax: (02) 35-96-49-08
Email: abbaye@st-wandrille.com, cellererie@st-wandrille.com
Web site: www.st-wandrille.com

Originally founded in 649, today the Abbey of Saint Wandrille is home to a community of Benedictine monks who belong to the Congregation of Solesmes. Visitors are welcome to join the monks in their daily life of prayer, which includes the singing of the Liturgy of the Hours and Mass in Gregorian chant. Guided tours of the monastery are also available (a visit can be organized anytime during the year prior to your visit). Among the most popular items available at the abbey gift shop are the Gregorian chant CDs and cassette recordings.

Where to stay? Guestrooms are available for men at the abbey, while the Saint Joseph House provides accommodation for women and couples. To make reservations for women and couples, email: st.joseph@ st-wandrille.com. Groups and other individuals, email: hotellerie@ st-wandrille.com.

How to get there? Rouen is twenty-six miles from Saint-Wandrille-Rançon. The nearest rail stations are at Yvetot, Rouen, or Le Havre. Take a taxi from any of the train stations to reach the abbey.

MONASTÈRE DE LA NATIVITÉ
105, rue Victor-Guichard
89100 Sens
Tel: (03) 86-65-13-41 • Fax: (03) 86-65-73-49

Founded in 1920, the Monastery of the Nativity is home to a community of Dominican monks. As well as attending religious services, visitors can spend time in the crypt praying before the fifteenth-century miraculous statue of Our Lady of Graces. Among the most popular products at the gift shop are the abbey's chocolates.

Where to stay? A guesthouse is available to those individuals and groups who are seeking a few days of prayer and reflection.

How to get there? Sens is easily accessible by train or bus. Take a taxi to arrive at the monastery.

ABBAYE SAINTE-LIOBA
530 chemin des Mérentiers
Quartier Saint-Germain
13109 Simiane-Collongue
Tel: (04) 42-22-60-60 • Fax: (04) 42-22-79-50
Email: benedictins@lioba.com
Web site: www.lioba.com; www.lioba-artisanat.com

Founded in 1987, the Abbey of Sainte-Lioba is home to a community of Benedictine monks and nuns. Visitors are welcome to participate in the prayer life of the community, which includes both their Mass and the Liturgy of the Hours (sung in French and Gregorian chant).

Where to stay? A guesthouse is available to those individuals seeking spiritual refreshment and solitude in a monastic environment. Groups of young people (eighteen to thirty-five years old) are especially welcome and many activities are provided. To make reservations by email, visit the Web site and fill out the online email form.

How to get there? Simiane-Collongue is located fourteen miles from Marsailles; continue by bus or taxi to the abbey. The abbey itself is about one mile from the village of Simiane. Simiane is accessible by train and is on the Marseilles-Aix line.

ABBAYE SAINT-PIERRE DE SOLESMES

1 place Dom Guéranger
72300 Solesmes
Tel: (0243) 95-03-08 • Fax: (0243) 95-03-28, 95-68-79
Email: abbaye@solesmes.com
Web site: www.solesmes.com

Refounded by Dom Guéranger in 1837, the renowned Abbey of Saint Peter today serves as a worldwide center for Gregorian chant and spirituality. Home to a community of almost ninety Benedictine monks, the abbey has gained international recognition for their recordings and publications of Gregorian chant. All visitors are welcome to join the monks in their daily life of prayer, which includes the singing of the Divine Office and Mass in Latin Gregorian chant. All of Solesmes's Gregorian chant recordings (on CD or cassette) can be purchased at the abbey gift shop, as well as throughout the world at many Catholic and secular book and music stores.

Where to stay? Guestrooms, located within the monastic enclosure, are available to those men who seek a place of retreat and prayer. Meals are taken with the monks. To make reservations, email: hospes@solesmes.com. For more information about other places to stay at Solesmes, see the story about the Benedictine Congregation of Solesmes in Part 2 of this book, titled, "Standing on Holy Ground."

How to get there? Please see the story about the Benedictine Congregation of Solesmes in Part 2 of this book, titled, "Standing on Holy Ground." All necessary information regarding location and directions is included in the story.

ABBAYE SAINTE-CÉCILE

Abbaye La Trappe
61380 Soligny-La-Trappe
Tel: (02) 33-84-17-00, 33-84-17-01 • Fax: (02) 33-34-98-57, 33-84-17-08
Web site: www.latrappe.fr

A world-famous monastery, the Abbey of La Trappe is home to a community of Cistercian-Trappist monks who started the Cistercian Reform movement in the early nineteenth century. All visitors, however, are warmly invited to participate in Mass and vespers. You can purchase some of the abbey's products, including yogurt, cheese, milk, cream, milk-based desserts, and fruit preserves.

Where to stay? Only men (individually or in groups) can be accommodated in the monastic guesthouses. Maximum stay is eight days. To make reservations, email: hotelier@latrappe.fr; Tel: (02) 33-84-17-05. For groups or young people, you can stay at the nearby La Bergerie, which receives about two thousand guests each year with capacity for fifty guests. To make reservations at this place, contact Les Amis de La Bergerie, Abbaye de La Trappe, 61380 Soligny La Trappe; Tel: (02) 33-84-17-67; Fax: (02) 33-24-55-10; Email: bergerie@latrappe.fr.

How to get there? Alencon is about thirty miles from Soligny-La-Trappe. Nearest Train Station: L'Aigle.

MONASTÈRE DE LA VISITATION
Domaine de Guerre
84700 Sorgues
Tel: (04) 90-83-31-14

Founded in 1624, the monastery is home to a community of Visitation monks. All religious services are open to the public and are sung in French. Many pilgrims come to pray before the tomb of Saint Maxima, a young girl who died as a martyr during the reign of Diocletian.

Where to stay? Seventeen guestrooms are available to those individuals who are seeking a time of prayer and quiet.

How to get there? Avignon is seven miles from Sorgues. Avignon is accessible by train and bus; continue by taxi to the monastery. Another nearby rail station is at Sorgues Chateaune.

ABBAYE SAINT-MICHEL-DE-FRIGOLET
13150 Tarascon-sur-Rhône
Tel: (04) 90-95-70-07 • Tel (guesthouse): (04) 90-90-52-70
Fax: (04) 90-95-75-22
Email: abbayedefrigolet@frigolet.com
Web site: www.frigolet.com

Founded in 1133, the Abbey of Saint-Michel-de-Frigolet is home to a community of Premonstratensian Canons (Norbertine Fathers). As well as taking guided tours of the thirteenth-century cloister, Saint Michael Church, and Our Lady of Good Remedy Chapel, visitors can attend religious services. Great celebrations take place at the monastery on the feast day of Our Lady of Good Remedy, which is the first Sunday after May 15. An excellent gift shop can be found on the premises.

Where to stay? The monastery guesthouse provides accommodations for both men and women who wish to participate in a personal retreat at the abbey. Maximum stay is one week. For groups of young people, ask about staying at the "Ferme" (former abbey farm), which can hold up to sixteen people in three rooms. Couples may wish to stay at the L'Evêché/The Bishopric. To make reservations, contact Norbertine comunity guesthouse for retreat, Tel: (04) 90-95-70-07; Fax (04) 90-90-79-23. Sisters of Saint-Charles's community, Tel: (049) 90-95-79-50; Fax: (04) 90-90-79-23. Hôtel Saint-Michel, Tel: (04) 90-90-52-70; Fax: (04) 90-95-75-22.

How to get there? Eyguieres is located about seven miles from Tarascon-sur-Rhône, which is accessible by train.

ORDRE DE LA VIERGE MARIE
38, rue J-F Marmontel
94320 Thiais
Tel: (01) 48-84-75-58, (01) 48-53-27-37
Tel (community): (01) 48-84-75-58
Fax (monastery): (01) 48-52-24-98
Web site: www.annonciade.org
Email: contact@annonciade.org

Founded in 1501, the monastery is home to members of the Order of the Virgin Mary. All are invited to attend the religious services of the community.

Where to stay? A guesthouse with twenty rooms is available to those individuals who are seeking a time of prayer and reflection (groups, youth, couples, etc.). To make a reservation, you can email the monastery: economat-thiais@annonciade.org.

How to get there? Paris is twelve miles from Thiais. From Paris, take a taxi to the monastery.

ABBAYE NOTRE-DAME DE TOURNAY

65190 Tournay
Tel: (05) 62-35-70-21 • Fax: (05) 62-35-25-72
Email: contact@abbaye-tournay.com
Web site: www.abbaye-tournay.com

Founded in 1935, the Abbey of Notre-Dame de Tournay is home to a community of Benedictine monks who belong to the Congregation of Subiaco. Visitors are welcome to join the monks in their prayer life, which includes daily recitation of the Liturgy of the Hours and celebration of Mass (both are said in French). Ceramics, candies, fruits, and religious books are just a few of the items available in the abbey gift shop.

Where to stay? Those who desire to participate more fully in the prayer life of the monastery may be accommodated in one of the abbey's guestrooms (thirty rooms for men, twelve for women). To make reservations, contact the guesthouse at Tel: (05) 62-35-28-43; Fax (06) 63-64-17-59.

How to get there? Tournay is located twenty-five miles northwest of the world famous pilgrimage destination and city of Lourdes. Tournay is accessible by train.

ABBAYE NOTRE-DAME-DE-SAINT-JOSEPH

Soeur Hôtelière, Abbaye Cistercienne
88130 Ubexy
Tel: (03) 29-38-25-70, 29-38-04-32 • Fax: (03) 29-38-05-90
Email: abbaye.ubexy@wanadoo.fr
Web site: www.abbaye-ubexy.com.fr

Founded in 1841, the Abbey of Notre-Dame-de-Saint-Joseph is home to a community of Cistercians monks. All visitors are invited to attend religious services, which include Mass and vespers.

Where to stay? Both individuals and groups (maximum twenty people) who wish to participate more fully in the prayer life of the monks can be accepted into the guesthouse.

How to get there? Ubexy is located about thirty miles south of Nancy. The nearest train station is at Charmes (Vosges) and Vincey. Continue by bus or taxi for the remaining three miles to the abbey (from the Charmes train station).

ABBAYE NOTRE-DAME-DE-BELLOC

64240 Urt
Tel: (05) 59-29-65-55 • Fax: (05) 59-29-44-08
Email: belloc.abbaye@wanadoo.fr
Web site: www.belloc-urt.org; www.belloc-urt.org/belloc

Founded in 1875, the Abbey of Notre-Dame-de-Belloc is home to a community of Benedictine monks who belong to the Congregation of Subiaco. Daily offices are sung in French and Latin, with Mass in Gregorian chant. A gift shop on the premises sells the monastery's cheese.

Where to stay? Individuals and groups (including couples) who desire a deeper experience of monastic life may be accommodated in the abbey guesthouse. In total, the guesthouse has eighteen single rooms, ten double rooms, and four dormitories, as well as guest lounges, a library, and chapel choir. Conferences and meeting facilities are available. Maximum stay is six days. Nearby is the Benedictine Monastery of St. Scholastica, which also offers hospitality. You can contact them at Tel: (05) 59-70-20-28; By mail: Monastère Sainte-Scholastique, 64240 Urt.

How to get there? Biarritz is located about twenty-three miles from Urt, the latter which is accessible by train. Note: Do not confuse the village of Bellocq (which is close to Orthez) and the actual monastery of Belloc, which is in/near the city of Urt.

ABBAYE NOTRE-DAME-DU-PRÉ

12, rue Raoul Auvray
76540 Valmont
Tel: (02) 35-27-34-92 • Fax: (02) 35-27-86-21
Email: economat.ndp@wanadoo.fr

Founded in 1011, the Abbey of Notre-Dame-du-Pré is home to a women's community of Benedictine monks. All visitors are invited to participate in religious services, which include the celebration of Mass and the Divine Office (said/sung in French and Gregorian chant).

Where to stay? The monastery guesthouse is open to both individuals and groups who seek a place of prayer and solitude.

How to get there? Valmont is located about thirty-two miles from Le Havre. Nearest rail stations: Fecamp and Yvetot.

ABBAYE SAINT-LOUIS-DU-TEMPLE

Limon
91430 Vauhallan (Essone)
Tel (abbey): (01) 69-85-21-00 • Tel (guesthouse): (01) 69-85-21-20
Email: m.abbesse@wanadoo.fr
Web site: www.abbaye-limon-vauhallan.com

Founded in 1789, the Abbey of Saint-Louis-du-Temple is home to a community of Benedictine monks. As well as touring the abbey museum and grounds, visitors can attend religious services, which are sung in both French and Gregorian chant. Many of the abbey's farm products are available at the gift shop.

Where to stay? With excellent guesthouse facilities, the abbey has thirty rooms, several meeting rooms, and a small library. To make reservations, Tel/Fax: (01) 69-85-28-96; Email: accueil@abbaye-limon-vauhallan.com.

How to get there? Paris is located about fifteen miles from Limon. Nearest rail station: Igny, serviced by Paris RER (Massy-Palaiseau). The Igny train station is located about two miles from the abbey.

ABBAYE SAINT-NICOLAS

124, rue de la Place-Notre-Dame
B.P. 236
27132 Verneuil-sur-Avre
Tel: (02) 32-32-02-94 • Fax: (02) 32-32-72-46
Email: verneuil@paindevie.fr
Web site: www.aux4coinsdumonde.net/abbaye

Founded in 1627, the abbey of Saint-Nicolas is home to a community of Benedictine monks. As well as touring the fifteenth-century Gothic church, visitors can join the monks in their celebration of Mass and the Divine Office (which are both sung in Gregorian chant according to the Order of Solesmes).

Where to stay? The guesthouse is available only for men who wish to stay within the enclosure.

How to get there? Verneuil-sur-Avre is located about seventy-two miles from Paris. Verneuil-sur-Avre is accessible by train.

ASSOCIATION JÉRUSALEM VEZELAY
Presbytère
89450 Vézelay
Tel: (03) 86-33-39-50 • Fax: (03) 86-33-36-93
Email: basilique@vezelay.cef.fr
Web site: http://vezelay.cef.fr

Founded in 1975, the monastery is home to the Monastic Fraternity of Jerusalem. As well as praying before the relics of Saint Mary Magdalene in the crypt of the abbey basilica, visitors can attend religious services with the monks, which are sung in polyphony and French. Many of the abbey's products and artworks are available in the gift shop (which is located at 78, rue Saint-Pierre).

Where to stay? The monks operate two guesthouses, one of which provides accommodations for twenty people (Béthanie des Fraternités), and the other which accommodates up to thirty-five people (Centre Pax Christi).

How to get there? Vézelay is located about thirty-five miles south of Auxerre; the village is located at the crossing of D951 and D957 between Avallon and Clamecy. There are three possibilities by train: (1) the rail station of Sermizelles-Vézelay, which is about seven miles from Vézelay; (2) the rail station at Avallon, which is about ten miles from the monastery; (3) the train station at Montabard.

MONASTÈRE DE LA VISITATION
Montée de l'Uriol
38450 Vif
Tel: (04) 76-72-51-18

Founded in 1645, the monastery is home to a community of Visitation monks. Every day, visitors are welcome to join the monks in the abbey chapel for Mass and the Liturgy of the Hours, which are both sung in French.

Where to stay? A guesthouse with thirty-five rooms provides accommodation to both men and women, individuals and groups.

How to get there? Vif is located about eleven miles from Grenoble, the latter which is accessible by train.

ABBAYE NOTRE-DAME-D'ACEY

39350 Vitreux
Tel: (03) 84-81-04-11 • Fax: (03) 84-70-90-97
Email: monastere.acey@wanadoo.fr
Web site: http://acey.eglisejura.com

Founded in 1136, the Abbey of Notre-Dame-d'Acey is home to a community of Cistercian-Trappist monks. The abbey church, built in the twelfth century, is a historical monument. The abbey operates a factory that works with silver and gold.

Where to stay? Fifteen guestrooms are available to individuals and couples, and the abbey's dormitory can accommodate up to fifty-two people. To make reservations, email: hotelier.acey@orange.fr.

How to get there? Vitreux is located between Lyon and Strausbourg, and is about twenty-five miles from Besancon. Nearest rail stations: Ranchot and Dijon, which is one hour from Ranchot.

MONASTÈRE DU CHALAIS

B.P. 128 Chalais
38340 Voreppe
Tel: (04) 76-50-02-16 • Fax: (04) 76-50-22-23
Email: accueil.chalais@orange.fr

Originally founded at the end of the sixteenth century, today the Monastery of Chalais is home to community of Dominican nuns. As well as spending time in the chapel, visitors can join the sisters in religious services.

Where to stay? Two guesthouses are available including "Petite Hôtellerie" and "Ermitage." The first hotel can accommodate groups of about twenty people and has meeting facilities/rooms. The second guesthouse can accommodate about twenty people and also includes a dining room and meeting room. Maximum stay is eight days. Bring warm clothing, a raincoat, and good shoes, due to the altitude and surrounding area.

How to get there? The Chalais monastery is located near Grenoble by the town of Voreppe. Train stations are in Voreppe, Voiron, and Grenoble. Although Voreppe is the closest train station, fewer trains stop there. Bus service is available to Voreppe, Voiron, and Grenoble. Taxi is the only way to reach the monastery.

ABBAYE SAINT-PAUL
rue de l'Ecole
62219 Wisques
Tel: (03) 21-95-11-04, 21-12-28-78, 21-12-28-50
Fax: (03) 21-38-19-40, 21-12-28-79, 21-12-28-51
Email: info@abbaye-wisques.com (Web site has an online email form.)
Web site: www.abbaye-stpaul-wisques.com

Founded in 1889, the Abbey of Saint-Paul is home to a community of Benedictine monks who belong to the Congregation of Solesmes. Visitors are welcome to join the monks in their daily life of prayer, which includes the singing of the Divine Office and Mass in Gregorian chant. The abbey gift shop sells a number of religious art ceramics, as well as Gregorian chant CDs.

Where to stay? The abbey's guesthouse has twenty-eight rooms open to both individuals and groups.

How to get there? Wisques is about twenty-five miles from Calais. Nearest rail station: Saint-Omer.

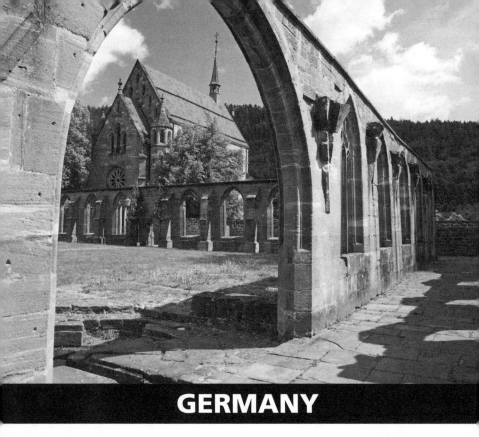

GERMANY

ABTEI SANKT ERENTRAUD

Kellenried 3
88276 Berg (Ravensburg)
Tel: (07505) 956-60 • Tel (guesthouse): (07505) 1261, 1620
Fax: (07505) 1260
Email: info@abtei-kellenried.de
Web site: www.abtei-kellenried.de

Founded in the eighteenth century, the Abbey of Sankt Erentraud is home to a community of Benedictine nuns. Visitors can tour the abbey church (which was restored after World War II). Both the Liturgy of the Hours and Mass are sung in Latin and German.

Where to stay? Since 1962, the monks have operated a twenty-three-room guesthouse (singles and doubles) which provides accommodations for those individuals who wish to participate in the prayer life of the nuns. The guesthouse features a dining room, community room, gardens, roof terrace, and a small meditation room. A library is avail-

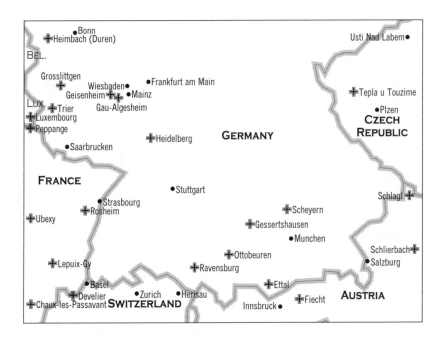

able for guests. To make a reservation, email: gaestehaus@abtei-kel-lenried.de; Tel: (07505) 1261.

How to get there? Berg is located eleven miles east of Ravensburg and about one hundred miles west of Munich. Ravensburg is accessible by train; once in Ravensburg, you can take a taxi or local bus (bus #10; stop #13) to arrive at the abbey.

BENEDIKTINERABTEI ETTAL
Kaiser-Ludwig-Platz 1
82488 Ettal
Tel: (08822) 740 • Fax: (08822) 74-228
Fax (Guesthouse): (08822) 74-480
Email: hotel@kloster-ettal.de; verwaltung@kloster-ettal.de
Web site: www.kloster-ettal.de

Founded in 1330, today the Abbey of Ettal is home to a community of Benedictine monks. A place of pilgrimage for many centuries, the monastery still remains one of the most famous abbeys in Germany and is known for its history, architecture, and art. Visitors can participate in the prayer life of the monks by attending Mass and the Divine

Office, as well as taking guided tours of the abbey. Guests can stay at the Ludwig der Bayer Hotel, which has very comfortable rooms. The abbey produces its own beer, which visitors can purchase.

Where to stay? The hotel also has a number of modern facilities, including an indoor pool, sauna, tennis courts, big breakfast buffet, television room, and a restaurant featuring the region's finest cuisine. Conference rooms are available for groups.

How to get there? Ettal is located about fifty miles southwest of Munich via the A95. Nearest rail station: Garmisch (Garmisch-Parten Kirchen).

BENEDIKTINERMISSIONARE
Kloster Jakobsberg
55435 Ockenheim (Gau-Algesheim)
Tel: (06725) 304-0, 304-111 • Fax: (06725) 304-100
Web site: www.klosterjakobsberg.de

Founded in 1720, the Abbey of Jakobsberg is home to a community of Benedictine monks. Mass and the Liturgy of the Hours are celebrated daily in the abbey church, which all visitors are welcome to attend. The two major feast days at the abbey are those dedicated to Saint Christopher (July 25) and Saint Barbara (December 4).

Where to stay? Guestrooms (singles and doubles) are available for individuals and small groups, but you must come with the intention of participating in the prayer life and work of the monastery.

How to get there? Ockenheim and Gau-Alesheim are located about forty miles west of Frankfurt via the A3/A60 and B41. Gau-Algesheim and Ockenheim are accessible by train. The abbey lies in Ockenheim.

KLOSTER MARIENTAL
65366 Geisenheim (Mayence)
Tel: (06722) 99-580 • Fax: (06722) 99-5813
Email: marienthal@franziskaner.de

Founded in 1309, the Cloister of Mariental is home to a community of Franciscan priests and brothers. Visitors can join the Franciscans in Mass and the Liturgy of the Hours, as well as spend time in the Room of Meditation, which lies inside the monastery.

Where to stay? Guesthouse accommodations are available for those individuals who wish to join the community in their prayers, work, and meditation (guesthouse visitors must be at least eighteen years of age).

How to get there? Geisenheim is located forty miles west of Frankfurt via the A3. Geisenheim is accessible by train.

ABTEI OBERSCHÖNENFELD

86459 Gessertshausen (Augsburg)
Tel: (08238) 962-50, 37-30 • Fax: (08238) 600-65, 37-00
Email: abtei@abtei-oberschoenenfeld.de
Web site: www.abtei-oberschoenenfeld.de

Founded in 1211, the Abbey of Oberschönenfeld is home to a community of Cistercian monks. Religious services are open to the public and are sung in Gregorian chant. Some of the monks' artistic works, which are available for purchase, include handcrafted furniture, wooden statues, candles, and embroidered items.

Where to stay? The abbey operates a guesthouse, which provides comfortable rooms to young people, men, women, individuals, groups, and families (including children) who wish to participate in a personal monastic environment retreat. To make reservations, Tel: (08238) 9625-27 or (08238) 9625-0; Fax: (08238) 60065; Email: anmeldung@abtei-oberschoenenfeld.de.

How to get there? Gessertshausen is located sixty miles northwest of Munich and ten miles west of Augsburg via the B300. Augsburg and Gessertshausen are accessible by train. Take a taxi for the remaining one to two miles to the abbey.

ABTEI HIMMEROD

Himmerod 3
54534 Grosslittgen (Koblenz)
Tel (abbey): (06575) 9513-0, 9513-12
Tel (guesthouse): (06575) 9513-20, 9513-17 • Fax: (06575) 9513-39
Email: verwaltung@kloster-himmerod.de
Web site: www.abtei-himmerod.org

Founded in 1134, the Abbey of Himmerod is home to a community of Cistercian monks. Every day, the monks celebrate Mass and the Divine Office in the abbey church.

Where to stay? The monastery offers two guesthouses (guestwings), which together can welcome men, women, families, married couples, and people of any age, including children.

How to get there? Grosslittgen is located one hundred thirty miles west of Frankfurt via the A3/A48. Himmerod, which is where the abbey is located, is situated 2.5 miles west of Grosslittgen. Nearest rail station: Wittlich.

ABTEI NEUBURG
Stiftweg 2
69118 Heidelberg
Tel: (06221) 895-0 • Fax: (06221) 895-166
Email: kloster@abtei-neuburg.de
Web site: www.stift-neuburg.de

Founded in 1130, the Abbey of Neuburg is home to a community of Benedictine monks. As well as touring the eighteenth-century abbey church, visitors can stroll in the monastery's grand garden. Mass is celebrated daily, and the two major feast days of Saint Benedict (March 21 and July 11) bring a large number of pilgrims. The monks produce excellent jams, which are available for visitors and tourists to purchase.

Where to stay? The abbey operates a simple and peaceful guesthouse, which is open to men who seek a spiritual retreat. Meals are taken with the monks. Small groups are welcome based on availability. To make a reservation, call, fax, or email: gaestehaus@abtei-neuburg.de.

How to get there? Heidelberg is located fifty-five miles south of Frankfurt via the A5. Heidelberg is accessible by train; once in Heidelberg, you can take a taxi or bus (bus #34).

ABTEI MARIAWALD
Gästehaus
52396 Heimbach/Eifel (Duren)
Main Tel: (02446) 95-06-0 • Fax: (02446) 95-06-30
Cloister Tel: (02446) 9506-16 • Fax: (02446) 9506-211
Likörfabrik Tel: (02446) 9506-18 • Fax: (02446) 9506-218
Web site: www.kloster-mariawald.de

Founded in 1470, the Abbey of Mariawald is home to a community of Cistercian monks. Visitors are welcome to join the monks in religious services, including Mass and the Liturgy of the Hours.

Where to stay? The monks operate a contemplative guesthouse, which is open only to men who wish to experience a time of prayer and silence. To make reservations, contact Porter/Guesthouse, Tel: (02446) 9506-16, 9506-0; Fax: (02446) 9506-211, 9506-30; Email: pforte@kloster-mariawald.de.

How to get there? Heimbach (Duren) is located about forty-five miles west of Bonn and ninety miles north of Trier, via B265. Heimbach/Duren is accessible by train and bus; once in Heimbach, take a taxi or local bus to the abbey.

NEUZELLE KLOSTER
Foundation pen Neuzelle
Collegiate Course 7
15898 Neuzelle (Frankfurt-an-der-Oder)
Tel: (033652) 81-40 • Fax: (033652) 81-419
Email: info@stift-neuzelle.de
Web site: www.kloster-neuzelle.de

Founded in 1268, the Cloister of Neuzelle is home to a community of Premonstratensian Canons (Norbertine Fathers). Inside the artistically rich abbey church, visitors can join the monks in their daily lives of prayer, including Mass. There are concerts featuring both classical and sacred music throughout the year at the abbey. Guided tours are available by appointment only.

Where to stay? A diocesan guesthouse is located near the abbey, providing accommodations to both men and women who are visiting the monastery.

How to get there? Neuzelle is in northeast Germany, about four hundred miles east of Frankfurt and eighty miles southeast of Berlin via the A12/B112/B246. Neuzelle is accessible by train and bus.

BENEDIKTINERABTEI
Sebastian-Kneipp-Str. 1
87724 Ottobeuren
Tel: (08332) 79-80 • Fax: (08332) 798-125, 798-120
Email: bildungshaus@abtei-ottobeuren.de
Web site: www.abtei-ottobeuren.de

Founded in the eighth century, Ottobeuren Abbey is home to a community of Benedictine monks. Welcoming visitors and tourists from all over the world, the abbey features a vast basilica that is virtually unmatched for its interior beauty and majestic spaciousness. As well as exploring the immense church, the faithful can spend time in the well-appointed museum, attend religious services, and visit the abbey gift shop. Guided tours of the abbey are available, but you should make reservations in advance.

Where to stay? Although guestrooms are not available, there is a tourist office located across the street that can help arrange accommodations close to the monastery. For more information, contact Kurverwaltung-Haus des Gastes, Marktplatz 14, 87724 Ottobeuren; Tel: (08332) 92-19-52, 92-19-53, 92-19-50; Fax: (08332) 92-19-92; Email: touristikamt@ottobeuren.de; Web site: www.ottobeuren.de.

How to get there? Ottobeuren is located about seventy-two miles west of Munich and six miles southeast of Memmingen. Memmingen is accessible by train, and then you can switch to local bus or taxi to reach Ottobeuren. From the Memmingen bus station, there are regular departures from platform #1 for Ottobeuren Abbey.

BENEDIKTINERABTEI ZUM HEILIGEN KREUZ
Schyrenplatz 1
85297 Scheyern (Pfaffenhofen)
Tel (abbey): (08441) 752-0;
Tel (guesthouse): (08441) 752-210, 752-230
Fax: (08441) 752-210
Email: info@kloster-scheyern.de
Web site: www.kloster-scheyern.de

Founded in 1119, the Abbey of Heiligen Kreuz is home to a community of Benedictine monks. Visitors are welcome to join the monks at religious services in the abbey church, as well as participate in the summertime processions to honor the Holy Cross. Concerts featuring both classical and sacred music take place throughout the year at the abbey.

Where to stay? The monastery operates an excellent guesthouse called Schyren-Hof, which provides accommodations for both men and women, as well as for groups. To make a reservation, Tel: (08441) 7520; Fax: 752210; Email: info.@monastery scheyern.de.

How to get there? Scheyern is located about thirty-four miles north of Munich via the A9. Nearest rail station: Pfaffenhofen; then switch to bus to reach Scheyern.

BENEDIKTINERABTEI ST. MATTHIAS

Matthiasstrasse 85
54290 Trier
Tel: (0651) 1709-0, 31-079 • Fax: (0651) 1709-243, 359-69
Email: Benediktiner@AbteiStMatthias.de
Web site: www.abteistmatthias.de

Founded in 1148, the Abbey of Saint Matthias is home to a community of Benedictine monks. Located on the outskirts of Trier, the monastery receives thousands of pilgrims annually for one main reason—the sacred relics of the apostle Saint Matthias are enshrined here. As well as attending religious services with the monks, the faithful can visit the abbey museum, which houses an extensive collection of artifacts, paintings, and historical documents. The feast day of Saint Matthias is celebrated annually on May 14, with many pilgrims arriving for the great day of festivities.

Where to stay? The abbey provides a guesthouse for men. To make reservations, email: gaesteempfang@abteistmatthias.de.

How to get there? Trier is located about one hundred forty-five miles west of Frankfurt near the Luxembourg border. Trier is easily accessible by train and bus.

GREECE

SERVING AS THE CENTER of Eastern Orthodox monasticism, Mount Athos has long been considered one of the most famous monastic sites in Europe. With only monks registered as its permanent residents, today the city is the only place in Greece to be completely dedicated to prayer and the worship of God. Covering an area of approximately two hundred square miles, Mount Athos lies on the beautiful Halkidiki peninsula in the northeastern section of the country, and is comprised of about twenty monasteries.

According to Orthodox Christian tradition, the founding of Mount Athos dates back to the first century. It is said that Apostle John the Evangelist and the Virgin Mary discovered the area when they were forced to take refuge there during a storm on their travels to Cyprus to visit Lazarus. Struck by the beauty of the land, the Virgin Mary asked God to offer the mountain to them as a gift. After presenting the petition to the Lord, she then heard God reply: "Let this place be your lot, your garden and your paradise, as well as a salvation, a haven for those who seek salvation." Ever since that time, Mount Athos has been referred to as *The Garden of the Virgin Mary.* However, it wasn't until the fifth century that the first monks arrived at Mount Athos to establish their monasteries.

Today, Mount Athos serves as a self-governed city in Greece, but it is subject to the Ministry of Foreign Affairs in political matters, and subject to the Ecumenical Patriarch of Constantinople in religious matters. The entire municipality is divided into twenty self-governed territories, each one consisting of a cardinal monastery with other monastic establishments surrounding it (cloisters, cells, cottages, hermitages, and so on).

Each monastery is governed by a superior who presides over the affairs of the community and is elected for life. The superiors are also members of the Holy Assembly, which exercises its legislative authority over all of Mount Athos. Within each monastery, the activities of the monks are performed in community, including the liturgy, prayer, manual labor, housing, and eating.

In compliance with a long-standing tradition, only men are allowed to visit Mount Athos (and its monasteries). In order to visit the city, you must first apply for a permit and then make reservations with one of the following:

1. Pilgrim's Office of Athos, 109 Egnatia Str., Thessaloniki; Tel: (2310) 252-578, (031) 861-611; Fax: (031) 861-811; Web site: www.monachos.net/library/Visiting_Mount_Athos.

2. American Consulate General, 43 Tsimiski, 7th Floor, 54623 Thessaloniki; Tel: (031) 242-905/6/7; Fax: (031) 242-927); Email: info@usconsulate.gr; Web site: www.usconsulate.gr; http://thessaloniki.usconsulate.gov/contact-us.html.

3. U.S. Embassy Athens, 91 Vasilisis Sophias Avenue, 10160 Athens; Tel (Main Switchboard/Info): (210) 721-2951; Tel: (01) 721-2951; Fax: (01) 645-6282; Email: AthensAmEmb@state.gov; Web site: http://athens.usembassy.gov/contact-us.html.

4. Contact the Greek National Tourist Organization within your country to obtain the latest phone and fax numbers (and email addresses) of those offices providing the permits.

Bookings must be made at least two weeks prior to your visit, since the number of visitors to Mount Athos is limited. Once your reservation is confirmed, you will receive a code number which will serve as your permit. The number of permits issued daily is limited to about one hundred and twenty.

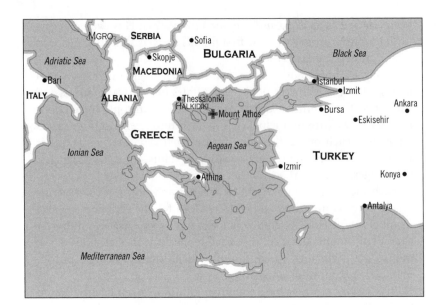

The Pilgrim's Office charges a fee for the permit, which usually allows for a three-night stay and includes both lodging and food at the monasteries. Overnight stays are allowed only for those individuals with a proven religious or scientific interest in the area and who are over eighteen years of age.

To obtain more detailed information about Mount Athos, be sure to visit the following Web sites:

- www.athosfriends.org/PilgrimsGuide
- www.macedonian-heritage.gr/Athos/General/visiting.html
- www.monachos.net/library/Visiting_Mount_Athos

HOW TO GET TO MT. ATHOS?

Mt. Athos is accessible by boat with daily departures from Ouranoupolis and Ierissos to Daphne, the sea port of Mount Athos. The boat trip is about two hours long. To reach Ouranoupolis from Thessaloniki, you can travel by taxi or bus (KTEL buses: contact the Prefect of Chalkidiki, 68 Karakasi St., Thessaloniki; Tel: 2310/924-444). Once in Daphne, you can take a bus (thirty-five minutes) to reach Karies, the capital of Mount Athos.

WHERE TO STAY?

The following is a brief outline of each of the twenty Mount Athos monasteries listed in their respective hierarchical order. Please note the phrase "second account" included with some entries, which indicates that an alternate source provided additional/contradictory information:

1. Holy Monastery of Megisti Lavra
   Foundation: AD 963
   Founder: monk Athanasios
   Dedication: Dormition of Athanasios
   Rank: first in the hierarchical order
   Celebration: July 5
   Location: southeast end of the Athos Peninsula
   Special note: home to the most monks of all the monasteries (approximately three hundred monks live here)
   Accommodation: welcoming guesthouse

2. Holy Monastery of Vatopedion
   Foundation: fourth century
   Founder: Emperor Theodosios A'
   Dedication: to the Annunciation of the Mother of God
   Rank: second in the hierarchical order
   Location: northeastern part of the Athos peninsula
   Celebration: March 25

   (Second account)
   Foundation: between 972 and 985
   Founders: monk Athanasios, monk Nikolaos, monk Antonios
   Accommodation: large guesthouse

3. Holy Monastery of Iviron
   Foundation: tenth century
   Founders: Ioannis the Ivir and Ioannis the Tornikios
   Dedication: to the Assumption of the Mother of God
   Rank: third in the hierarchical order
   Location: northeast side of the peninsula
   Celebration: August 15

4.   Holy Monastery of Helandarion
     Foundation: tenth century
     Founder: Helandarios
     Dedication: to the Presentation of the Virgin Mary
     Rank: fourth place in the hierarchical order
     Location: northeast side of the peninsula
     Celebration: November 21
     Accommodation: large guesthouse

5.   Holy Monastery of Dionysos
     Foundation: fourteenth century
     Founders: Saint Dionysios
     Dedication: to the birth of the honorable
     Saint John the Baptist
     Rank: fifth in the hierarchical order
     Celebration: June 24
     Location: southwest side of the peninsula
     Accommodation: very comfortable guesthouse with meals
     served in the monks' splendid refectory

6.   Holy Monastery of Koutloumousion
     Foundation: tenth century
     Founder: Koutloumous
     Dedication: to the Transfiguration of Christ
     Rank: sixth in the hierarchical order
     Location: northeastern side of Mount Athos
     (very close to Karyes)
     Celebration: August 6
     Special note: considered to be one of the most magnificent
     of all Mt. Athos monasteries
     Accommodation: large guesthouse

7.   Holy Monastery of Pantokrator
     Foundation: fourteenth century
     Founders: monk Alexios and monk Ioannis
     Dedication: to the Transfiguration of Christ
     Rank: seventh in the hierarchical order
     Location: eastern side of the peninsula
     Celebration: August 6
     Accommodation: large guesthouse

8. Holy Monastery of Xiropotamos
   Foundation: fifth century
   Founder: Empress Pulcheria
   Dedication: to the forty martyrs
   Rank: eighth in the hierarchal order
   Celebration: March 9
   Location: southwest side of the Athos peninsula

   (Second account)
   Foundation: tenth century
   Founders: monk Pavlos Xeropotaminos
   Accommodation: large guesthouse

9. Holy Monastery of Zografos
   Foundation: tenth century
   Founders: monk Moses, monk Aaron and monk Ioannis
   Dedication: to Saint George
   Rank: ninth in the hierarchical order
   Celebration: April 23
   Location: southwest side of the peninsula
   Special note: All the monks are Bulgarian,
   and all services are performed in Bulgarian
   Accommodation: large guesthouse

10. Holy Monastery of Dochiarios
    Foundation: tenth century
    Founder: monk Efthimios
    Dedication: to the Archangels Michael and Gabriel
    Rank: tenth in the hierarchical order
    Celebration: November 8
    Location: west side of the promontory
    Accommodation: modest guesthouse

11. Holy Monastery of Karakalos
    Foundation: third century
    Founder: Empress Karakalla
    Dedication: to Peter and Paul, Apostles
    Rank: eleventh in the hierarchical order
    Location: east of the peninsula
    Special note: The monastery was destroyed in 1988
    by a fire, but has been completely rebuilt
    Celebration: June 29

    (Second account)
    Foundation: eleventh century
    Founder: monk Karakalas
    Accommodation: large guesthouse

12. Holy Monastery of Filotheos
    Foundation: tenth century
    Founder: Saint Filotheos
    Dedication: to the Annunciation of the Mother of God
    Rank: twelfth in the hierarchical order
    Location: east side of the peninsula
    Celebration: March 25
    Accommodation: large guesthouse

13. Holy Monastery of Simon Petras
    Foundation: thirteenth century
    Founder: Saint Simon
    Dedication: to the birth of Jesus
    Rank: thirteenth in the hierarchical order
    Celebration: December 25
    Accommodation: guesthouse has spectacular
    panoramic views

14. Holy Monastery of Saint (Agios) Pavlos
    Foundation: eighth century
    Founder: Saint Pavlos
    Dedication: to the Candlemas of Jesus
    Rank: fourteenth in the hierarchical order
    Celebration: February 2

(Second account)
Foundation: tenth century
Founder: Pavlos Xeropotaminos
Accommodation: comfortable guesthouse

15. Holy Monastery of Stayronikitas
Foundation: tenth century
Founder: Nikiforos Stavronikitas
Dedication: to Saint Nikolaos
Rank: fifteenth in the hierarchical order
Celebration: December 6

(Second account)
Founder: patrician Nikitas
Accommodation: large guesthouse

16. Holy Monastery of Xenophon
Foundation: tenth century
Founder: Saint Xenophon
Dedication: to Saint George
Rank: sixteenth in the hierarchical order
Celebration: April 23
Location: southwest side of the Athos peninsula
Accommodation: large guesthouse

17. Holy Monastery of Gregorios
Foundation: fourteenth century
Founder: Gregory of Sinai
Dedication: to Saint Nikolaos
Rank: seventeenth in the hierarchical order
Celebration: December 6
Special note: recognized as one of the most organized and
strict coenobitic (communal) monasteries
Location: southwest side of Mount Athos

(Second account)
Founder: Gregorios from Syriana
Accommodation: large guesthouse

18. Holy Monastery of Esfigmrnos
    Foundation: fifth century
    Founders: Emperor Theodosios B'
    Dedication: to the Ascension of Jesus Christ
    Rank: eighteenth in the hierarchical order
    Location: northeast side of the peninsula
    Celebration: forty days after Easter

    (Second account)
    Foundation: tenth century
    Accommodation: large guesthouse

19. Holy Monastery of Panteleimon
    Foundation: eleventh century
    Founders: Russian monks
    Dedication: to Saint Panteleimon
    Rank: nineteenth in the hierarchal order
    Celebration: July 27
    Location: southwest side of the peninsula
    Accommodation: guesthouse;
    Russian pilgrims especially welcome

20. Holy Monastery of Kastamonitis
    Foundation: fourth century
    Founder: Constantine the Great
    Dedication: to Saint Stephen
    Rank: twentieth in the hierarchical order
    Celebration: December 27

    (Second account)
    Foundation: eleventh century
    Founder: monk Kastamonitis
    Accommodation: large guesthouse

HUNGARY

JÉZUS SZIVE NOVERÉK TÁRSASÁGA

Wlassics Gyula u. 84/b
1181 Budapest
Tel/Fax: (01) 290-9674
Email: SDSHhun@dpg.hu

Founded in 1993, this Hungarian abbey is home to the newly established Society of Adoration of the Sacred Heart monks. As well as spending time in the church, the faithful can join the monks in Mass and eucharistic adoration.

Where to stay? Students, families, groups, and consecrated religious are all welcome to stay for a few days in the guesthouse (if available).

How to get there? Budapest is the capital city of Hungary and is accessible by train and bus. Once inside Budapest, the easiest way to reach the abbey is by taxi.

CISZTERCI NOVÉREK BOLDOGASSZNOY HÁZA MONOSTOR

2623 Kismaros (Vác)
Tel: (027) 350-306, 350-307 • Fax: (027) 350-029

Founded in 1955, the abbey is home to a community of Cistercian monks. Annually, the monastery receives several thousand students and pilgrims who come to attend religious services with the monks and to pray in the fairly newly built monastery church (1993).

Where to stay? Guests traveling independently or in groups can be accommodated in the abbey guesthouse, but they must come with the desire to participate more fully in the prayer life of the monastery.

How to get there? Kismaros is located about thirty-five miles north of Budapest via E71/E77. Kismaros is accessible by train.

IRELAND

SAINT BENEDICT'S PRIORY
The Mount
Cobh
Co. Cork

Founded in 1916, Saint Benedict's Priory offers the visitor an incredible array of monastic hospitality. As well as spending time in retreat, guests can visit the Irish Monastic Heritage Center, the Bible Garden, and the shrine of Saint Oliver Plunkett. The Bible Garden contains more than an acre of species of trees, shrubs, plants, and flowers that are named in the Bible. Time can also be spent praying the monastic Liturgy of the Hours with the Benedictine Oblate sisters, as well as attending Mass and eucharistic adoration.

Where to stay? The monastic guesthouse has six single rooms and two double rooms.

How to get there? Cobh is located about one hundred sixty miles southwest of Dublin via M7/N8. Nearest rail station: Cork.

ST. MARY'S PRIORY
Dominican Retreat Centre
Tallaght Village, Dublin 24
Tel: (353) 1- 40-48-100; (01) 404-8189
Fax: (353) 1-45-96-784; (01) 459-60-80
Email: retreats@DominicansTallaght.org
Websites: www.prioryinstitute.com;
www.goodnews.ie/tallaghthome

Founded in 1865, the Convent of Saint Mary Immaculate is home to a community of Dominican nuns. Visitors can attend Mass in the convent chapel (built in 1886) and join in one of many prayer groups. The feast days of Saint Thomas Aquinas (January 28), Saint Dominic (August 8), and Our Lady of the Rosary (October 7) are celebrated at the chapel.

Where to stay? The nuns operate an excellent guesthouse called The Dominican Retreat and Pastoral Center, which has forty bedrooms (thirty-five singles, five doubles), a conference room, restaurant, and garden. Men, women, and young people are welcome to stay at the guesthouse, which include facilities for the handicapped. Concerts of both classical and sacred music take place throughout the year at the convent.

How to get there? Dublin is the capital city of Ireland and is easily accessible by train and bus. The easiest way to reach the convent is by taxi.

CISTERCIAN MONKS OF BOLTON ABBEY
Bolton Abbey
Moone, Co. Kildare
Tel: (0507) 241-02; (05986) 24-102 • Tel/Fax: (0507) 24-309
E-mail: boltonabbey@eircom.net; enquiry@boltonabbey.ie
Web site: www.boltonabbey.ie

Founded in 1965, Bolton Abbey is home to a community of thirteen Cistercian monks, whose primary means of livelihood is dairy farming. As well as spending time in retreat and attending the monks' Liturgy of the Hours, guests can visit the remains of the Celtic monasteries of Moone and Castledermot—famous for their high crosses—which is close by.

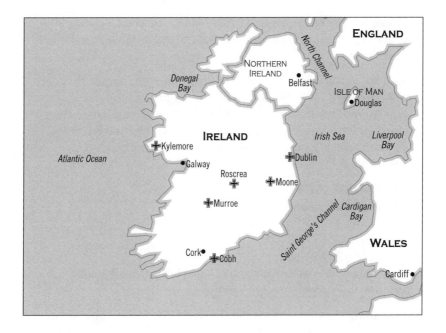

Where to stay? Accommodation in one of the eight monastic guestrooms should be confirmed with the guestmaster at least one month before the expected date of arrival. The most convenient times for phoning/faxing the monastery are between 10:30 and 11:30 AM and 6:00 and 7:00 PM, Irish time).

How to get there? Moone is located about forty miles southwest of Dublin via E20. Nearest rail station: Athy.

GLENSTAL ABBEY
Murroe
Co. Limerick
Tel: (061) 386-103 • Fax: (061) 386-328
E-mail: monks@glenstal.org; guestmaster@glenstal.org
Web site: www.glenstal.ie

Originally founded in 1927, the Benedictine abbey of Glenstal has continued to grow over the years and today houses almost fifty monks. Among their numerous apostolic works, the monks run a large farming enterprise which is primarily devoted to milk production.

Where to stay? Also involved in academics and lecturing, the monks operate a twelve-room guesthouse that can accommodate more than three thousand visitors each year.

How to get there? Murroe is located about one hundred twenty miles southwest of Dublin and twelve miles east of Limerick. Nearest rail station: Limerick. From Glenstal, there is one bus connection a day to Limerick, which is seventeen miles away. The nearest airport is Shannon, which is one hour from the monastery by taxi.

KYLEMORE ABBEY
Kylemore (Connemara)
Co. Galway
Tel: (095) 411-46 • Fax: (095) 411-23
Tel/Fax: (01) 289-94-87
E-mail: bbrew@kylemoreabbey.ie; oflaherty@cyberclub.iol.ie
Web site: www.kylemoreabbey.com

Welcoming visitors from around the world, Kylemore Abbey is home to a community of Irish Benedictine nuns whose founding dates back to 1665. A popular destination for both tourists and religious pilgrims, the abbey features a visitors' center, craft and pottery shop, restaurant, and beautiful gardens. The visit is self-guided and takes about two hours. There is a video presentation about the history every thirty minutes in the video room. There is also a craft shop and a restaurant facility (self service).

Where to stay? A number of hotels are located near Kylemore Abbey.

How to get there? Connemara/Kylemore is located about one hundred eighty miles west of Dublin and forty-five miles west of Galway. The nearest rail station is at Galway; local bus or taxi service is available to Connemara.

MOUNT SAINT JOSEPH ABBEY
Roscrea (Limerick)
Co. Tipperary
Tel: (0505) 21-711 • Fax: (0505) 22-198
Email: info@msjroscrea.ie
Web site: www.msjroscrea.ie

Located in the midst of many ancient Celtic monastic sites and medieval ruins, Mount Saint Joseph Abbey was founded in 1878 by thirty Cistercian monks. Today, the monks operate a farm and boarding school. Fresh home-baked bread is just one of the many ways the monks extend a hearty welcome to all who come to spend a few days in retreat and participate in their daily lives.

Where to stay? The guesthouse accommodates about forty people. A wonderful and popular waterfall is located on the grounds near the guesthouse. Individuals or groups can stay up to a week. It is possible to speak with the monks for counseling purposes and spiritual guidance.

How to get there? Roscrea is located about seventy-five miles west of Dublin via M7. Roscrea is accessible by train and bus.

ITALY

ABBAZIA DI MONTE OLIVETO MAGGIORE
Località Chiusure—Monte Oliveto
53020 Asciano (Siena)
Tel: (0577) 707-017, 707-611, 70-76-52 • Fax: (0577) 707-070, 70-76-44
Email: abbazia@monteolivetomaggiore.it; foresteria@
monteolivetomaggiore
 Web site: www.monteolivetomaggiore.it

Recognized as one of the early foundations of the Benedictine Olivetan Order, the abbey of Monte Oliveto Maggiore dates back to 1313.
For centuries, the monastery has held a foremost position in the fields
of science and art. Recently, they opened a school for the restoration
of old books. An abbey restaurant is on the premises.

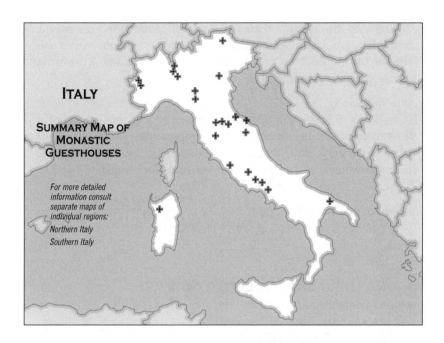

Where to stay? Ten guestrooms are available to those individuals or groups who wish to participate in a spiritual retreat or personal days of reflection. The guesthouse is closed during the winter. To make reservations, Tel: (0577) 707018.

How to get there? Asciano is located about seventy-five miles south of Florence and one hundred thirty miles north of Rome. Asciano is accessible by train (via the line Florence and Rome/Florience-Siena-Grosseto). Once in Asciano, taxi is the best way to reach the abbey.

ABBAZIA SACRA DI SAN MICHELE
Padri Rosminiani
Via alla Sacra, 14
10057 Avigliana (SantíAmbrogio di Torino)
Tel/Fax: (011) 939-130 • Fax (011) 93-97-06
E-mail: info@sacradisanmichele.com
Web site: www.sacradisanmichele.com

An architectural and natural wonder, the abbey and shrine of Saint Michael today serves as one of the most famous Benedictine monasteries from Medieval Europe, dating back almost one thousand years.

Sitting atop the rocky, chiseled summit of Mount Pirchiriano, the monastery has a number of sites to interest the religious visitor, including the Monk's Tomb, the Stairway of the Dead, and the Primitive Shrine of Saint Michael.

Where to stay? Since the abbey can only accommodate two or three visitors at a time (men or women), guests must stay for a period of at least three to five days and be willing to participate in the prayer life of the monastery. Only Italian is spoken at the abbey. The guesthouse is open throughout the year, except between the periods of July 1 to September 15 and December 15 to January 15.

How to get there? Avigliana/Sant'Ambrogio di Torino is located about eighteen miles west of Turin via A32. Avigliana is accessible by train.

MONASTERO SAN VINCENZO MARTIRE
Monaci Benedettini Silvestrini
Via San Vincenzo, 88
01030 Bassano Romano (VT)
Tel: (0761) 634-007, 634-086, 175-1616
Fax: (0761) 634-734, 1760-286
E-mail: sanvincenzo@silvestrini.org
Web site: http://sanvincenzo.silvestrini.org

Built in 1630, the monastery of Benedettini Silvestrini is home to a community of Benedictine monks. As well as spending time in the abbey, visitors can pray at the shrine of Santo Volto, a center for spirituality, which is located next to the monastery.

Where to stay? The monks operate a vast guesthouse which provides accommodations for more than three hundred people. Conference facilities can accommodate two hundred people. To make reservations, email: ospitalita@silvestrini.org; Fax: (0761) 1760-286.

How to get there? Bassano Romano is located about thirty-five miles north of Rome via SS2. Bassano Romano is accessible by bus and train (Rome- Viterbo). Other nearby train stations include Ostiense and Oriolo.

▼ ITALY NORTH

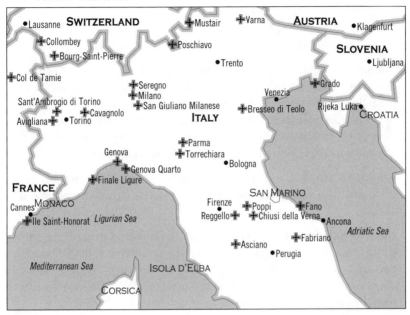

- Lausanne **SWITZERLAND**
- Collombey
- Bourg-Saint-Pierre
- Col de Tamie
- Mustair
- Varna
- **AUSTRIA**
- Klagenfurt
- Poschiavo
- **SLOVENIA**
- Ljubljana
- Trento
- Seregno
- Milano
- Sant'Ambrogio di Torino
- San Giuliano Milanese
- Grado
- Venezia
- Cavagnolo
- Avigliana
- Torino
- **ITALY**
- Bresseo di Teolo
- Rijeka Luka
- **CROATIA**
- Parma
- Torrechiara
- Genova
- Genova Quarto
- Finale Ligure
- Bologna
- **FRANCE**
- Cannes **MONACO**
- Ile Saint-Honorat *Ligurian Sea*
- **SAN MARINO**
- Firenze
- Reggello
- Poppi
- Chiusi della Verna
- Fano
- Ancona
- *Adriatic Sea*
- Fabriano
- Asciano
- Perugia
- *Mediterranean Sea*
- **ISOLA D'ELBA**
- **CORSICA**

ITALY SOUTH ▼

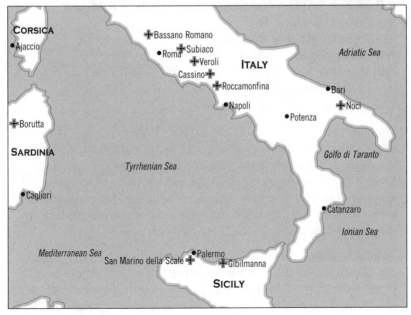

- **CORSICA**
- Ajaccio
- Bassano Romano
- Subiaco
- Roma
- Veroli
- **ITALY**
- *Adriatic Sea*
- Cassino
- Roccamonfina
- Bari
- Napoli
- Noci
- Potenza
- Borutta
- **SARDINIA**
- *Golfo di Taranto*
- *Tyrrhenian Sea*
- Cagliari
- Catanzaro
- *Ionian Sea*
- *Mediterranean Sea*
- San Marino della Scale
- Palermo
- Gibilmanna
- **SICILY**

ABBAZIA DI SAN PETRO DI SORRES

Località San Pietro di Sorres
07040 Borutta (Sassari) Sardinia
Tel: (079) 824-001, 824-001 • Fax: (079) 824-019, 824-01

Founded in the eleventh century, the Abbey of San Petro di Sorres is home to a community of monks who belong to the Benedictine Congregation of Subiaco. The faithful can participate in the liturgical life of the monks, including Mass and the Liturgy of the Hours. Major feast days celebrated at the monastery include Saint Peter (June 29), Saint Benedict (July 11), and the Birth of the Virgin Mary (September 8).

Where to stay? About thirty guestrooms are available to those individuals who wish to participate in a personal retreat of prayer and silence.

How to get there? Borutta is located on the Island of Sardinia. Sardinia is accessible by ferry or air from the mainland of Italy. Once in Sardinia, take SS131 to the junction of Bonnanaro; exit at Borutta. The nearest bus station is located at Torralba and Giave; continue by local bus or taxi to the abbey.

ABBAZIA SANTA MARIA ASSUNTA DI PRAGLIA

Via Abbazia di Praglia, 16
35033 Bresseo di Teolo (Padova)
Tel: (049) 99-00-010, 99-99-300, 99-99-322
Fax: (049) 99-02-740, 99-99-344
E-mail: abbazia@praglia.it
Web site: www.praglia.it

Founded in the twelfth century, Saint Mary's Abbey is home to a community of forty Benedictine monks. As well as visiting the vast monastery, the faithful can spend time in retreat by attending the monks' Liturgy of the Hours (sung in Gregorian chant). At the abbey gift shop, visitors may purchase such items as honey, herbs, ointments, soaps, cosmetic creams, and liqueurs, most of which are produced by the monks themselves.

Where to stay? Men wishing to participate in the life of the monks can stay in one of the guestrooms, which are located on the interior of the monastery, while women and groups can stay in one of the ten small "apartments" on the exterior with fifteen beds, kitchen, and living room. To make a reservation, email the guestmaster at foresteria@ praglia.it.

How to get there? Bresseo di Teolo is located about forty-five miles west of Venice via A13. The nearest train station is at Padua; continue by taxi to the abbey or by taking the bus for Teolo-Vò Euganeo-Noventa Vicentina. Exit the bus at San Biagio.

ABBAZIA DI MONTECASSINO

03043 Cassino (Frosinone)
Tel: (0776) 311-529 • Fax: (0776) 312-393, 311-643
Email info@montecassino.it
Web site: www.officine.it/montecassino; www.montecassino.it

Founded by Saint Benedict about the year 529, the Abbey of Montecassino has, through the centuries, garnered a worldwide reputation for being a place of holiness, culture, and art. Many great historic figures have visited the monastery, including Charlemagne who, in 787, bestowed many privileges and gifts upon the abbey. Reduced to rubble during World War II, the abbey was quickly rebuilt in accordance with the ancient architectural pattern. For guided tours of the abbey, Tel: (388) 1915720; Email: ilsentierocooperativa@yahoo.it; Web site: www.ilsentierocoop.it.

Where to stay? Only men can be accommodated in the guestrooms; advance reservations are required.

How to get there? Cassino/Monte Cassino is about sixty-five miles north of Rome via A1. Cassino is accessible by train and bus.

ABBAZIA DI SANTA FEDE

Via Santa Fede 92
10020 Cavagnolo (Torino)
Tel: (011) 915-11-24

Founded in the twelfth century, the Abbey of Santa Fede is home to a community of Marist Fathers.

Where to stay? Visitors can be accommodated in one of the guestrooms and are invited to participate in the spiritual retreats of the house.

How to get there? Cavagnolo is located about twenty-eight miles east of Turin via A4. Nearest train station: Cavagnolo-Brusasco.

CONVENTO-SANTUARI DE LA VERNA

Località La Verna
52010 Chiusi della Verna (Arezzo)
Tel: (0575) 5341 • Fax: (0575) 599-320

Founded in 1213, the Convent and Sanctuary of Verna is home to a community of Franciscan Minors. Among the most famous site to visit at the monastery and shrine is the renowned Chapel of the Stigmata. Religious celebrations and eucharistic processions are held throughout the year. Organ concerts take place in July and August at the shrine.

Where to stay? The Franciscans operate a very large guesthouse, which is open to both men and women (one hundred twenty beds are available).

How to get there? Chiusi della Verna is located about seventy-five miles south of Florence A1/SR71. Nearest rail station: Arezzo.

MONASTERO DI SAN SILVESTRO

Via San Silvestro Abate 66
60044 Fabriano (Ancona)
Tel: (0732) 216-31
Fax: (0732) 216-33
Email: sansilvestro@silvestrini.org
Web sites: www.silvestrini.org; http://sansilvestro.silvestrini.org

Founded in 1231, the Monastery of San Silvestro is home to a community of Benedictine monks. As well as touring the abbey, visitors can attend Mass in the monastery church.

Where to stay? A modern, well-equipped guesthouse provides accommodation (thirty-five rooms) to those individuals who wish to participate in a personal retreat of prayer and recollection.

How to get there? Fabriano is located about one hundred thirty-five miles southeast of Florence. Fabriano is accessible by train (Rome-Ancona line).

EREMO DI MONTE GIOVE

Via Rosciano 90
61032 Fano (Pesaro-Urbino)
Tel (hermitage): (0721) 864-090 • Tel (guesthouse): (0721) 864-603
Fax: (0721) 864-603, 868-588
Web site: www.eremomontegiove.it

Built in the seventeenth century, the hermitage of Monte Giove is home to a community of Benedictine monks. Visitors are welcome to join the monks at Mass, the Liturgy of the Hours, spiritual retreats, and in days of prayer. Among the most popular feast days at the abbey are those celebrations that honor Saint Benedict (March 21 and July 11), Saint Romuald (June 19), and the Feast of the Transfiguration (August 6).

Where to stay? A guesthouse with forty rooms is available only to those individuals and groups (maximum twenty people) who want to participate in the prayer life of the hermitage. One week is maximum stay.

How to get there? Fano is located one hundred seventy miles east of Florence via A14. Take the train to Fano, then transfer to local bus #6.

ABBAZIA DI SANTA MARIA

Via Santuario 59—Finale Pia
17024 Finale Ligure
Tel: (019) 601-700, 604-391 • Fax: (019) 601-912, 604-3924
Web site: www.finalpia.it

Founded in 1477, the Abbey of Santa Maria is home to a community of monks which belong to the Benedictine Congregation of Subiaco. Visitors can tour the beautiful abbey church which has a number of frescoes and sculptures, as well as other religious artwork. The faithful are invited to join the monks at Mass and to participate in the abbey's conferences and spiritual retreats.

Where to stay? The monastery guesthouse, Villa Enrichetta, provides accommodations for those individuals and families who are seeking a time of prayer and silence. It is recommended to book in advance and in writing, not by phone.

How to get there? Finale Ligure is located about one hundred twenty miles southwest of Milan via A7 and 15 miles south of Savona. Finale Ligure is accessible by train; transfer to a local bus (orange one) to Calvisio; exit at the bus stop opposite the abbey church.

CONVENTO DI SANT'ANNA
Piazza Sant'Anna 8
16125 Genova
Tel: (010) 277-0433 • Fax: (010) 251-3281
E-mail: carmelo@split.it

Founded in 1584, the Convent of Sant'Anna is home to a community of Carmelite monks. Visitors are invited to attend religious services, which include Mass and the Liturgy of the Hours. Among the most important feast days celebrated at the abbey are those honoring Our Lady of Mount Carmel (July 16), Saint Anne (July 26), Saint Thérèse of Lisieux (October 1), Saint Teresa of Avila (October 15), and Saint John of the Cross (December 14). Organ concerts are given throughout the year, especially during the community's major feast days.

Where to stay? Individuals and small groups can be accommodated in the Carmelite guesthouse, which has ten rooms. Singles, small groups, and young people are welcome.

How to get there? Genova is located about ninety miles southwest of Milan via A7. Genova is accessible by train; then transfer to Bus #33 until you reach Magenta. Continue to the elevator door at the convent.

ABBAZIA S. MARIA DELLA CASTAGNA
Via Romana della Castagna, 17
16148 Genova-Quarto
Tel: (010) 399-0996 • Fax: (010) 377-8227
E-mail: abbazia.castagna@libero.it

Founded in 1843, the Abbey of Santa Maria della Castagna is home to a community of Benedictine monks. As well as touring the abbey church and grounds, visitors are invited to participate in the prayer life of the monks.

Where to stay? A guesthouse provides accommodation for twenty-one people (seven singles, seven doubles).

How to get there? Genova-Quarto is located about ninety miles southwest of Milan via A7. Rail station: Genova-Quarto Dei Mille.

CONVENTO CAPPUCCINI

Santuario Maria SS. di Gibilmanna
90010 Gibilmanna-Cefalù (Palermo)
Tel: (0921) 421-835 • Fax: (0921) 422-221
E-mail: gibilmanna.sanctuario@tiscalinet.it

Founded in 1535, the Convent and Sanctuary of Maria Santissima di Gibilmanna is home to a community of Capuchin Friars Minor. As well as praying before a miraculous image of the Virgin Mary located inside the shrine, visitors can join the monks in their daily life of prayer in the abbey church. Many musical concerts, Marian processions, and religious celebrations take place throughout the year at both the sanctuary and abbey.

Where to stay? The Saint Clare guesthouse is open to all individuals, families, and groups who wish to embark on a spiritual retreat or a time of prayer and solitude.

How to get there? Gibilmanna is located on the Island of Sicily, about five hundred fifty miles south of Rome. One of the most convenient ways to reach Sicily is by train. Travel to Reggio di Calabria, situated at the southern end of Italy. As the train arrives at the port of Villa San Giovanni in Calabria, it will move onto barge for the one-hour crossing into eastern Sicily. Passengers will not even leave their seats during the short voyage across the Strait of Messina. Once on the island, the train will transfer back on to a track and continue to the main station in Palermo. From Rome to Palermo takes around twelve hours and from Naples to Palermo takes ten hours. The nearest train station to Gibilmanna is at Cefalu. Sicily is also accessible by bus.

CONVENTO-SANTUARIO DELLA MADONNA DI BARBANA

Isola de Barbana
34073 Grado (Gorizia)
Tel: (0431) 804-53

Founded in 582, the Convent of Madonna di Barbana is home to a community of Franciscan Minors. Welcoming thousands of pilgrims annually, the Franciscans serve as custodians of this Marian shrine, which houses a miraculous image of the Virgin Mary. Many religious processions and celebrations are held throughout the year at the shrine.

Where to stay? The Franciscans also operate the Pilgrim's Guesthouse, which provides accommodation for both individuals and groups (twenty-four rooms are available).

How to get there? Grado is located about eighty-five miles east of Venice via A13. Nearest rail station: Gorizia-Centrale.

ABBAZIA DI CHIARAVALLE
Via San Arialdo 102
20139 Milano
Tel: (02) 574-03-404; Fax: (02) 5393544
E-mail: s.m.chiaravalle@libero.it

Founded by Saint Bernard of Clairvaux in 1135, the Abbey of Chiaravalle is home to a community of twenty-two Cistercian monks. As well as touring the beautiful abbey church with its many frescoes and works of art, visitors can attend religious services with the monks. Annually, on August 20, there is a solemn High Pontifical Mass to honor Saint Bernard.

Where to stay? Since the twelve guestrooms are located inside the monastic enclosure, only men can be housed for an overnight stay.

How to get there? Milan is located in Northern Italy and is accessible by train and bus. To reach the abbey, take a taxi.

ABBAZIA MADONNA DELLA SCALA
Contrada Z.B. 58
70015 Noci/Walnuts (Bari)
Tel: (080) 847-5838, (080) 847-5839
Email: abate@abbazialascala.it; lascala@abbazialascala.it
Web site: www.abbazialascala.it

Founded in 1930, the Abbey of Madonna della Scala is home to a community of monks that belong to the Benedictine Congregation of Subiaco. Religious services, including Mass and the Liturgy of the Hours, take place in the abbey church and are open to the public.

Where to stay? Only men can be accommodated in the abbey guestrooms, since they are located inside the monastic enclosure. Courses to learn Gregorian chant are offered during the summer. To make a reservation, email accoglienza@abbazialascala.it.

How to get there? Noci is located about three hundred fifteen miles southeast of Rome via A1/A16/A14. Noci is accessible by train. The abbey is located about five miles from Walnuts.

ABBAZIA DI SAN GIOVANNI EVANGELISTA
Piazzale San Giovanni Evangelista 1
43100 Parma
Tel: (0521) 235-592, 235-311

Founded in 1144, the Abbey of San Giovanni Evangelista is home to a community of Benedictine monks. As well as touring the impressive abbey church, the faithful are invited to participate in the prayer life of the monks.

Where to stay? Only those men who seek a time of personal retreat in a monastic environment can be accommodated.

How to get there? Parma is located about eighty miles south of Milan via A1 and sixty-five miles north of Bologna. Parma is accessible by train.

MONASTERO DI CAMALDOLI
Località Camaldoli
52010 Poppi (Arezzo)
Tel: (0575) 556-012 • Fax: (0575) 556-001
E-mail: camaldoli@camaldoli.com, sangregorio@camaldoli.it
Web site: www.camaldoli.it

Founded almost a thousand years ago, the Abbey of Camaldoli is home to a community of Camaldolese Benedictine monks. Visitors are invited to attend religious services with the monks and to participate in the many retreats and seminars that are held each year at the monastery, which are based upon the theme of ecumenism and interreligious dialogue.

Where to stay? A well-appointed guesthouse is available to anyone who wishes to participate in either a traditional silent retreat or a course offered by the monks.

How to get there? Poppi is located about thirty-five miles from Florence. Poppi is accessible by train.

ABBAZIA DI VALLOMBROSA
Località Vallombrosa
50060 Reggello/Vallombrosa (Firenze)
Tel (Abbey): (055) 862-029, 862-251, 862-252-29, 862-074
Tel (guesthouse): (055) 862-074, 86-20-36
(only available during the summer)
Email: info@evallombrosa.it
Web site: www.monaci.org

Founded in 1028, the Abbey of Vallmobrosa is home to a community of Benedictine monks. Guided tours of the abbey are available to groups during the summer. All visitors are welcome to attend religious services with the monks in the church. Organ concerts are held during the months of July and August.

Where to stay? The monks operate a very large guesthouse (63 rooms) called "The Forest" for those individuals and groups. Private bathrooms, private telephone, room service are included. To make reservations, contact "The Forest," St. John Gualberto 2, 50066 Vallombrosa (FI), Tel: (055) 86-21-81; Fax: (055) 86-21-61; Email: info@ albergolaforesta.it.

How to get there? Reggello/Vallombrosa is located about twenty-five miles southeast of Florence via A1. The nearest train station is at Vallombrosa; continue to the abbey by taxi.

CONVENTO-SANTUARIO
DI SANTA MARIA DEI LATTANI
Località Monte Lattani
81035 Roccamonfina (Caserta)
Tel: (0823) 921-037

Founded in 1430, the Convent of Santa Maria dei Lattani is home to a community of Franciscan Minors. Many pilgrims come here annually to pray in the abbey shrine, which has a miraculous image of the Blessed Virgin Mary.

Where to stay? Men can be accommodated in the monastery guesthouse, while women and families can be accommodated in the nearby sanctuary hotel. All are invited to participate in religious services at the abbey and sanctuary.

How to get there? Roccamonfina is located about one hundred ten miles south of Rome via A1. The nearest train station is at Caserta.

ABBAZIA DI SAN MICHELE
Sacra di San Michele
10057 Sant'Ambrogio di Torino (Torino)
Tel: (011) 939-130; Fax (011) 93-97-06
Email: info@sacradisanmichele.com
Web site: www.sacradisanmichele.com

Founded almost a thousand years ago, the Abbey of San Michele is home to a community of Rosminiani Fathers. Visitors and guests are welcome to attend Mass as well as the spiritual conferences held at the monastery throughout the year.

Where to stay? Faithful to its vocation, the abbey offers excellent accommodations for those individuals who wish to participate in a spiritual retreat. Reservations are recommended, since there are only four or five rooms available.

How to get there? Sant'Ambrogio di Torino is located about twenty miles west of Turin via A32. Sant'Ambrogio di Torino is accessible by train (Turin-Modane).

ABBAZIA DEI SANTI PIETRO E PAOLO IN VIBOLDONE
Via della Abbazia 6
20098 San Giuliano Milanese (Milano)
Tel: (02) 984-1203 • Fax: (02) 982-2409-43

Originally founded in 1176, today the abbey of Santi Pietro e Paolo is home to a community of Benedictine monks who revived the monastery in 1941. The faithful are welcome to join the monks in their daily life of prayer in the abbey church, which includes Mass and the

Liturgy of the Hours. Many organ, Gregorian chant, and polyphonic music concerts are held at the abbey throughout the year.

Where to stay? Ten guestrooms are available to individuals and small groups who wish to spend time in prayer and reflection in a monastic environment.

How to get there? San Giuliano Milanese is located about ten miles south of Milan via SS9. Milan is easily accessible by train and bus. The local train Milan/Piacenza arrives at S. Giuliano rail station, which is less than one mile from the abbey. Local bus service is also available to S. Giuliano.

ABBAZIA DI SAN MARTINO DELLE SCALE
Piazza Platani 5
90040 San Marino delle Scale (Palermo)
Tel: (091) 418-104
Web site: www.abbaziadisanmartino.it

Founded in 590, the Abbey of San Martino delle Scale is home to a community of monks who belong to the Benedictine Congregation of Monte Cassino. As well as exploring the ancient abbey church, all visitors are invited to participate in religious services, which include Mass and the Divine Office (sung in Gregorian chant). During July and August, symphonic concerts are held within the abbey cloister, and organ concerts are held in the church.

Where to stay? Individuals and small groups seeking a spiritual retreat are welcome to spend several days at the abbey (ten guestrooms are available inside the monastic enclosure and five guestrooms on the exterior).

How to get there? San Marino delle Scale is located on the island of Sicily, about five hundred fifty miles south of Rome. One of the most convenient ways to reach Sicily is by train. Travel to Reggio di Calabria, situated at the southern end of Italy. As the train arrives at the port of Villa San Giovanni in Calabria, it will move onto a barge for the one-hour crossing into eastern Sicily. Passengers will not even leave their seats during the short voyage across the Strait of Messina. Once on the island, the train will transfer back on to a track and continue to the main station in Palermo. From Rome to Palermo takes around twelve hours and from Naples to Palermo takes ten hours. The nearest train station is at Palermo. Sicily is also accessible by bus from the mainland of Italy.

ABBAZIA S. BENEDETTO

Via Stefano da Seregno, 100
20038 Seregno (Milano)
Tel: (0362) 23-95-11, (0362) 268-911
Fax: (0362) 32-11-30
Web site: www.monaci-benedettini-seregno.com

Founded in the fourteenth century, today Saint Benedict's Abbey is home to a community of Benedictine monks. All visitors are invited to participate in the prayer life of the monks, which includes both Mass and the Liturgy of the Hours. Honey, jelly, liquors, and medicines are all available at the porter's lodge.

Where to stay? Guestrooms located on the exterior of the monastery are available, while guestrooms inside the monastery are occasionally available to young people who wish to experience the monastic life firsthand. If this is the case, as a requirement for admission, a letter from a priest explaining your intention must be sent to the Father Abbot prior to your visit.

How to get there? Seregno is located about sixteen miles north of Milan via SS36. Seregno is accessible by train.

MONASTERO S. SCOLASTICA

Casa per Esercizi Spirituali
Località Santa Scholastica
00028 Subiaco (Roma)
Monastery St. Scholastica Tel: (0744) 82-421 • Fax: (0744) 824-397
E-mail: monastero@benedettini-subiaco.it
Web site: www.benedettini-subiaco.it
Subiaco: (0744) 85-5-69 • Fax: (0744) 82-28-62
Monastery S. Benedict/Holy Grotto Tel: (0774) 85-039
Fax: (0744) 819-800
E-mail: sacrospeco@tiscali.it

Serving as one of the thirteen monasteries founded by Saint Benedict (480-547) in the area of Subiaco, the abbey of Saint Scholastica is one of Europe's most famous monastic pilgrimage sites. Subiaco is actually home to two different monasteries, but one community. The first house is the Monastery of St. Scholastica and the second is The Sanctuary at the Holy Grotto.

Where to stay? The monastery's guesthouse offers very comfortable accommodations and excellent hospitality to independent or group travelers who wish to participate in the spiritual exercises and life of the monks. To make reservations, contact Foresteria-Ospitalità, Tel: (0774) 85-569; Fax: (0774) 822-862; Email: foresteria@benedettini-subiaco.it.

How to get there? Subiaco is located about forty-five miles from Rome via A24. The nearest train station is located at Roviano. Subiaco is accessible by bus from Rome.

MONASTERO DI SANTA MARIA DELLA NEVE
43010 Torrechiara (Parme)
Tel: (052) 355-178

Founded in 1471, the Monastery of Santa Maria della Neve is home to a community of monks who belong to the Benedictine Congregation of Subiaco. Visitors are welcome to participate in religious services, which include Mass and the Liturgy of the Hours. The major annual religious celebrations at the abbey are March 21 and July 11, the feast days of Saint Benedict.

Where to stay? The monastery guesthouse has more than twenty-four rooms for adults, as well as a dormitory for groups of young people.

How to get there? Torrechiara is located about eighty miles south of MIlan via A1 and eighty miles northwest of Bologna via A14/A1. Nearest rail station: Parma.

BILDUNGSHAUS KLOSTER NEUSTIFT
Stiftstrasse. 1
39040 Vahrn/Varna (Neustift)
Tel: (0472) 83-61-89, 835-588 • Fax: (0472) 83-73-05, 838-107
Email: info@kloster-neustift.it
Web site: www.kloster-neustift.it

Founded in 1142 as the region's spiritual and religious center, this Augustinian monastery has, for centuries, attracted large numbers of pilgrims who seek lodging while on their journeys to either the Holy Land or Rome. On a tour, guests can visit the abbey's famous cloister, library, church, museum, and wine cellar. Although there is no gift shop, you can purchase the abbey's wines and herb teas.

Where to stay? The monastery's convention and education center provides housing (forty-nine beds) to those groups who either give their own seminars or to individuals who join the in-house courses and events. Contact the convention and education center at: Bildungshaus Kloster Neustift, Stiftstraße 1, 39040 Vahrn, Tel: (0472) 83-55-88, 83-61-89; Fax: (0472) 83-81-07, 83-73-05; Email: bildungshaus@kloster-neustift.it.

How to get there? Varna is located about sixty-five miles north of Trent via A22. Nearest rail station: Bressanone.

ABBAZIA DI CASAMARI
Frazione di Casamari
03020 Veroli/Casamari (Frosinone)
Tel: (0775) 282371, 282-800 • Fax: (0775) 283215
Email: abatedicasamari@virgilio.it; lucamolignini@virgilio.it
Web site: www.casamari.it

Built in 1035, today the Abbey of Casamari is home to a community of Cistercian monks. As well as taking tours of the ancient and beautiful church, visitors can attend religious services with the monks.

Where to stay? Although only men can be accommodated inside the monastic enclosure, women can be accommodated in a nearby guesthouse (reservations are required for both). Music concerts and exhibitions are held throughout the year at the monastery. Reservations are required; call (0775) 332-371.

How to get there? Veroli/Casamari is located sixty-five miles southeast of Rome via A1. Nearest rail station: Frosinone (Rome-Frosinone-Naples). Frosinone is also accessible by bus (direction Veroli).

LUXEMBOURG

ABBAYE SAINT-MAURICE
9737 Clervaux
Grand-Duché de Luxembourg
Tel: (0352) 921-027 • Fax: (0352) 920-144
Web site: www.abbayesaintmaurice.org

Refounded in 1890, the Abbey of Saint Maurice is home to a community of Benedictine monks who are a part of the Congregation of Solesmes. All are invited to participate in the monks' daily life of prayer, especially Mass and Liturgy of the Hours, which are sung in Gregorian chant. Visitors can purchase such items as books, religious art, Gregorian chant CDs, and cassettes at the abbey gift shop.

Where to stay? Twenty guestrooms are available for men inside the abbey, and housing is also available outside the abbey grounds for youth and groups. The latter is ideal for group retreats and camps and can accommodate groups of about fifty people. It includes a kitchen, meeting room, and thirteen rooms, seven of which each feature six bunk beds.

How to get there? Clervaux is located about forty miles north of Luxembourg city via E421/N7. Clervaux is accessible by train (Liege-Luxembourg; Clervaux-Luxembourg). The train station is about twenty minutes by foot from the abbey; hence, some people take a taxi.

CARMEL
10, rue Sainte-Thérèse-d'Avila
1152 Luxembourg
Tel: (0352) 43-16-31 • Fax: (0352) 42-18-28
Email: carmel@pt.lu

Founded in 1889, this Luxembourg convent is home to a community of Carmelite nuns. Visitors are welcome to attend Mass and the Divine Office, which are said in French, in the convent chapel.

Where to stay? Four guestrooms are available to those individuals who want to participate in a personal retreat of prayer and silence.

How to get there? Luxembourg is accessible by train and bus. To reach the convent, take a taxi.

MONASTÈRE DES BÉNÉDICTINES DU SAINT-SACREMENT
3, rue Saint-Benoît
3391 Peppange
Tel: (0352) 51-10-61 • Fax: (0352) 51-06-08

Founded in 1875, the Monastery of Saint-Sacrement is home to a community of Benedictine monks. The abbey's Mass and Liturgy of the Hours are open to the public; all visitors are welcome to attend.

Where to stay? A limited number of guestrooms are available to those individuals who wish to participate in a personal retreat of prayer and silence.

How to get there? Peppange is located about seven miles south of Luxembourg city via A3. Nearest rail station: Bettenbourg. Once in Luxembourg city, it's easiest to simply take a taxi for the seven miles to the monastery.

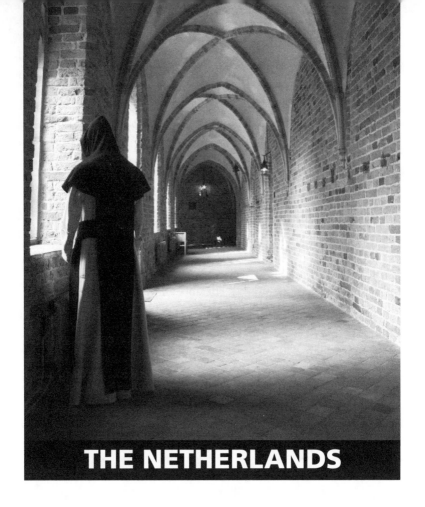

THE NETHERLANDS

ABDIJ O.L. VROUW VAN KONINGSHOEVEN

Notre-Dame de Koningshoeven
Eindhovenseweg 3
5056 RP Berkel-Enschot
Tel: (013) 543-61-24, 540-85-08 • Fax: (013) 544-36-78
Email: info@koningshoeven.nl
Web site: www.abdijkoningshoeven.nl

Founded in the nineteenth century, the Abbey of Koningshoeven is home to a community of eleven Trappist monks. Since the monastery is situated on land that was not originally suitable for farming, early on, the monks resorted to brewing beer for their livelihood. Today, their brewery remains the single most important source of revenue for the abbey.

Where to stay? About thirty guestrooms are available to men and women who wish to participate in the prayer life of the monks and spend a few days in personal retreat. Both individuals and groups are welcome (maximum twenty people). Conference facilities and meeting rooms are available. Monks are available for spiritual guidance and counseling. The guesthouse is closed on Mondays.

How to get there? Berkel-Enschot is located about seventy miles south of Amsterdam via A2/A65/N65. From A65, the highway turns into A58 near Tilburg, from which you can proceed to the Abbey by following the signs. The nearest train station is at Tilburg (five miles from the abbey); from Tilburg take bus #141 in the direction of Eindhoven. Get off the bus at the stop in front of the Abbey Gatehouse (first stop after crossing the bridge that goes over the canal).

SINT WILLIBRORDSABDIJ
Slangenburg, Abdijlaan 1
7004 JL Doetinchem
Tel: (0315) 29-82-68
Web site: www.willibrords-abbey.nl

Founded in 1945, the Benedictine Abbey of Saint Willibrords lies in a beautiful setting of forest and woods. As well as leading a contemplative life of prayer, study, and hospitality, the monks devote themselves to the manufacture of liturgical vestments and the preservation of valuable and rare old religious books.

Where to stay? The abbey features two guesthouses. The first includes the guesthouse inside the enclosure; only men can stay here. The second guesthouse is the Castle Slangenburg.

How to get there? Doetinchem is located about eighty miles east/southeast of Amsterdam via the A1/A12. Doetinchem is accessible by train; take a taxi to reach the abbey. If traveling by bus, take Bus #74 and for the castle exit at Castle Slangenburg.

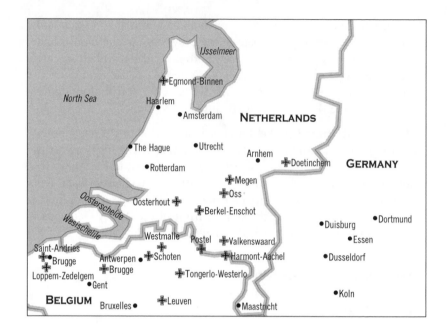

SINT ADALBERTABDIJ

Benedictijner Monniken
Abdijlaan 26
1935 BH Egmond-Binnen
Tel: (072) 506-14-15, 506-2786 • Fax: (072) 506-48-34, 506-6254
E-mail: klooster@abdijkaarsen.nl; abdij@abdijkaarsen.nl
Web site: www.abdijkaarsen.nl; www.abdijvanegmond.nl

Founded in 950, the Abbey of Saint Adalbert is home to a community of
Benedictine monks. As well as visiting the large and austere monastery
church, visitors can participate in religious services with the monks, including Mass. The most popular feast days at the abbey include celebrations honoring Saint Benedict (March 21 and July 11), Saint Adalbert
(June 20), and the Consecration of the Monastery (October 7).

Where to stay? The monastery operates a guesthouse with twelve
rooms. It is available to those individuals who wish to participate
more fully in the prayer life of the monks. One of the major activities
of the monks is the production of candles.

How to get there? Egmond-Binnen is located about twenty-five miles
northwest of Amsterdam via N8. Nearest rail station: Haarlem.

KLOOSTER SINT JOSEPHSBERG
Clarastraat 2
5366 AK Megen
Tel: (0412) 46-23-14 • Fax: (0412) 46-31-20
Web site: www.clarissen.nl

Founded in 1721, the Convent of Saint Josephberg is home to a community of Poor Clare nuns. Mass is celebrated daily, and the most popular feast day at the chapel is August 11 (Saint Clare of Assisi).

Where to stay? The nuns operate a small guesthouse with eight rooms for women who seek a place of prayer and silence. Young women discerning their vocation can stay for three months or longer.

How to get there? Megen is located about seventy miles southwest of Amsterdam via A2. Nearest rail station: Nijmegen.

PRIORIJ FONS VITAE
Benedictuslaan 7
5343 NB Oss
Tel: (0412) 451-1245 • Fax: (0412) 45-36-01

Founded in 1952, the Priory of Fons Vitae is home to a community of Benedictine monks of the Holy Sacrament. Candles, ceramics, and religious icons are just a few of the items that you may purchase at the priory.

Where to stay? A guesthouse is available to those individuals who wish to participate in a personal retreat in a monastic environment. Only five or six people can be accommodated at one time, and everyone is expected to join the monks in their prayer life, which includes Mass and the Divine Office.

How to get there? Oss is located about sixty-five miles southwest of Amsterdam via A2. Nearest rail station: Eindhoven.

SINT-PAULUS ABDIJ
Hoogstraat 80
4901 PK Oosterhout
Tel: (0162) 45-33-94, 451-001 • Fax: (0162) 42-53-11
Web site: www.paulusabdij.nl

Founded in 1907, the Abbey of Sint-Paulus is home to a community of Benedictine monks. Visitors are welcome to attend Mass in the chapel, as well as the Liturgy of the Hours. The monks produce artistic ceramics.

Where to stay? Since the guesthouse is very small, only men who want to spend a few days in prayer and silence can be accommodated. Small groups are welcome.

How to get there? Oosterhout is located about sixty miles south of Amsterdam via A2/A27. Nearest rail station: Breda.

SAINT BENEDICTUS ABDIJ DE ACHELSE KLUIS
Abdijweg 50
5556 VE Valkenswaard
Tel (abbey): (011) 800-760, 800-766, (40) 206-9955
Tel (guesthouse): (011) 800-766
Fax: (011) 648-130
Email: webmaster@achelsekluis.org webmaster
Web site: www.achelsekluis.org

Founded in 1686, the Abbey of Achelse Kluis is home to a community of Cistercian monks. Serving as a place of prayer and contemplation, the monastery invites all visitors to join them in the chapel for Mass and the singing of the Divine Office.

Where to stay? The monastery guesthouse receives both men and women, providing an opportunity for individuals to join the monks in their daily life. Although the abbey does not organize retreats, it does accept already prepared/organized retreats by groups. Individuals and groups may stay for a week. The guesthouse is closed every fourth weekend of the month.

How to get there? Valkenswaard is located about eighty-five miles south of Amsterdam via A2. Nearest rail station: Gorinchem. Valkenswaard is accessible by bus lines 171 and 172; then switch to local bus 276 (Valkenswaard-Achel).

NORWAY

LUNDEN KLOSTER
Monastery of the Annunciation
Ovre Lunden 5
0598 Oslo
Tel: (047) 23-19-44-20, 22-64-18-20
Fax: (047) 23-19-44-21, 22-65-57-90
Email: kloster@lunden.katolsk.no
Web site: http://lunden.katolsk.no

Founded in 1951, the Monastery of the Annunciation is comprised of nine nuns who belong to the contemplative branch of the Dominican Order and who come from France, Germany, Italy, Norway, and Poland. Visitors are encouraged to participate in the daily office, which is sung in both Norwegian and Gregorian chant. You may purchase candles, icons, rosaries, cards, books, and other religious articles from the sisters.

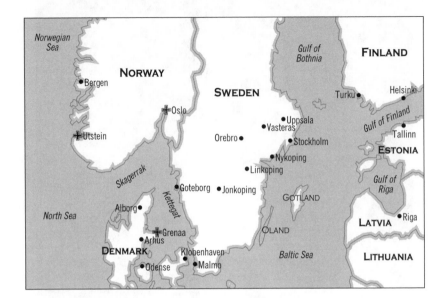

Where to stay? The monastery has a guesthouse with six rooms.

How to get there? The Monastery of Lunden is located in the capital city of Norway: Oslo. The best way to reach the monastery is by taxi.

UTSTEIN KLOSTER

4000 Utstein (Stavanger)
Tel: (04) 51-72-47-05 • Fax: (04) 51-72-47-08
Email: info@utstein-kloster.no
Web site: www.utstein-kloster.no

Originally founded in 1270, then restored in 1965, the Abbey of Ut-stein is home to a community of Augustinian monks. As well as attending religious services with the monks, visitors can spend time in the church to explore some of its ancient ruins (such as the original baptismal font which dates back to the thirteenth century).

Where to stay? A comfortable guesthouse, which can accommodate up to thirty people, is located on the monastery grounds. To make reservations, email: booking@utstein-kloster.no.

How to get there? Utstein is located about three hundred thirty-five miles from Olso. Nearest rail station: Stavanger.

POLAND

JASNA GÓRA—SANCTUARY OF THE POLISH NATION MONASTERY OF THE PAULINE FATHERS

ul. O. A. Kordeckiego 2
42225 Częstochowa
Tel: (034) 3-777-777, 365-66-88 • Fax: (034) 365-67-28
Email: klasztor@jasnagora.pl; sanktuarium@jasnagora.pl;
information@jasnagora.pl; centrum.informacji@jasnagora.pl
Web site: www.jasnagora.pl

Founded in 1383, the Cloister of Paulin—w is home to a community
of Pauline Fathers, who serve as custodians of one of Eastern Europe's
most famous Marian Shrines—Our Lady of Częstochowa. As well as
praying before the miraculous image of the Blessed Virgin Mary, visitors can attend the many daily religious services that take place in the
renowned pilgrimage church. Some of the sanctuary's most popular
feast days are May 3 (Virgin, Queen of Poland), August 15 (The Assumption), August 26 (Black Madonna), September 8 (Birth of the
Blessed Virgin Mary), and the first Sunday of October (Our Lady of
the Rosary).

Where to stay? The Pauline Fathers operate the Pilgrim's House, which has more than one hundred comfortable rooms, as well as a restaurant. For more information or to make a reservation, contact Dom Pielgrzyma im. Jana Palwa, II (Pilgrim's House), Ul. Kard. Wyszyńskiego 1/31, 42-225 Częstochowa 25, Tel: (034) 324-70-11; Fax: (034) 365-18-70; Email: dp@jasnagora.pl.

How to get there? Częstoçhowa is located in south central Poland and accessible by train and bus. If traveling by road from Krakow, take 4/E40 west to Katowice and 1/E75 north to Częstoçhowa.

KLASZTOR OJCÓW BERNARDYNÓW
Ulica Bernadynska 46
34130 Kalwaria Zebrzydowska (Kraków)
Tel: (033) 87-66-304 • Fax: (033) 87-66-641

Founded in 1603, the Monastery of the Virgin of the Angels is home to a community of Bernardine Fathers, who serve as custodians of Poland's second most famous shrine—Kalwaria Zebrzydowska. A dynamic place of pilgrimage, the monastery is home to numerous celebrations, processions, and daily religious activities. One of the most prominent sites is the Zebrzydowski Chapel with its miraculous painting of the Blessed Virgin. Often referred to as the "Polish Jerusalem," the sanctuary is known for its annual Passion plays. The site was Pope John Paul's favorite boyhood shrine: he grew up just five miles from here.

Where to stay? The monastery operates a guesthouse (called Pilgrim's House/Dom Pilegrzyma), which welcomes both individuals and groups.

How to get there? Kalwaria Zebrzydowska is located about twenty miles southwest of Krakow in the Beskidy Mountains. From Krakow, take 7/E77 south and then head east on 96. Kalwaria Zebrzydowska is accessible by train and bus.

OPACTWO BENEDYKTYNÓW

Ul. Benedyktynska 37
30-375 Kraków-Tyniec
Tel: (012) 688-52-00, 2675-526, 2675-977
Fax: (012) 688-52-01, 2619-000
Email: tyniec@benedyktyni.pl
Web site: www.tyniec.benedyktyni.pl

According to local tradition, King Casimir founded the Abbey of Tyniec in 1044, which is now home to a community of Benedictine monks. Visitors are welcome to visit the abbey and participate in the monastic religious services, including Mass and the Liturgy of the Hours. Vespers and the Sunday Mass are sung in Gregorian chant. The monastery operates a small gift shop, as well as a publishing house.

Where to stay? Guestrooms can accommodate thirty-five individuals, mostly men, but mixed groups may also be accepted. Polish, English, German, French, Italian, and Russian are spoken at the abbey. To make a reservation, contact the guestmaster at Benedictine Abbey in Tyniec, Visitor's Prefect, ul. Benedyktynska 37, 30-375 Krakow, Poland, Tel: (012) 2675-977, 2675-526; Fax: (012) 268-08-01; Email: tyniec@benedyktyni.pl.

How to get there? Krakow is accessible by bus and train. To reach the monastery, take a taxi.

SANKTUARIUM BOŻEGO MILOSIERDZIA— SHRINE OF DIVINE MERCY

ul. Siostry Faustyny 3
30-420 Kraków-Łagiewniki
Tel: (012) 252-33-11, 252-33-33 • Fax: (012) 263-79-97
Email: pielgrzymki@milosierdzie.pl
Web site: www.milosierdzie.pl

Home to a community of the Sisters of Mercy, this convent is the site where Christ appeared to Saint Faustina between the years 1931 and 1938, entrusting her with the mission to spread devotion to his divine Mercy. Today, the shrine welcomes pilgrims and visitors throughout the year who come to pray at the renowned sanctuary. The largest crowds arrive on the first Sunday after Easter, which is the Feast of the Divine Mercy.

Where to stay? The sisters operate a guesthouse for those men and women who are seeking a place of spiritual refreshment and solitude. Reservations must be made well in advance.

How to get there? Krakow is accessible by train and bus. The shrine itself is located south of Old Town Krakow. The basilica is a five-minute walk from the Krakow Lagiewniki station.

KLASZTOR KARMELITOW BOSYCH

Ulica Swietoduska 14
20082 Lublin
Tel: (081) 53-202-44 • Fax: (081) 53-444-60
Email: wsdlublin@karmel.pl

Founded in 1624, the Cloister of Bosych is home to a community of Carmelite monks. Visitors are welcome to attend daily Mass in the abbey church, as well as the sacred music concerts that are held throughout the year. You may purchase Gregorian chant and other sacred music tapes at the abbey.

Where to stay? Guestrooms are available to those men who wish to participate in a personal retreat of prayer and silence.

How to get there? Lublin is located about one hundred ninety miles northeast of Krakow. Lublin is accessible by train and bus.

KLASZTOR OJCÓW FRANCISZKANÓW
Niepokalanów
96-515 Teresin k. Sochaczewa
Tel: (046) 864-22-22, 861-37-01 • Fax: (046) 861-34-90, 861-37-59
Email: niepokalanow@op.pl
Web site: www.niepokalanow.pl

Founded in the late 1920s by Saint Maximilian Kolbe, the small town and friary of Niepokalanów is home to a community of Franciscan friars. Open throughout the year, the shrine has many activities and exhibits related to the life of its founder, who died a martyr at Auschwitz. As well as attending religious services with the friars, pilgrims and tourists can visit the shrine's museum, Saint Maximilian's first room, the statue of the Immaculata (the first object placed on the soil in 1927), and a puppet show depicting the history of Christianity in Poland.

Where to stay? The friars operate two large guesthouses, which provide accommodations for approximately one hundred and eighty people.

How to get there? Niepokalanów is located about twenty-three miles west of Warsaw along 2/E30. Niepokalanów is accessible by train and bus.

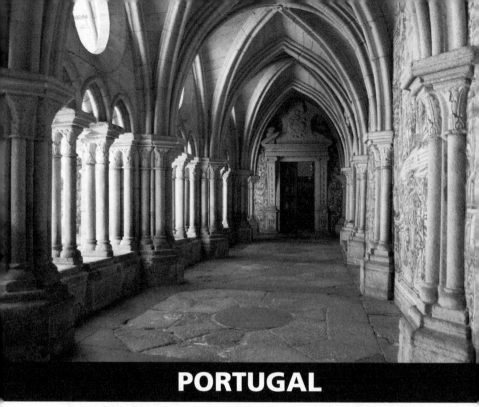

PORTUGAL

CASA DAS IRMAS DOMINICANAS
Rua Francisco Marto 50
2495 Fatima
Tel: (0249) 533-317 • Fax: (0249) 532-688
Email: casa-ir-dominicanas@clix.pt

Founded during the twentieth century, the convent is home to a community of Dominican nuns. The convent and guesthouse is located near the world famous shrine of Our Lady of Fatima, where the Virgin Mary appeared to three small children in 1017. All guests are welcome to join the nuns in religious services, including Mass, the Liturgy of the Hours, and the rosary.

Where to stay? The convent operates a guesthouse which provides hospitality and overnight accommodations to visiting pilgrims. Serving as a very comfortable and well-organized guesthouse, the Casa das Irmas Dominicanas has more than forty rooms that are available to both individuals and groups. An excellent restaurant is located on the premises. Conference facilities are also available.

How to get there? Fatima is located about seventy-five miles north of Lisbon. Fatima is accessible by train; however, as the rail station is situated about fifteen miles from the shrine, you will need to take a local bus or taxi. Fatima is also accessible by bus from throughout Portugal.

CONVENTO DE SAO FRANCISCO
Rua de São Francisco
2400-234 Leiria
Tel: (0244) 32754

Founded in 1902, the Convent of Saint Francis is home to a community of Franciscan Minors. All visitors can participate in religious services, which include Mass and the Liturgy of the Hours. Two of the most important feast days celebrated at the chapel are those honoring Saint Anthony (June 13) and Saint Francis (October 4).

Where to stay? The friars operate a very large hotel, which welcomes individuals, families, and groups for prayer and reflection.

How to get there? Leiria is located about ninety miles north of Lisbon. Leiria is accessible by train and bus.

SANTUÁRIO E CONVENTO NOSSA SENHORA DE BALSAMAO

Balsamao-Macedo de Cavaleiros
5340-091 Chacim
Tel: (0278) 468010 • Fax: (0278) 468028

Founded in the seventeenth century, the convent of Nossa Senhora de Balsamao is now home to a community of Marian Fathers who serve as custodians of the famous Marian shrine located here. As well as attending the convent's religious services, the faithful can pray before the shrine's miraculous image of the Blessed Virgin Mary.

Where to stay? The fathers operate a well-established guesthouse, which has thirty-seven rooms and an excellent restaurant. Banquet rooms with a capacity of two hundred people are available.

How to get there? Chacim is located about two hundred eighty-five miles north of Lisbon. Balsamão, the location of the monastery, is located about ten miles from Macedo de Knights and two miles from Chacim. Chacim is accessible by bus; the best way to reach the monastery is by taxi.

MOSTEIRO DE SANTA ESCOLASTICA

4795-311 Roriz (Santo Tirso-Porto)
Tel: (0252) 941-232, 871-655 • Fax: (0252) 881-525
Email: monjas.beneditinas@clix.pt

Founded in 1938, the Monastery of Santa Escolastica is home to a community of Benedictine monks. All visitors are welcome to join the monks in daily religious services, including Mass and vespers. A highlight for visitors is eating and purchasing the monks' famous "homemade" chocolates.

Where to stay? Thirteen guestrooms are available to families and young people. Some people who are embarking on the journey to Santiago de Compostela stay overnight at the guesthouse.

How to get there? Roriz is located about two hundred ten miles north of Lisbon and one hundred thirty miles south of Santiago de Compostela. Nearest rail station: Porto.

SCOTLAND

IONA ABBEY

Nunraw, Haddington EH41 4LW
Tel: (01620) 830-223, 83-228 • Fax: (01620) 830-304
E-mail: abbot@nunraw.org.uk
Web site: http://www.isle-of-iona.com/abbey.htm

Dating back to early Christian Europe, Iona Abbey was founded in AD 563 by Saint Columba, one of the most influential Celtic saints originally from Ireland. The Celtic monastery developed into a thriving Christian community and served as a key foundation and gathering point for spreading the faith throughout the country. In time, the abbey become one of the most prominent places of pilgrimage throughout Europe and still remains today Scotland's most sacred and historical site.

Where to stay? Iona Abbey Centre provides lodging and accommodations for individuals and groups up to fifty people. Or you can stay at the Bishop's House accommodation: www.a1tourism.com/uk/bishops.html.

How to get there? Iona Abbey is located on the western coast of Scotland near the Isle of Mull. Arriving at the abbey takes several forms of transportation. First, travel to Oban by train, bus, or road.

From Oban, ferry across to Craignure on the Isle of Mull, where you then switch to a bus to Fionnphort for your final leg of the journey—a ferry ride to Iona. Oban and Fionnphort are about one hundred and one hundred fifty miles respectively from Glasgow.

SANCTA MARIA ABBEY

Nunraw, Haddington EH41 4LW
Tel: (01620) 830-223, 83-228 • Fax: (01620) 830-304
E-mail: abbot@nunraw.org.uk
Web site: www.nunraw.org.uk

Founded in 1946, Sancta Maria Abbey is the thriving home of the Cistercian monks in Scotland, and one of the three principal abbeys belonging to the order in Great Britain. As well as daily prayer, the monks devote their time to raising cattle in order to finance the monastery. The abbey is surrounded by more than thirteen hundred acres of woodlands and wildlife.

Where to stay? The guesthouse accommodates fifty beds in single rooms and more than six hundred people overnight at the guesthouse each year. A variety of informal retreats are offered and individuals can often meet with a monk for counseling. Visitors can help the monks with daily chores including dish washing, food preparation, and maintaining the grounds. Contact the guesthouse at Tel: (01620) 830-228; Email: domdonald@yahoo.co.uk.

How to get there? The Sancta Maria Abbey and Guesthouse is located twenty-five miles east of Edinburgh in Nunraw near Haddington. Haddington is accessible by train and bus; take a taxi to the abbey.

PLUSCARDEN ABBEY
The Guestmaster
St. Benedict's or St. Scholastica's Retreat
Elgin, Morayshire IV30 3UA
Fax: (01343) 890-258
Email: Visit Web site for email form
Web site: www.pluscardenabbey.org

Founded in 1230, today Pluscarden Abbey is home to a community of twenty-seven Benedictine monks. Offering an authentic monastic experience, visitors are welcome to attend the monks' Mass and Liturgy of the Hours, which are sung in Gregorian chant. The abbey gift shop carries a variety of books, gifts, souvenirs, as well as honey from the monks' apiary, bees-wax polish, and fresh fruit from their garden. Gregorian chant CDs and cassette tapes of the Pluscarden monks are available, both at the gift shop and over the Internet (visit their Web site).

Where to stay? Women are housed in St. Scholastica's Retreat House (twelve comfortable bedrooms with modern facilities), while men are housed in the newly built wing of the abbey (fourteen bedrooms). Guests are invited to share lunch and supper with the monks in the refectory. All guests are expected to help out with routine chores. Silence is expected throughout much of your monastic retreat here. To make a reservation, visit the abbey Web site and fill out the online email application.

How to get there? Elgin is located about one hundred eighty miles north of Edinburgh. The abbey is located six miles west of Elgin, forty miles east of Inverness and about seventy miles west of Aberdeen (both cities have airports). From the south, take the A9 to Inverness and the A96 to Forres or Elgin, or take the A92 to Aberdeen and the A96 to Elgin for the simplest routes. Elgin is accessible by rail and bus. Bus service from Elgin to the abbey is not frequent, so you will usually need to take a taxi.

SPAIN

MONASTERIO SANTA MARÍA LAS HUELGAS

Las Huelgas
09001 Burgos
Tel: (0947) 201-630, 206-045 • Fax: (0947) 273-686
E-mail: ocsosmrlh@planalfa.es
Web site: http://www3.planalfa.es/lashuelgas

Founded in 1187, the Monastery of Santa María las Huelgas is home to a community of Cistercian monks. Mass is celebrated daily. The most important feast days at the abbey are those honoring Our Lady of Mount Carmel (July 17) and Saint Elie (July 20).

Where to stay? Only women can be accommodated at the guesthouse. Ten rooms are available and the cost is by donation.

How to get there? Burgos is a large city situated in Northern Spain and located one hundred fifty miles north of Madrid. Burgos is easily accessible by train and bus.

MONASTERIO SAN PEDRO DE CARDEÑA

09193 Castrillo del Val (Burgos)
Tel: (0947) 290-033 • Fax: (0947) 290-075
E-mail: ocsocardena@planalfa.es; spc-secretaria@hotmail.com;
Guestmaster: spc-hospederia@hotmail.com
Web site: www.cardena.org

Founded in 899, the Monastery of San Pedro de Cardeña is home to a community of Cistercian monks. The monastery is located in a spectacular setting and is home to a very impressive structure. The monks themselves carry a very rich spiritual tradition, which they warmly share and welcome all visitors to participate in.

Where to stay? The guesthouse includes fifteen (single) rooms; a minimum of two nights is required with a maximum of ten days allowed. To make reservations, Tel: (0947) 290-033 or (0677) 632-886, Monday through Friday, 10:00 AM to 1:00 PM and 4:00 PM to 6:00 PM. You can also contact the guestmaster by email: spc-hospederia@hotmail.com.

How to get there? Castrillo del Val is located about six miles southeast of downtown Burgos. Burgos is accessible by bus and train. Once in Burgos, the best way to reach the monastery is by taxi.

MONASTERIO DE SAN JERÓNIMO DE YUSTE

10430 Cuacos de la Vera (Cáceres)
Tel: (0927) 172-130 • Fax (0927) 172-130

Founded in 1408, the Monastery of San Jerónimo de Yuste is home to a small community of Spanish monks. The Monastery of the Order of Jerónima Cuacos de Yuste (Caceres) is where the Emperor Charles I retired, died, and was buried. The monastery is considered a historic and artistic monument. When touring the abbey grounds, you can visit the monastery cloister, refectory, and attend Mass in the Gothic church.

Where to stay? Since the guesthouse has just four rooms, only men can be accommodated for an overnight stay.

How to get there? Cuacos de la Vera is located about eighty-five miles southwest of Madrid. Nearest rail station: Caceres.

REAL MONASTERIO DE SANTA MARÍA DE EL PAULAR

28741 El Paular (Rascafría)
Tel: (091) 869-1425 • Fax (091) 869-1015
Email: elpaular@monasterioelpaular.com
Web site: www.monasterioelpaular.com

Founded in 1153, the Monastery of Santa María de El Paular is home to a community of Benedictine monks. As well as touring the abbey and surrounding area, visitors are welcome to attend the abbey's Mass, which is sung in Gregorian chant.

Where to stay? Although the monastery can only accommodate men, there is a hotel nearby which can provide excellent accommodations. You can contact them at the Sheraton Santa María de El Paular, Tel: (091) 869-1011; Fax: (091) 869-1006.

How to get there? Rascafría is located about forty miles north of Madrid. Travel along the N-1 motorway towards Burgos and exit at 69, following the signs for M-604 Rascafría/Lozoya. Almost immediately, you will come to a roundabout; follow the signs for M-604 Rascafría. Nearest train station: Puerto de Cotos (eight miles).

MONASTERIO DE SAN BENITO

31200 Estella (Navarra)
Tel: (0948) 550-882

Founded in 1616, the Monastery of San Benito is home to a community of Benedictine monks. Both the monastery's celebration of Mass and the Liturgy of the Hours are open to the public. Several different cassettes of the monks' recorded music can be purchased at the monastery.

Where to stay? Guestrooms are available to accommodate those individuals who wish to embark on a monastic retreat of prayer and silence.

How to get there? Estella (Navarra) is located about one hundred twenty miles east of Burgos. The nearest rail station is in Navarra and Estella is accessible by local bus.

MONASTERIO DE NUESTRA SEÑORA DEL OLIVAR

44558 Estercuel (Teruel)
Tel: (0978) 752-300, 72-70-09 • Fax (0978) 727-009, (0978) 75-23-00
E-mail: elolivar@arrakis.es
Web site: info@monasterioelolivar.com;
www.monasterioelolivar.com

Founded in the early thirteenth century, the Monastery of the Virgin of the Olive Grove is home to a famous Marian shrine and miraculous statue. According to legend, a small hermitage was first built at the site where a wooden statue of the Virgin Mary was discovered. As the popularity of the image grew, the Order of Mercy Friars were invited to act as custodians of the newly established shrine. Today, the monastery serves not only as the novitiate and training house for the Order of Mercy Friars, but also as a pilgrimage site. Visitors are welcome to join in the prayer life of the monks. Annually, on September 24, the abbey attracts thousands of pilgrims when the shrine celebrates the Feast of Our Lady of Mercy.

Where to stay? A guesthouse with thirty guestrooms (doubles and individuals) is available to accommodate visiting pilgrims (open to men, women, and children). The monastery also includes conference halls, spiritual retreats, and a dining room for about seventy-five people. Monks are available for spiritual guidance.

How to get there? Estercuel is located about eighty miles south of Zaragoza. Nearest rail station: Teruel.

ABADÍA DE SANTA CRUZ DEL VALLE DE LOS CAÍDOS
Carretera de Guadarrama/El Escorial
28029 Guadarrama/Valle de Cuelgamuros (Madrid)
Tel: (091) 890-5411, 890-13-98 • Fax: (091) 890-55-44, 890-55-94
E-mail: abadia-valle@ctv.es

Founded in 1958, the Abbey of Santa Cruz del Valle de los Caídos is home to a community of Benedictine monks. The abbey attracts both pilgrims and tourists alike for its spectacular and imposing basilica, which includes a crypt carved out of the rock itself. Tours are available for visitors.

Where to stay? Accommodation is available in either of the two separate guesthouses. In the guesthouse located inside the monastery, men can be accommodated in sixteen rooms. In the other guesthouse, which is located at the exterior, both men and women can be accommodated in one hundred and ten rooms. For further information about the latter, Tel: (091) 890-5492; Fax (091) 896-1542.

How to get there? Guadarrama is located about thirty miles northwest of Madrid and the abbey is situated along the A-6 road from Madrid to El Escorial. The abbey is accessible by bus line 660: Escorial-Valle de los Caídos.

PADRE HOSPEDERO
Monasterio de Santa María de la Vid
Ctra. De Soria, s/n.
09491 La Vid de Aranda (Burgos)
Tel: (0947) 530-510, 530-051-4 • Fax: (0947) 530-429
E-mail: licet@mx3.redestb.es
Web site: www.monasteriodelavid.org

Founded in 1162, the Monastery of Santa María de la Vid is home to a community of Augustinian monks. As well as participating in religious services in the abbey, visitors can tour the church, cloister, funeral chapel, refectory, library, and the ancient hotel that was used for pilgrims who were traveling to Santiago de Compostela. Annually, on June 1, a large Marian procession is held at the abbey.

Where to stay? A guesthouse with fifty-four rooms (singles and doubles) and a capacity for seventy-five people provides accommodations to both men and women who are seeking a time of spiritual refreshment in a monastic environment. The minimum stay is two days, except during the summer, which requires a week stay. A youth guesthouse, complete with kitchens, meeting rooms, chapel, and much more, can accommodate one hundred fourteen people.

How to get there? La Vid de Aranda (Aranda de Duero) is located sixty miles north of Madrid. The monastery can be reached along N-122 if coming from Valladolid. The nearest rail station is Burgos. Although a long drive, taxi from Burgos is essentially the best and most efficient way to reach the monastery by public transportation.

MONASTERIO DE SANTA TERESA DE ÁVILA
20210 Lazkao (Gipuzkoa)
Tel: (0943) 88-01-70 • Fax: (0943) 16-08-68
E-mail: benedictinos@euskalnet.net

Founded in 1640, the Monastery of Santa Teresa de Ávila is home to a community of Benedictine monks. Mass is celebrated daily in the abbey chapel, which all are invited to attend.

Where to stay? Those who wish to participate more fully in the prayer life of the community can ask to be accommodated in one of the monastery guestrooms. There are twenty rooms for men and eight for families.

How to get there? Lazkao is located about one hundred fifteen miles northeast of Burgos and thirty miles from San Sebastian. Nearest train station: Beasain (one mile).

MONASTERIO NUESTRA SEÑORA DEL ESPINO
Santa Gadea del Cid.
09200 Miranda de Ebro (Burgos)
Tel: (0947) 332-712 • Fax (0947) 332-652

Originally founded in 1443, the Monastery of Nuestra Señora del Espino is home to a community of Redemptorist Fathers. As well as touring the vast abbey church, visitors can participate in religious services with the community.

Where to stay? Only groups can be accommodated in the guesthouse, which is located inside the monastery. There is another hotel located at the exterior of the monastery, which accepts young people. For reservations, Tel: (0947) 35-90-15.

How to get there? Miranda de Ebro is located about fifty miles northeast of Burgos. Miranda de Ebro is accessible by train (the railway station is one of the oldest in Spain).

CONVENTO-SANTUÁRIO DE NUESTRA SEÑORA DE MONTESCLAROS
39417 Montesclaros (Santander)
Tel: (0942) 770-559, 770-553

Founded in the sixteenth century, the convent and shrine of Nuestra Señora de Montesclaros is home to a community of Dominican monks. A popular pilgrimage site, the monastic sanctuary has a miraculous image of the Blessed Virgin Mary that dates back to the eighth century. As well as attending the many processions and celebrations that are held at the shrine annually, the faithful can also participate in daily religious services in the chapel.

Where to stay? A guesthouse with forty rooms is available to pilgrims and retreat participants.

How to get there? Montesclaros is located about eighty-five miles southwest of Madrid. Nearest rail station: Santander.

DESPATX DE LA BASILICA
08199 Montserrat
Tel: (093) 877-77-66 (ext. 1503) • Fax: (093) 877-77-50
Booking & Information Office:
Tel: (093) 877-77-01 • Fax: (093) 877-77-24
E-mail: reserves@larsa-montserrat.com, serveidepremsa@abadiamontserrat.net
Web site: www.abadiamontserrat.net

Founded in the eleventh century, the renowned abbey and sanctuary of Our Lady of Montserrat is home to a community of Benedictine monks. For centuries, this monastery has served as one of Europe's most important places of pilgrimage, since, within its walls, it possesses a twelfth-century miraculous statue of the Blessed Virgin Mary. One million pilgrims and visitors travel here annually, not only to pray before the beloved image, but also to hear one of the country's oldest and most famous boys' choirs—the Escolania. As well as the activities associated with the shrine, visitors are invited to attend the Liturgy of the Hours and Mass with the monks in the abbey church.

Where to stay? Since the monastery offers several types of accommodation, it is best to contact them in advance to make reservations (or visit their Web site). The two main types of accommodations are the hotel and apartments. The Hotel Abat Cisneros features eighty-two rooms and is a three-star hotel located in a historic building next to the monastery. The hotel can accommodate about one hundred fifty guests. The Abat Marcet Apartments include ninety-two apartments, which can accommodate up to two hundred sixty people.

How to get there? Montserrat is located about thirty-five miles west of Barcelona and is accessible by train and bus. An aerial cable car connects travelers with the monastery at the top of the mountain.

MONASTERIO DE SAN BENET
08199 Montserrat (Barcelona)
Tel: (093) 83-50-078 • Fax (093) 828-42-29
Email (Mother Abbess): montserrat@benedictinescat.com,
Monastery: stbenet@benedictinescat.com
Web site: www.benedictinescat.com/Montserrat

Founded in 1954, the Monastery of San Benet is home to a community of Benedictine monks. Mass is celebrated daily. Many pilgrims visit the abbey for the two feast days of Saint Benedict (March 21 and July 11).

Where to stay? The guesthouse features eight (double) rooms. To make reservations, email: hostatgeria.sb@benedictinescat.com.

How to get there? The monastery is located on the mountain at Montserrat. See previous entry regarding information on arriving at Monserrat.

MONASTERIO DE OSEIRA

32135 Oseira (Ourense)
Tel: (0988) 282-804, 282-004 • Fax: (0988) 282-528
Email: cisteroseira@planalfa.es

Founded in 1137, the Monastery of Oseira is home to a community of Cistercian monks. As well as visiting the abbey church, the faithful can join the monks for the daily celebration of Mass and the Liturgy of the Hours.

Where to stay? Fourteen guestrooms are available to those men and women who wish to embark on a monastic retreat of prayer and silence. Meals are shared with the monks in the refectory.

How to get there? Oseira is located about fifty miles southeast of Santiago de Compostela. Nearest rail station: Ourense (twenty miles).

MONASTERIO DE SAN PELAYO

Calle San Vicente 11
33003 Oviedo (Principado de Asturias)
Tel: (0985) 218-981 • Fax: (0985) 222-442
E-mail: mspelayo@telefonica.net; mspelayo@las.es
Web site: www.monasteriosanpelayo.com

Founded in the ninth century, the Monastery of San Pelayo is home to a community of Benedictine monks. Mass is celebrated daily in the chapel with chant.

Where to stay? Ten guestrooms are available for individuals and groups. Meeting rooms are available for parishes, catechesis groups, and Christian communities.

How to get there? Oviedo is located about two hundred fifty miles east of Santiago de Compostela. Oviedo is accessible by train and bus.

MONASTERIO DE SAN SALVADO

Plaza Del Monasterio, 1
09132 Palacios de Benaver (Burgos)
Tel: (0947) 45-02-09 • Fax: (0947) 45-02-62

Founded in 834, the Monastery of San Salvador is home to a community of Benedictine monks. As well as praying in the chapel, visitors can attend Mass and the Liturgy of the Hours, which are sung in Gregorian chant.

Where to stay? The guesthouse features twenty-four rooms (singles and doubles), as well as a dormitory of twelve beds. The guesthouse is open to receiving individuals and groups, who can meet for spiritual exercises and retreats. Meals are eaten with the monks, which enriches your visit to the monastery.

How to get there? Palacios de Benaver is located about fifteen miles west of Burgos. The most efficient way to reach the monastery from Burgos is by taxi. Burgos is accessible by train or bus.

MONASTERIO DE SANTA MARÍA LA REAL Y SAN BERNARDO
Camino de la Real 3
07010 Palma de Mallorca
Tel: (0971) 75-04-95 • Fax: (0971) 76-44-12

Founded in 1232, the Monastery of Santa María la Real y San Bernardo is home to a community of Missionary Fathers of the Sacred Heart. Although people come throughout the year, the most popular day is August 20 (the feast day of Saint Bernard), when numerous celebrations take place.

Where to stay? Both men and women (traveling independently or in groups) are welcome to remain for a short stay in the abbey guesthouse, which has twenty-six rooms.

How to get there? Palma de Mallorca is the port city on the island of Majorca, located about two hundred fifteen miles east of Valencia (in eastern Spain). The island is accessible by ferry from Barcelona and Valencia.

CONVENTO-SANTUARIO DE NUESTRA SEÑORA DE CURA
07629 Randa (Mallorca)
Tel: (0971) 66-09-94 • Fax: (0971) 66-20-52

Founded in the twelfth century, the convent and sanctuary of Our Lady of Cura is home to a community of Franciscan friars. As well as enjoying the beautiful panoramic view of the surrounding countryside, the faithful can spend personal time in the chapel (which is filled with Baroque statues), visit the library-museum, and attend religious services.

Where to stay? A guesthouse with twenty-five rooms provides accommodations for both men and women.

How to get there? Randa is located on the island of Majorca, about two hundred fifteen miles east of Valencia (in eastern Spain). The island is accessible by ferry from Barcelona and Valencia. Take local taxi service to the monastery.

ABADÍA DE RONCESVALLES (ABBAYE DE RONCEVAUX)
31650 Roncesvalles (PA)
Tel: (0948) 76-00-00 • Tel (Guesthouse): (0948) 76-02-25
Fax: (0948) 79-04-50

Founded in 1127, the Abbey of Roncesvalles is home to a community of Canons Regular. Roncesvalles is popular for serving as the starting point of the Way of St. James route for many (the Santiago de Compostela pilgrimage). Visitors can tour the ancient abbey church.

Where to stay? A guesthouse is available to those individuals who wish to spend personal time in retreat.

How to get there? Roncesvalles is located about three hundred miles northeast of Madrid and thirty miles northeast of Pamplona. Nearest train station: Pamplona. From Pamplona, take a taxi to Roncesvalles.

MONASTERIO DE SAN JULIÁN DE SAMOS
Calle San Benito
27620 Samos (Lugo)
Tel: (0982) 54-60-46 • Fax: (0982) 54-61-82

Originally founded in the sixth century, the Monastery of San Julián de Samos is now home to a community of Benedictine monks. Mass is celebrated daily. The most important feast days celebrated at the monastery are those honoring Saint Julian (January 9) and Saint Benedict (March 21 and July 11). Organ concerts are held at certain times of the year.

Where to stay? Forty guestrooms are available to those individuals who wish to participate more fully in the prayer life of the community.

How to get there? Samos is located a little more than one hundred miles east of Santiago de Compostela and two hundred thirty miles west of Burgos. Nearest train station: Lugo.

MONASTERIO DE SANTA MARÍA DE HUERTA

42260 Santa María de Huerta (Soria)
Tel: (0975) 327-002 • Fax: (0975) 327-397
Email: huerta@monasteriohuerta.org
Web site: www.monasteriohuerta.org

Founded in 1162, the Monastery of Santa María de Huerta is home to a community of Cistercian monks. Visitors can tour parts of the abbey as well as take part in religious services with the monks. Items available at the abbey gift shop include cheese, wine, meat, honey, books, and the liquor called "Tizona."

Where to stay? Twelve guestrooms are available to those individuals who seek a place for prayer and silence and who wish to experience monastic life firsthand. Short spiritual courses on prayer and the monastic life are available at certain times of the year. For more information about these courses or to inquire about reservations, Tel: (0620) 13-22-23.

How to get there? Santa María de Huerta is located about one hundred miles northeast of Madrid along the A-2 (Madrid-Zaragoza). Santa Maria de Huerta is accessible by bus and train.

ABADIA BENEDICTINA DE SANTO DOMINGO DE SILOS

Hospedería "Maison d'Accueil Spirituel"
09610 Santo Domingo de Silos
Tel: (0947) 39-00-68, 39-00-49 • Fax: (0947) 39-00-33
Web site: www.abadiadesilos.es

Located in north-central Spain, the monastery of Santo Domingo de Silos is home to a community of Benedictine monks. In the mid 1990s, this abbey gained international fame for their recordings of Gregorian chant which "hit number one" on the European pop charts and made a great impression in the United States. Pilgrims and visitors are invited to attend religious services with the monks, which include a morning High Mass and singing of the canonical hours. Guided tours of the abbey are also available.

Where to stay? A guesthouse (Hospedería) is located next to the monastery, providing accommodations to both men and women.

How to get there? Santo Domingo de Silos is located in north central Spain, about one hundred miles north of Madrid via the N1. Santo Domingo de Silos is not accessible by train; the nearest rail station is located in Burgos, forty miles to the north. To arrive at Santo Domingo de Silos, you must take either a bus or a taxi to the monastery from Burgos.

MONASTERIO DE SANTA MARÍA DEL PARRAL
Subida del Parral 2
40003 Segovia
Tel: (0921) 43-12-98 • Fax: (0921) 42-25-92
E-mail: oshsmparral@planalfa.es
Web site: www3.planalfa.es/msmparral/parral/fondo.htm

Founded in 1454, the Monastery of Santa María del Parral is home to a community of Herminite monks. All visitors are welcome to tour parts of the abbey, which was declared a national monument in 1914. Mass is chanted in the chapel daily. The most important feast days celebrated at the abbey are September 8 (Saint Mary of Parral) and September 30 (Saint Jerome).

Where to stay? Men may stay at the twenty-three room guesthouse for a maximum of seven days. Participation in all monastic activities is required. For more information or to make reservations, contact the monastery by mail, phone: (918) 691-425 or (0616) 099-803, or email: oshsmparral@planalfa.es.

How to get there? Segovia is located about fifty-five miles northwest of Madrid. Segovia is easily accessible by train or bus.

MONASTERIO SAN JUAN DE LA CRUZ
Calle Cardenal Zuniga
Alameda de la Fuencisla
40003 Segovia
Tel: (0921) 412-410, 43-13-49, 43-19-61 • Fax: (0921) 43-16-50

Founded in 1586, the Monastery of San Juan de la Cruz is now home to a community of Carmelite monks. Pilgrims come throughout the year to pray before the relics of the great mystic, Saint John of the Cross. Along with visiting the museum, which is dedicated to the life of the saint, the faithful are invited to join the Carmelites for Mass in the chapel.

Where to stay? A guesthouse with forty rooms provides accommodations to both men and women.

How to get there? Segovia is located about fifty-five miles northwest of Madrid via M50, A6, and A61. Segovia is accessible by train and bus.

MONASTERIO CASA DE LA TRINIDAD
39150 Suesa (Cantabria)
Tel: (0042) 510-021
Email: montrini@terra.es
Web site: www.parrocchie.it/civo/suesa

Founded in 1887, the monastery is home to a community of Holy Trinity monks. Everyone is welcome to attend religious services with the monks, which include Mass and the Liturgy of the Hours.

Where to stay? The fourteen-room guesthouse, which was recently restored, can accommodate up to thirty-five people.

How to get there? Suesa is located about one hundred fifty miles north of Burgos and ten miles from Santander along the A8/370 (Santander-Bilbao road). Santander is accessible by train or bus; to reach the monastery and Suesa, take a taxi.

MONASTERIO SANTA MARÍA DE LA CARIDAD
31522 Tulebras (Navarra)
Tel: (0948) 851-475 • Fax: (0948) 850-012
E-mail: ocsocari@planalfa.es

Founded in 1147, the Monastery of Santa Maria de la Caridad is home to a community of Cistercian monks. In addition to exploring the abbey church and museum, visitors are invited to attend the daily celebration of Mass with the monks.

Where to stay? Only those men and women who seek to participate more fully in the prayer life of the monks can be accepted for an overnight stay in the small guesthouse, which can accommodate twenty people.

How to get there? Tulebras is located about one hundred eighty miles northeast of Madrid. Nearest rail station: Tudela.

ABADÍA DE SAN SALVADOR DE LEYRE
31410 Yesa (Navarra)
Tel (Abbey): (0948) 884-011, (0948) 884-150
Fax (Abbey): (0948) 884-230
Tel (Guesthouse): (0948) 884-100 • Fax (Guesthouse): (0948) 884-137
Email: info@monasteriodeleyre.com
Web site: www.monasteriodeleyre.com

Situated at the top of a mountain and offering spectacular views of the valley below, the Abbey of Saint Salvador of Leyre was founded in the ninth century and is now home to a community of Benedictine monks. Visitors can tour the abbey and attend religious services with the monks, which include the singing of the Liturgy of the Hours and Mass in Gregorian chant.

Where to stay? Guestrooms are available for men within the walls of the monastery. All others, whether traveling independently or in groups, are welcome to stay in the monastic hotel located next to the monastery. As such, all guests are expected to participate in the daily life of the monastery and respect the hours of silence. To make reservations, contact the monastery guesthouse by email: hotel@monasteriodeleyre.com or by phone: (0948) 884-100; Fax: (0948) 884-137.

How to get there? Yesa is located about two hundred sixty miles northwest of Madrid and thirty miles southwest of Pamplona along N-240. Although Pamplona is accessible by train and bus, Yesa is accessible by taxi only.

SWITZERLAND

HOSPICE DU GRAND-SAINT-BERNARD

1946 Bourg-Saint-Pierre
Tel: (027) 787-12-36 • Fax: (027) 787-11-07
Email: hospicestbernard@gsbernard.ch
Web site: www.saint-bernard.ch

Founded by Saint Bernard of Menthon, the Grand-Saint-Bernard Hospice is home to a community of Benedictine monks who have provided food and shelter to pilgrim travelers at the Swiss-Italian border for almost a thousand years. Located high in the European Alps, this is where the monks first bred Saint Bernard dogs, later training them to rescue stranded and lost travelers.

Where to stay? Today, many pilgrims and groups still visit the hospice to share in the simple religious services with the monks and refresh themselves with the beautiful scenery of the Swiss Alps. Overnight visitors include pilgrims, youth/school groups, cyclists, skiers, and many others who simply wish to experience the special atmosphere of the Grand-Saint-Bernard Hospice.

How to get there? The Great St. Bernard Pass is located near the intersection of the borders of France, Italy, and Switzerland, about fifteen miles northwest of Aosta and fifteen miles east of Chamonix. The Great St. Bernard Pass is located on the international road from Martigny, Switzerland, to Aosta, Italy. The road has no access from mid-October until mid-June. The Great St. Bernard Pass is not accessible by train; the nearest train station is at Orsieres. To arrive at Orsieres, take the local "Saint Bernard Express" from the city of Martigny. From the train station at Orsieres, take the bus that goes to the Great St. Bernard Pass.

MONASTÈRE SAINT-JOSEPH

1868 Collombey (Valais)
Tel: (024) 471-23-69 • Fax: (024) 472-29-04

Founded in 1629, the Monastery of Saint-Joseph is home to a community of Bernardine monks. The monks celebrate Mass and the Liturgy of the Hours daily in the abbey chapel, which all visitors are invited to attend. Religious services are sung in both French and Gregorian chant. The major apostolic work of the monks includes making hosts, liturgical vestments, and chaplets.

Where to stay? A guesthouse is available to both men and women, with special accommodations for groups of young people.

How to get there? Collombey is located about seventy miles east of Geneva and is accessible by road and bus. Nearest rail station: Corbier

MONASTÈRE DU CARMEL

Notre-Dame de l'Unité
2802 Develier
Tel: (032) 422-82-21 • Fax: (032) 422-82-24
Email: carmeldevelier@mocad.ch

Founded in 1946, this monastery is home to a community of Carmelites. The Mass and Liturgy of the Hours are celebrated in French; all visitors are welcome to attend religious services with the monks.

Where to stay? There are only two guestrooms available to those individuals who seek a personal retreat of prayer and silence.

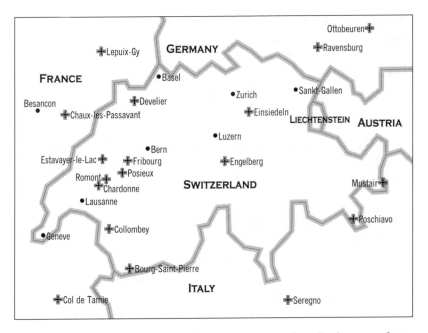

How to get there? Develier is located about one hundred twenty-five miles northeast of Geneva. Nearest rail station: Delemont; take a bus to Develier.

KLOSTER EINSIEDELN

8840 Einsiedeln (Schwyz)
Tel: (055) 418-61-11, 526-240 • Fax: (055) 418-61-12
E-mail: einsiedeln@kath.ch; kloster@kloster-einsiedeln.ch
Web site: www.kath.ch/einsiedeln

Founded in 934, the Abbey of Einsiedeln is home to a community of Benedictine monks. Serving as one of Switzerland's most famous places of pilgrimage, the monastery is home to a miraculous image of the Blessed Virgin Mary, which is located in the Chapel of Our Lady. Down through the centuries, the abbey has retained its processions, solemn liturgies, and tradition of sacred music, with orchestral Masses still performed occasionally during the High Mass. Many religious services take place in the abbey church daily, including Mass, the Liturgy of the Hours, and the rosary. Most prayers are sung in Gregorian chant. The monks from this abbey have gained international attention for their sacred music.

Where to stay? Guestrooms are available to individuals and groups who seek to spend a few days in prayerful retreat; however, one must reserve a room well in advance of arrival. Close to the monastery, there are also a large number of bed-and-breakfast inns that can provide accommodations for both visitors and pilgrims. To make reservations at the abbey, Tel: (055) 418 62 40; Fax: (055) 418 64 25; Email: gast@kloster-einsiedeln.ch.

How to get there? Einsiedeln is located about twenty-five miles southeast of Zurich and about forty miles from Lucerne. Einsiedel is accessible by train, but not by bus.

BENEDEKTINER ABTEI
6390 Engelberg (Sarnem)
Tel: (041) 639-61-61 • Fax: (041) 630-61-13

Founded in 1120, the Abbey of Engelberg is home to a community of Benedictine monks. Guided tours of both the abbey and church are available; all visitors can participate in the prayer life of the monks, which includes Mass and the Liturgy of the Hours.

Where to stay? Since the abbey has just a few guestrooms, only men can be accommodated.

How to get there? Engelberg is located sixty miles south of Zurich. Engelberg is accessible by train.

MONASTÈRE NOTRE-DAME-DE-L'ASSOMPTION
Grand Rue 3,
1470 Estavayer-le-Lac (Fribourg)
Tel: (026) 663-42-22 • Fax: (026) 663-54-39
Email: dominicaines.estavayer@bluewin.ch

Founded in 1280, the Monastery of Notre-Dame-de-l'Assomption is home to a women's community of Dominican monks. As well as exploring the abbey church, visitors can join the monks in religious services, including Mass and the Liturgy of the Hours, which are sung in French and Gregorian chant.

Where to stay? The guesthouse has fifteen rooms (six rooms with two beds, eight rooms with one bed, and one room with four beds). The guesthouse is closed in January.

How to get there? Estavayer-le-Lac is located about one hundred ten miles southwest of Zurich. Nearest rail station: Fribourg.

ABBAYE NOTRE-DAME-DE-LA-MAIGRAUGE
2, chemin de l'Abbaye
1700 Fribourg
Tel: (026) 309-21-10, 322-91-50 • Fax: (026) 309-21-15, 322-91-55
Email: contact@maigrauge.ch
Web site: www.maigrauge.ch

Founded in 1284, the Abbey of Notre-Dame-de-la-Maigrauge is home to a community of Cistercian monks. Central to the life of the monks is the Mass and the Liturgy of the Hours, which are sung in French and Gregorian chant.

Where to stay? A small guesthouse with ten rooms provides accommodation for those who wish to embark on a personal retreat in a monastic environment.

How to get there? Fribourg is about ninety-five miles northwest of Geneva. Fribourg is accessible by rail and bus. Once in Fribourg, take a taxi to the abbey.

MONASTÈRE SAINT-JOSEPH-DE-MONTORGE
Chemin de Lorette 10
1700 Fribourg
Tel: (026) 322-35-36 • Fax: (026) 322-35-58

Founded in 1628, the monastery is home to a women's community of Capuchin monks. The Liturgy of the Hours and Mass are said in French; all visitors are welcome to join the nuns in the abbey church for religious services. The nuns' major apostolic work includes the production of liturgical vestments, as well as making hosts.

Where to stay? A small guesthouse provides accommodations only to women and young girls who wish to participate more fully in the prayer life of the monastery.

How to get there? Fribourg is about ninety-five miles northwest of Geneva. Fribourg is accessible by rail and bus. Once in Fribourg, take a taxi to the monastery.

MONASTÈRE DE LA VISITATION
Rue de Morat, 16
1700 Fribourg
Tel: (026) 347-23-40 • Fax: (026) 347-23-49

Founded in 1635, the Monastery of the Visitation is home to a women's community of the Visitation Order. Both Mass and the Liturgy of the Hours are celebrated in the abbey church, which all are invited to attend.

Where to stay? The guesthouse is open only to women and young ladies who wish to join the nuns in their monastic life of prayer.

How to get there? Fribourg is about ninety-five miles northwest of Geneva. Fribourg is accessible by rail and bus. Once in Fribourg, take a taxi to the monastery.

MONASTÈRE SAINTE-CLAIRE ("LA GRAND-PART")
Chemin des Crosettes 13
1805 Jongny (VD)
Tel: (021) 921-21-77 • Fax: (021) 922-07-35
Email: Courrielgrantpart@hotmail.com

Founded in 1424, the Monastery of Sainte-Clare is home to a community of Poor Clare nuns. All visitors are welcome to participate in the prayer life of the nuns, which includes the celebration of Mass and the Liturgy of the Hours in the chapel (recited in French).

Where to stay? Individuals seeking a place for prayer and silence can ask to be accommodated in one of the abbey guestrooms.

How to get there? Jongny is located about fifty miles northwest of Geneva along the A1. Take the train to Vevey and then the bus to Jongny.

KLOSTER SANKT JOHANN BAPTIST

7537 Müstair (Davos)
Tel: (081) 858-52-65

Founded in the ninth century, the Cloister of Saint John the Baptist is home to a community of Benedictine monks. As well as visiting the various historic chapels in the abbey church, pilgrims and tourists can attend religious services with the monks, which are open to the public.

Where to stay? Since there are only six guestrooms available, only those men and women who are willing to participate in the prayer life of the monastery during their stay can be accommodated.

How to get there? Müstair is located one hundred thirty-five miles southeast of Zurich. Nearest rail station: Davos.

CHEMIN DE L'ABBAYE 19

1725 Posieux
Tel: (026) 409-71-00, 409-71-02, 402-17-83
Fax: (026) 401-71-01, 401-10-53
Email (General): communaute@abbaye-hauterive.ch;
secretariat@abbaye-hauterive.ch
Email (Hostel): accueil@abbaye-hauterive.ch
Web site: http://abbaye-hauterive.ch

Founded in 1138, the Abbey of Hauterive is home to a community of Cistercian monks. Guided tours of the thirteenth and fourteenth church and cloister are available during the week, and also after High Mass on Sundays. Mass and the Liturgy of the Hours are sung in Gregorian chant, while the regular presentations given by the monks are in French.

Where to stay? Seventeen guestrooms are available for men, six guestrooms for women, and a dormitory room with eight beds for groups of young people. The length of a stay is two to seven nights. Participation in the monastic life is required, including silence during meals. To make a reservation , email: accueil@abbaye-hauterive.ch.

How to get there? Posieux is located about eighty miles northeast of Geneva. Exit motoway A12 (exit "Matran") and travel in the direction of Fribourg; continue in the direction of "Bulle-Posieux" and follow the signs to "Abbaye d'Hauterive." Take the bus from Fribourg (#336) to Posieiux via Le Bry, exiting at "Grangeneuve-Institue Agricole" bus stop. Walk down to the abbey from there.

MONASTERO DI SANTA MARIA PRESENTATA
Via di Santa Maria ai Pioppi
7742 Poschiavo (Pontresina)
Tel: (081) 844-02-04 • Fax: (081) 844-32-11

Founded in 1629, the Monastery of Santa Maria Presentata is home to a women's community of Augustinian monks. In 1972, the ancient monastery was replaced by a more modern one. The most popular days at the abbey church are the feast days honoring Saint Bernard (August 20) and Saint Augustine (August 28).

Where to stay? Since the nuns have just a few guestrooms, only women may be accommodated.

How to get there? Poschiavo is located about one hundred fifty miles southeast of Zurich. Poschiavo is accessible by rail.

ABBAYE DE LA FILLE-DIEU
1680 Romont
Tel: (026) 651-90-10, 651-90-12, 652-22-42
Fax: (026) 651-90-11, 652-23-15
E-mail: abbaye.fille-dieu@romont.ch;
office@Fille-Dieu.ch, info@fille-dieu.ch
Web site: www.fille-dieu.ch

Founded in 1268 by the Trappists, the Abbey of Fille-Dieu is now home to a women's community of Cistercian monks. In 1996, the monks reconsecrated the beautifully restored abbey church to honor the 650th anniversary of its original construction in 1346. Those visiting the monastery can attend Mass, which is sung in Gregorian chant, and the Liturgy of the Hours, which is sung in French.

Where to stay: Individuals who wish to participate in a silent monastic retreat may be accommodated in one of the abbey's guestrooms.

How to get there? Romont is located about sixty miles northeast of Geneva. Romont is accessible by train or bus.

PART 4

Appendices

MONASTIC-RELATED WEBSITES

MONASTERY GUESTHOUSE LINKS

For an extensive listing of monasteries, visit the "Trip Planning Resources" section of the official Web site for the World Religious Travel Association: www.religioustravelassociation.com. Please note that you will need a password to access "Trips Planning Resources," which will be provided complimentary with your registration.

MONASTIC AND RELIGIOUS ORDERS LINKS

Augustinian Order: www.osanet.org
Benedictine Order: www.osb.org
Capuchins: www.capuchins.org
Carmelite Order: www.ocarm.org
Carthusian Order: www.chartreux.org
Cistercian Order of the Strict Observance (Trappists): www.ocso.org
Conventual: www.ofmconv.org
Discalced Carmelite Order: www.ocd.pcn.net
Dominican Order: www.op.org
Franciscan Order: www.ofm.org
Orthodox Monasteries: www.orthodox-monasteries.com

TRIP PLANNING TOOLS & RESOURCES

GENERAL TRIP PLANNING

Airline (group booking specialists): www.objectix.com
Airline complaints (delays, baggage): http://airconsumer.ost.dot.gov
Airline delays: www.fly.faa.gov/flyfaa/plaintext.html
Airline flight status: www.flightstats.com
Airline seats: www.seatguru.com
Airline tickets: www.kayak.com; www.sidestep.com
Airline toll free numbers: www.tollfreeairline.com
Airline tracker: www.flightarrivals.com
Airports (information, maps): www.airports.com
Airport parking: www.parkrideflyusa.com: http://www.flyrideusa.com
Airport security wait times: http://waittime.tsa.dhs.gov

Bus and subway directions: www.hopstop.com

Calendar and holidays: www.timeanddate.com/calendar
Calling codes: www.countrycallingcodes.com
Country facts: www.cia.gov/library/publications/the-world-factbook/
   index.html
Currency converter/foreign exchange data: www.oanda.com;
   www.xe.com
Customs (USA): www.customs.ustreas.gov

Department of Homeland Security: www.dhs.gov
Driving directions: www.mapquest.com; www.randmcnally.com;
   www.viamichelin.com; www.theaa.com; www.maps.google.com

Electric guide: www.kropla.com
Embassies: www.embassyworld.com; www.tripresource.com
   embassy.htm
Emergency/disaster information: www.redcross.org;
   www.disasternews.net; www.fema.gov
Emergency/health (personal): www.airambulancecard.com

FAA Air Traffic Control: www.faa.gov
Farecast: www.farecast.com
Flight delay information: www.fly.faa.gov/flyfaa/usmap.jsp
Flight tracker: www.flightview.com
Frequent flyer programs: www.webflyer.com

Group travel planners: www.grouptour.com;
    www.goexperience.com; www.glamer.com

Health (Travel Health Info): www.cdc.gov; www.who.int;
    www.who.org; www.passporthealthusa.com; www.tripprep.com
Hostel: www.hostels.com; www.hostelworld.com

Insurance (travel): www.travelguard.com, www.tripinsurance.com,
    www.airambulancecard.com
Internet access/hotspot: www.wi-fihotspotlist.com;
    www.wififreespot.com

Language translation (learning phrases):
    http://babelfish.altavista.com/tr
Last-minute travel planning: www.dontforgetyourtoothbrush.com
Lodging (Christian lodging): www.christian-hotel.com;
    www.christianhospitalitynetwork.org
Lodging (monasteries): www.monasterystays.com

Passports & Visas: www.embassy.com; www.projectvisa.com;
    http://travel.state.gov; http://travel.state.gov/passport;
    www.travisa.com
Physical disabilities & special needs travel: www.access-able.com

Rail Europe: www.raileurope.com

Time around the world: www.timeanddate.com/worldclock;
    www.worldtimezone.com; www.time.gov
Tipping guide: www.tipping.org
Tourist offices & embassies (worldwide): www.towd.com;
    www.embassyworld.com; www.tripresource.com/embassy.htm
Train travel: www.raileurope.co: www.cwrr.com;
    www.railagent.com; www.amtrak.com; www.railpass.com;
    www.eurail.com

Transportation Security Administration (TSA): www.tsa.gov
Transportation Security Administration traveler's tip:
    www.tsa.gov/travelers/index.shtm
Travel planning: www.worldtravelguide.net
Travel planning (religious sites): www.sacred-destinations.com;
    www.bibleplaces.com
Travel planning (USA): www.homeandabroad.com;
    www.planetware.com
Travel planning (Worldwide): www.homeandabroad.com;
    www.worldtravelguide.net
Trip planning tools & resources: www.religioustravelassociation.com
Traffic advisories: http://traffic.tann.net

U.S. State Department/travel warnings: http://travel.state.gov

Visas: (see Passports & Visas)

Weather around the world: www.weather.com;
    www.accuweather.com; www.intellicast.com
World Health Organization: www.who.int/eha/disasters

GETTING AROUND EUROPE

If you will be traveling independently in Europe (while visiting the monasteries and convents), you should plan to prepare your trip well in advance—especially in regards to your transportation means. First of all, if you plan to travel by rail, you can map out much of your trip by visiting the website: www.raileurope.com. You can also purchase your train tickets in advance via Rail Europe. If you plan to drive in Europe, you can map out your trip by using the following "driving directions" Web sites: www.mapquest.com; www.randmcnally.com; www.viamichelin.com; www.theaa.com; www.maps.google.com.

TRAVEL HEALTH, PASSPORT/ VISAS, & INSURANCE

HEALTH

If you plan to travel outside of the country, it is strongly recommended you contact a travel health provider about your trip plans (immediately upon booking your trip) and discuss what you must do to prepare and protect your health for each destination you plan to visit. Your health should not be taken lightly when embarking on a trip, for multiple reasons, ranging from the unpleasantry of being sick, to missing out on your vacation, to the potentially enormous costs of visiting hospitals and doctors overseas for medical or emergency purposes. For more information about travel health protection and requirements, visit the websites: www.cdc.gov; www.who.int; www.who.org; www.passporthealthusa.com; www.tripprep.com; www.airambulancecard.com.

PASSPORT & VISA INFORMATION

As passports and visa rules can change often, it is imperative that before making a trip reservation or booking, you learn the travel requirements of the foreign countries you plan to visit. Obtaining a passport and/or visa, as well as knowing whether you need one or not (and if so, to which countries), *is the responsibility of the traveler* and *not* the travel provider. Regarding passports, it is typically required that at least two blank pages are available, and that your passport is valid for at least six months beyond the conclusion of your trip. Regarding visas, it is the traveler's responsibility to contact the respective consulates or visa agencies to determine whether any visas are required. You should begin checking into passport and visa requirements about a year before a trip (or immediately upon booking a trip, if within one year of departure). Similar to traveler health requirements, obtaining the necessary travel documentation for your trip is not to be taken lightly or procrastinated. Without proper documentation, you risk forfeiting your entire trip, with no recourse to reimbursement. Worse yet, you could be advised, while traveling outside the United States, that you are not allowed entry into another country due to missing or inaccurate documentation. For more information about passports, visas, and travel documentation requirements, visit: www.embassy.com; www.projectvisa.com; http://travel.state.gov; www.travisa.com.

TRAVEL INSURANCE

No matter how well you plan your trip or vacation, things can go wrong. Trips can turn from life's most memorable moments into life's most challenging or even disastrous moments due to illness, medical emergencies, severe weather, missing or lost luggage, delayed flights, stolen passports or visas (or belongings of any kind), identity theft, security risks or change in political conditions, terrorism, or simply any other form of travel disruption. When such events happen, it's not uncommon for a trip to be altered, interrupted, or simply cancelled altogether. Not only can you risk losing your entire vacation investment, but you may even be forced to incur additional and potentially very large unplanned expenses. For these reasons and more, virtually every traveler should consider purchasing travel insurance. In cases where you will be traveling with a group such as your church or faith community, travel insurance should normally be mandatory, especially if it's an international trip or vacation. To learn more about travel insurance, contact your travel provider and/or a travel insurance company and specialist. To find a travel insurance provider, visit: www.religioustravelassociation.com (and then click on the travel insurance section in the directory). You can also research travel insurance providers on the Internet by searching for "travel insurance," "travel insurance directory," or "travel insurance providers."

TRAVEL MINISTRY RESOURCES AND MATERIALS

WORLD RELIGIOUS TRAVEL ASSOCIATION
Website: www.religioustravelassociation.com

The World Religious Travel Association (WRTA) is the leading organization dedicated to shaping, enriching, and expanding faith tourism and hospitality around the world. As a global network and community, WRTA's membership includes travelers, group planners, churches, pastors and clergy, ministry organizations, travel agents, travel suppliers, travel providers, and travel destinations. Any person or organization can join as an Associate or Active Level Member. The World Religious Travel Association serves as a "one-stop shop" for group planners and travelers; you can view and research vacation opportunities, travel companies, and travel agencies from throughout North America and around the world. In addition, as a complimentary associate, you can access the association's many valuable planning tools and resources specific to group planners and individual travelers.

WORLD RELIGIOUS TRAVEL EXPO & EDUCATIONAL CONFERENCE
Website: www.religioustravelexpo.com

Join hundreds of group planners, churches, travel agencies, tour operators, tourist boards, and travel companies at the annual World Religious Travel Expo and Educational Conference. Learn to develop or enrich your travel ministry by attending the educational seminars, while also meeting other leaders involved in travel ministry. At the tradeshow event, you can interact with hundreds of travel providers specializing in faith tourism by visiting their booths and exhibits. The World Religious Travel Expo is the single most important event of the year to attend for any church, organization, group planner, or religious/ministry leader involved in faith-based travel.

WRTA SOCIAL NETWORK
A social network for faith-based travelers, organizations, and travel providers
Website: www.faithtourismnetwork.com

Whether you are an individual traveler, group planner, religious leader, or travel provider, you can join the world's first-ever social network and community for faith-based travel at: www.faithtourismnetwork.com. You can post videos, photos, music, and blogs of your trips, while meeting other travelers with similar interests. You can also join groups or create your own. Possibly best yet, you can host your faith community or organization's travel ministry program on the network for free. Along with chatting and communicating with others on the network, you can research travel destinations, companies, agencies, and vacation options from around the world and view many travel photos and videos.

RELIGIOUS TRAVEL BUZZ
Keeping you abreast of faith tourism news, announcements, and press releases
As the official e-Newsletter publication of the World Religious Travel Association, *Religious Travel Buzz* keeps you abreast of the latest in faith travel news, events, and announcements. Each issue comes complete with stories of travel destinations, breaking news, company profiles, travel ministry tips, faith tourism conferences and events, and much more. To receive your free subscription, visit: www.religioustravelassociation.com or send an email to: info@religioustravelassociation.com. Ask to receive *Religious Travel Buzz*.

GOING ON FAITH
National newspaper for religious travel group planners: www.goingonfaith.com
Going On Faith is the international newspaper for faith-based travel groups. The publication also serves as the official newspaper and host of the Going On Faith Conference (www.gofconference.com), an annual gathering of its readership and subscribers. As the only publication written exclusively for the faith-based group travel planner, *Going On Faith* includes destination features, travel industry news, trip advice columns, and other tourism content, including a section dedicated to youth group travel ideas. The publication was founded in 1997 by publisher Mac Lacy and Charlie Presley. Each year's six issues are

read by more than fifty-five hundred subscribers to the print edition, in addition to a growing online readership.

CHURCH EXECUTIVE TRAVEL
Church Executive's publication for church group planners and travelers: www.churchexecutive.com

Church Executive Travel is the latest publication from Power Trade Media, publishers of *Church Executive* magazine. Through ongoing readership surveys and industry research, *Church Executive* focuses on the pulse of large church and megachurch issues, including the growing importance of religious group travel. The *Christian Travel & Cruise Guide* is specifically written for the pastor, church group travel planner, and leisure traveler. Each issue of the *Christian Travel & Cruise Guide* contains critical and informative must-read articles, including interviews, regional trip planner, theme trips, "how to" planning, and editorial features for the religious group travel planner.

LEISURE GROUP TRAVEL
The largest and oldest publication for group travel: www.leisuregrouptravel.com

Since 1994, group travel leaders, religious travel groups, tour operators, travel agents and other group travel organizers have relied on Leisure Group Travel, and now www.LeisureGroupTravel.com, to provide destination knowledge and "how-to" advice to help them plan better group trips. Each edition features a domestic city focus, state feature, cruise section, international destination, regular news brief columns, and a reference guide. *Leisure Group Travel* is distributed in print six times per year, with a special bonus issue each November. Web site content is updated weekly. Subscriptions to our magazine and *InSite* bi-weekly e-newsletter are free to qualified group travel organizers. You can also visit: www.grouptraveldirectory.com, a search engine for the group travel industry, representing over thirty thousand group-friendly suppliers and special group offers.

DOES YOUR CHURCH OR ORGANIZATION HAVE A TRAVEL PROGRAM?

EXPERIENCE YOUR FAITH FIRSTHAND

Every year millions of people travel throughout the world for religious or faith-based purposes. Many travel with their church, faith community, religious organization, or individually. These experiences are life-changing. There is no greater feeling than experiencing holy places firsthand such as monasteries and convents. Only through travel can you experience your faith in every way possible—physically, spiritually, socially, intellectually, and emotionally.

DOES YOUR CHURCH OR ORGANIZATION HAVE A TRAVEL PROGRAM?

As the majority of people travel every year on trips and vacations, ask yourself: Is your church or organization providing its members with faith-based travel options? The benefits of experiencing faith, fun, and fellowship together are priceless, and today more than fifty thousand churches feature travel programs. If your church or organization does not yet have a travel ministry, you might consider launching such a program for your faith community. Travel ministries can provide your members with life-changing experiences and vacations.

FOR MORE INFORMATION

Where can you learn more about starting a Travel Ministry? Visit: www.religioustravelassociation.com for excellent information, articles, and resources on launching such a program.

TOP TEN REASONS TO HOST A TRAVEL MINISTRY

1. Builds community
2. Deepens faith
3. Enriches lives
4. Provides opportunity to experience your faith and sacred sites firsthand
5. Makes history and culture come alive
6. Presents a wonderful way to vacation

7. Touches every human aspect of a person—spiritual, physical, intellectual, social, and emotional
8. Appeals to everyone—youth, young adults, singles, couples, families, baby boomers, retirees
9. Faith-based travel supports all other ministries
10. Makes for a great excuse to take time off from work!

INDEX

ABOUT THE AUTHOR

KEVIN J. WRIGHT is one of the world's most recognized faith tourism and hospitality authorities. A fifteen-year veteran of the travel profession, Kevin is founder and president of the World Religious Travel Association (WRTA)—the leading global community for the $18 billion and 300 million traveler faith tourism industry. The organization also hosts Faith Tourism Network, the world's first online social network for faith-based travel.

Kevin is also founder and chairman of the *World Religious Travel Expo*, an international trade show and educational conference for churches, organizations, group planners, travel providers, tourist boards, travel agencies, and individuals involved in faith tourism. In addition, Kevin is president of the Religious Marketing Consulting Group, a team of independent professionals who assist companies with entering or expanding their presence in faith-based travel and hospitality.

In the mid-1990s, Kevin introduced the first faith-based travel guidebook series, through Liguori Publications, and is today an award-winning author of four books, including his most recent: *The Christian Travel Planner*. In 2000, Kevin personally presented his travel guidebooks to Pope John Paul II at the Vatican. In 2004, he launched the high-profile religious travel division at Globus, one of the world's largest tour operators. Kevin has traveled to thirty countries and visited more than three hundred major places of pilgrimage, including monasteries and convents, while also writing for national publications and serving as an international guest speaker.

As one of the world's most sought after faith tourism authorities, Kevin has been interviewed by "The Early Show" (CBS), *TIME Magazine, USA TODAY, The Wall Street Journal, The New York Times, National Geographic,* the *Los Angeles Times,* and dozens of other media outlets around the globe.